D0151116

Social Work in a Risk Society

Also by Stephen A. Webb:

Information and Communication Technologies in Welfare Services
(co-edited with Elizabeth Harlow)

HV
40
.W385
2006

6213383O

Social Work in a Risk Society

Social and Political Perspectives

Stephen A. Webb

© Stephen Webb 2006

All rights reserved. No reproduction, copy or transmission of this publication may be made without written permission.

No paragraph of this publication may be reproduced, copied or transmitted save with written permission or in accordance with the provisions of the Copyright, Designs and Patents Act 1988, or under the terms of any licence permitting limited copying issued by the Copyright Licensing Agency, 90 Tottenham Court Road, London W1T 4LP.

Any person who does any unauthorised act in relation to this publication may be liable to criminal prosecution and civil claims for damages.

The author has asserted his right to be identified as the author of this work in accordance with the Copyright, Designs and Patents Act 1988.

First published 2006 by
PALGRAVE MACMILLAN
Houndmills, Basingstoke, Hampshire RG21 6XS and
175 Fifth Avenue, New York, N.Y. 10010
Companies and representatives throughout the world

PALGRAVE MACMILLAN is the global academic imprint of the Palgrave Macmillan division of St. Martin's Press, LLC and of Palgrave Macmillan Ltd. Macmillan® is a registered trademark in the United States, United Kingdom and other countries. Palgrave is a registered trademark in the European Union and other countries.

ISBN-13: 978–0–333–96361–6
ISBN 10: 0–333–96361–X

This book is printed on paper suitable for recycling and made from fully managed and sustained forest sources.

A catalogue record for this book is available from the British Library.

A catalog record for this book is available from the Library of Congress.

10   9   8   7   6   5   4   3   2   1
15   14   13   12   11   10   09   08   07   06

Printed in China

For Penni

and my parents, Mary and Philip Webb

Contents

Acknowledgements

This book has taken a long time to write and the ideas in it have been honed by contact and argument with many people. I would like to acknowledge my primary debt of gratitude to my long-time friend Graham McBeath whose assiduous reading and incisive commentary refined the text and forced me to address questions of which I was not even aware. He made many valuable suggestions, especially relating to the conceptual subject matter of the book. Harry Ferguson was encouraging about the initial topic and his natural enthusiasm prompted me to press ahead. My conversations with Brian Relph and Denis Jones have been immeasurably valuable in developing my views about social work practice. Brian's deep understanding helped shape my reading of managerial and organisational changes in social work. In addition I would like to express my gratitude to colleagues at the universities of Bradford and Sussex for their support. Their interest in this project has been invaluable. Imogen Taylor has been a constant source of encouragement and kindness. Colleagues at Sussex have all in their various ways confirmed my belief that collective association and critical dialogue can go hand in hand. I also want to acknowledge the contributions that social work students at Sussex have made over the past few years. Not only have they put up with my eccentricities but their commitment and intelligence have been a constant reminder of the value of social work. A special thank you must go to my friend Stephen Hudson, whose conversation provided a much needed diversion. I would also like to thank my sister Nicola Webb and brother Richard Webb for helping with family matters during difficult times.

Finally of course, this is a Palgrave Macmillan book and I found Catherine Gray to be an excellent editor, who has been supportive and extraordinarily patient. She made me think more carefully of the general audience I wish to reach. Catherine together with the anonymous readers also kept me (I hope) from being obscurely pedantic by weeding out clumps of verbiage and finding a clearer direction. I have benefitted enormously from working with Catherine and Sheree Keep at Palgrave Macmillan. I would like to thank Brian Morrison for excellent copy editing and indexing.

But my greatest thanks and gratitude go to Penni Adamson for her love, whole-hearted support and encouragement. Without her, it is not too much to say that I would not have survived to complete this book. How many times she heard the words 'it's almost finished' and compassionately let me think she believed it; this is in itself no small feat of generosity and companionship.

Setting the Scene

This opening chapter sets out the themes of the book highlighting my central preoccupation with the relation between current and past social work practice and the ever present phenomenon of risk. It is clear that social work needs to look for a new model of practice; one that is ethically valid as well as functionally accountable in terms of reasonable decision making procedures and interventions. There is a not entirely inappropriate perception that current social work has sunk into a 'managerialism' that is increasingly afraid of the complexity of risky situations and has become highly defensive. The latter has resulted in increasing dependence upon adherence to more and more elaborate rule systems, procedures and rule following. Thus there is a reduction of scope for social workers to develop competences of judgment, ethical insight, and holistic forms of practice. In effect social work is under threat of becoming a de-skilled profession. This book provides a diagnosis of the reasons for this vitiating process. But it is not merely cast in immediate terms of social work circumstances; rather it is located within an ecology of higher and lower level historical and contemporary political forces. Because of this we need to be tolerant of having to draw on social theory and sociology as well as material from professional and applied spheres. Here we will pay attention to the concepts of risk, governmentality, neo-liberalism and late modernity. The meaning and relations between these often opaque terms in relation to social work will it is hoped become apparent throughout the book.

One of the most powerful motives for innovation and change has been the search for absolute knowledge. The public's desire for omnicompetence on the part of central and local authorities and the impossible task of providing it in our complex modern world provoke a reactive politics. In Britain we can see concrete examples of this in child care deaths (e.g. Victoria Climbie), BSE, management of national exams systems, and the approach to paedophiles. Caught between an aspirational culture of individuals wanting a secure environment in which to execute their own life-plans and government's reactive responses to crises by creating more systems of accountability, paradoxically often farmed out to non-accountable private corporations, the public is made anxious and governments increasingly

1

authoritarian. The most obvious example here is post-September 11th USA which has seen substantial increases of government powers, e.g. 'Patriot Bills I and II'. British legislation governing asylum seekers and the use of surveillance systems extends powers of the state and ministerial fiat. In other words in a world that appears to be increasingly risky the public want to govern their own lives safely but freely, and governments at risk of blame try to assert control by authoritarian measures that may well compromise democracy.

The difficulties of building rule systems which can not only shape and control social problems but enable their prediction is a symbol of our being in a risk society. Unanticipated system failures combined with the public's persistent belief that governments should have anticipated them causes a spiralling of public fears about knowns and unknowns alike. Fear of crime is disproportionate to actual likelihood of being a victim, and in the nature of democracy governments have to respond to the fear as much as to the reality. That we deal more with images – 'simulacra' or the 'hyper-real' as Baudrillard calls the central idea of postmodern society – should act as a salutary warning about the creeping technologisation of risk society.

Dimensions of Risk Society

Ulrich Beck named these phenomena in his celebrated book of 1992: *Risk Society*. Here he links anxieties around particular risky activities in industry, chemicals, pollution, nuclear accident to our capacity to collectively mediate our fears through what he called 'reflexive modernisation'. For Beck this concept 'designates a developmental phase of modern society in which social, political, economic and individual risks increasingly tend to escape the institutions for monitoring and protection in society' (1992, p. 5) Here the concept of risk is connected to reflexivity because new anxieties about risks and the failure of experts and institutions to deal with them raise critical questions about current practices. Beck thinks of reflexive modernity as a new form of confrontation with the hazards and risk that are a by-product of modernity. We see the rise of social movements such as the Greens, Campaign against Climate Change, Friends of the Earth, People Not Profit, Amnesty International and anti-capitalist demonstrations, which democratise public understanding of the risks which they face. Thus, if a democracy is suffering a deficit in the traditional homes of politics e.g. Westminster, the Bundestag, the National Assembly, Congress and the Council Halls, it is benefitting from a surplus in the extra-parliamentary sphere of new social movements. So Beck's idea is that compensating forms of the rationalisation of risk emerge where existing forms have declined. We cope with our modern condition through emergent formations of reflexive monitoring as with 'identity politics' such as the disability rights, mental health service survivors, battered women's and justice for fathers movements and what has recently come to the fore, 'social capital' – community-based individuals' use of trusted collective or social knowledge. Increasingly user groups resist expert judgement and make claims to the right to self-definition and advocacy for those people whose identity has been denied by professionals, such as health and social care workers.

Re-configurations of the relation between state and people as a result of responses to uncertainty are particularly felt in the world of social work. This is because social care provision and social work deal with variably vulnerable populations under conditions of uncertainty, e.g. financial constraint, local government re-organisation and the constant re-structuring of public policy and local priorities. Under such conditions the opportunities for risky situations to arise are high, and knowing this social work attempts to develop ever more extensive management and 'actuarial' (accountability and insurance) systems. Social work in the last 15 years, damaged by successive child abuse scandals has embraced the language of risk and accountability much as have other public institutions. Targets, performance measures and lists of procedures issuing from central government have offered a 'calculative technology' for the assessment and constraining of risky situations. Of course the further burdening of already over-worked social care personnel leads to the opening up of more risk.

That the natural and the social worlds are risky is a given: hurricanes as well as family violence can lead to death. There are perhaps fewer and fewer areas of life in which the public believe that risk is unavoidable, and this view places enormous pressures upon public authorities which itself introduces new risks and challenges to democracy. At a crucial if local level social services and the subject of this book – social work – find themselves at the eye of the storm: the raging tumult of unrelenting contradictions between the often unpredictable emergence of risk within neo-liberal systems of governance that suggests risks are more effectively minimised through the self-regulating processes of the market than through the often spectacular failures of government planning.

Re-thinking Social Work in a Risk Society

This book began partly as a response to the perceived lack of conceptual meaning and professional engagement when it comes to thinking critically about risk and social work. Indeed, the wider relationship between social work and modern society, its politics, economics and social systems as effects of risk has barely been touched on in the literature. The book is thus a theoretical attempt to make sense of some of the broad currents of social and political change affecting social work in a risk society. It examines ways in which social work can be viewed through the theoretical lens of risk society, neo-liberalism and late modernity and offers some critical thoughts and recommendations on this complex configuration.

A key argument of the book is that social work needs to be analysed in terms of the political, social and economic changes, upheavals and displacements that have produced the insecurities and risks that mark this period of late modernity. From this vantage point it can be seen how the effects of these wider transformations feed into making a new paradigm for understanding social work (Macarov & Bearwald, 2001). Thus a central argument of the book is that the formation, shifts of attribution and structuring of social work take place within a complex system: this system includes a social dimension, that of risk society; a political dimension, that of advanced liberalism; and a cultural dimension, that of reflexive or late modernity.

The Governance of Risk

My analysis of social work is cast in terms of the logic of calculation and regulation as features of governing risk within advanced liberal political rule. The concepts of risk and neo-liberalism as they configure social work in new ways are examined in detail. It is shown how the preoccupation with risk and the problems which arise within neo-liberal risk society are translated into social work and how as a consequence risk is produced, prevented, minimised, dramatised, or channelled. The book illustrates how life planning in the face of crisis becomes crucial in this respect. A planned life is one that attempts to avert risk and uncertainty through reflexive forms of self-governance. We see how life planning in social work is normative in structuring life according to wealth, age, education, gender and status and in its expectations about an age-integrated life course for people. Many social work clients, especially unemployed people, single mothers, drug users and young people use social work as a temporary resource to re-orient themselves in fateful situations of personal crisis or when their own reflexive strategies fail or break down.

The book supports Hazel Kemshall's (2002) view that the role of social work has shifted from a preoccupation with need to one with risk, but wishes to extend her analysis by showing how risk and need are often conflated in assessing and determining service provision for users. This blending of risk and need is seen to be a reflection of a new hybridised form of risk as 'actuarial governance' in late modernity. Increasingly, actuarial risk, or the calculation of risk probabilities derived from statistical models based on aggregate populations is extended into social work.

This leads to a number of new and challenging questions about the role of social work in modern society. Rather than situating social work within a state or welfare society as a straightforward vehicle of social control, the key questions asked are: (1) as an organised knowledge and set of values, what role does it play, refuse to play, or aspire to play, in the constitution of risk society as a governable domain?; (2) how does social work reproduce the conditions necessary for its legitimation and its professional role in risk society?; (3) how do risk and its governance reconfigure the professional identity of social work?; (4) more practically, how do risk society and social governance impact on framing the stages of planning, implementing, evaluating, intervening and supporting in social work?; (5) and finally, what ethical practice might social work develop in response to these new conditions of risk and neo-liberal governance?

It will be seen how one of the most important features of social work – the social handling of risk – is also one of the least well understood. This book analyses and highlights social work's pivotal role of risk regulation and expert mediation for problematic populations and vulnerable people in risk society. Here the nature of risk in social work is analysed conceptually as formed between the twin rationalities of regulation and security. A tense relationship is shown to exist between security and regulation, instrumental and substantive rationality, as well as the emergence of the institutionalisation of risk in modern social work organisations, policy developments, and technologies of care. These tense relations are described as a general feature of ambivalence in late modernity. It is shown how social work's ambivalence is manifest through, on the one hand, its instrumental rationality, as complicity with calculating and regulatory practices, and on the other hand, its substantive rationality, in securing personal identity through its dialogic and expressive face-work. Garrett neatly captures this when he says there is a 'tension between the original ethical impulse and procedural execution [that] might be viewed as the focal point for a range of dilemmas which confront social workers' (2003c, p. 4) This ambivalence is shown not to be a matter of coincidence or compromise but something that grows out of the limitations and crisis of systems of governance in complex life-worlds.

Governance is becoming a widely used concept in defining key aspects of public sector provision and is described by Rhodes (1997) as '*a new* process of governing; or a *changed* condition of ordered rule; or the *new* method by which society is governed' (p. 46). Different networked relations of power and knowledge emerge out of this paradigm of governmentality, constructing relations between social workers and clients in novel ways. I think we can observe the opening up of new ways of practising and thinking, new authorities and mandates, new technologies and conceptions for regulating and controlling people in risk society. A new territory is emerging, after the welfare state, for the management of micro-sectors of society (anti-social behaviours, multiple problem families, 'at-risk' populations, attachment disorders, asylum seekers, emotional illiteracy) that social work is decisively involved in. The book shows how the new programme of 'actuarial practice' is configured alongside a rationality of risk, at the expense of more substantive ways of thinking about psychosocial problems. In trying to manage these micro-sectors on the edges of society social work increasingly comes to trust in scientific methods, forensic technologies and appeals to systematic evidence (Saleebey, 1992). It appeals to the authority and expertise of what Max Weber called an 'instrumental rationality' (*Zweckrationalität*) in which the boundaries of expert intervention become narrow and reductive, with the priority becoming one of selecting the appropriate means to the intervention's ends, whatever they happen to be. Throughout the book I show the limitations and problems associated with this type of rationality as it is increasingly deployed within social work. The recent elevated status of evidence-based practice, risk management and care management is addressed as a feature of the predominance of actuarialism in micro-management, policy formation and organisation of social work practice. Social work is increasingly organised and audited in ways that characterise this technological enframing whereby everything is regarded as a resource in a system that has to be calculated, regulated and controlled. Under the spell of instrumental reason, social work develops a certain kind of empirical 'knowledge production' whereby its practices are increasingly understood in terms of technical and functional means.

We also see how social workers like other public sector professionals increasingly resort to quasi-scientific methods as a means of legitimation and credentialism in hostile boundary wars with managers, governments and other professionals. Evidence-based practice, managed clinical care, knowledge management, decision analysis, competence learning and computerised assessment are all used to bolster professional judgement in the drive for effectiveness. Clear grids of intelligibility and specification are required as a rational response to risk. This is referred to in the book as the deepening of 'actuarial practice' in social work. Social workers are increasingly held accountable for their interventions and decisions in mechanistic ways. Within this accountability culture the high expectations of service users, management and government require social work to specify the limits and define the boundaries of intervention in a coherent way. Indices, rules and precision techniques are sought after as part of the legal and moral responsibility of social work in a society saturated by and obsessed with risk. The effectiveness, evidence-based, risk management and 'what works' movements in social work can be partly understood as a rational set of responses to these demands.

It is argued that social work is abandoning a holistic approach to working with clients in order to rationally align itself within the dominant politics of neo-liberal managed care. Thus social work is less concerned with addressing deeply rooted psychosocial problems than with the re-construction and re-generation of clients' life strategies. Strong economic motivators of competing self-interest come to dominate welfare policy in which a myopic short-run rationality of efficiency and performance dominates front-line practice. In Reich's analysis of child protection in Australia, for example, she explains how 'Neo-liberalism brought a proliferation of practices characteristic of [social governance] to child protection agencies – competition, the creation of markets, increased flexibility and the framing of social policy in terms of cost-effectiveness and efficiency criteria' (2000, p. 6). In a society that narrowly pursues material self-interest and individual choice adherence to an ethical stance is more radical than many people realise. For me this is one of the defining characteristics and distinctive features of social work and arguably its main strength. This book claims that the legitimacy of social work rests on exhortations that betray an ethical intent rather than a set of empirical or outcome-based possibilities. I claim that the return to ethics should be a major theme that characterises social work in the late modern scenario. I refer to this as the 'practice of value' and identify some key distinctive elements that legitimate an ethics of social work. If risk society necessitates a life without guarantees we require an ethical framework that acknowledges the continuity of care, recognition and strong values. We also need ethical relations that can deepen capacity building and mobilise social capital. Instead of trying to extend the ethical remit of social work into the political realm it is argued that the ethical in social work emerges as a fragile but necessary response to the politics of neo-liberal risk society.

Aims of the Book

This book develops an alternative and fresh analysis of social work which extends the critical social work tradition in challenging ways. With its reflections on politics, ethics, and critical ideas, this book may present for some, to borrow Nietzsche's phrase, a series of 'thoughts out of season'. By trying to identify the mechanisms underlying the changing nature of social work in contemporary society and the type of professional identity that emerges it breaks with many of the received ideas in social work. Equally it has a performative and re-constructive strand which I hope readers will find innovative and uncompromising. This reading of social work within the horizons of risk society and advanced liberalism requires re-thinking many of the received ideas that are associated with the theory and practice of social work. In critically situating social work within the contours of neo-liberal politics it is hoped to assist social workers to suspend residual categories and the busy-ness of instrumental life and material self-interest.

A good deal of the material used in this book is derived from the British context. This has proved necessary in order to demonstrate in some detail how social work can be understood in the context of specific economic, political and social transformations. This should not, however, limit the interest, relevance or applicability of the book to other contexts. Given the global phenomenon of 'high risk society' and neo-liberalism many of the themes, issues and arguments will be relevant to a wide international audience of readers (Beck, 1999; Mandel, 1996). The 'globalisation of risk' is about perceived shared threats and the expanding number of contingent events which affect very large numbers of people on the planet (Shaw, 1994). The book offers insights about social work and changes in welfare that are readily transferable to the Australasian, Canadian, European and US contexts and indeed, to any region that is exposed to the logic of advanced liberalism in risk society.

The book consists of seven chapters in addition to the present one. It begins in Chapter 1 with an introductory exposition drawing on recent sociological theory to examine the relationship between social work, risk society and modernity. Here modernity and its institutions, including social work, are represented as a complex network. Social work is portrayed as a practice that continuously re-creates itself and embodies itself in differentiating and constraining structures of modernity. The process of differentiation is central to the way in which social work plans, regulates and organises the life of clients. The chapter identifies two fundamental generative mechanisms of risk that are relevant for our understanding of social work in neo-liberal risk society. These are referred to as the logic of regulation and the logic of security which are shown to be a response to complexity and contingency in late modern societies. It is suggested that these two rationalities of risk modernity combine in a generative fashion to re-configure key aspects of social work under neo-liberal political rule.

Chapter 2 offers a detailed exploration of the rationality of regulation in social work. The changing British political and economic context of social work from the post-war period onwards is examined to help show how social work develops regulatory mechanisms involving the management of risk. It also contextualises British social work within the political arena of neo-liberal welfare endorsed by successive Conservative and Blairite New Labour governments and analyses the rise of neo-liberal social governance. Risk and regulation are shown to be inter-dependent concepts in shaping social work. The rise of risk management in social work is considered as typically involving four major components: risk identification; risk analysis; risk reducing measures and risk monitoring. The implications of the preoccupation with risk assessment and management in social work are addressed in terms of its changing professional identity, the push towards interprofessional collaboration, the greater involvement of service users, the emergence of 'proto professionals' and increasing workplace specialisation.

In Chapter 3 the relationship between security, trust and life planning within risk society is explored. The significance of these cornerstone concepts for social work is addressed by focusing on various policy and practice initiatives. The chapter details concrete examples of the social handling of security and life planning, and related metaphors of safety, protection, support and vulnerability that underpin this logic. The last part of the chapter examines the importance of trust in social work and the way in which it cuts through the practice agenda in a number of diverse ways, with institutionalised mechanisms of trust increasingly dominating the policy agenda. It is argued that the development of trust-based relations is more conducive to voluntary commitments and social proximity. The role and importance of voluntary agencies in social work are discussed in this context.

Chapter 4 examines the changing configurations of social work knowledge, intervention and value and the way changes in the macro-realm of government policy, collaborative work systems, and organisational policy translate to micro-levels of social work practice. It analyses the impact on perceptions of what counts as knowledge, the viability of direct work skills and intervention in social work. A core feature of the chapter charts the rise of empiricism in social work as related to changes in risk society and outlines various problems associated with this approach. This shift indicates a decline in intensive face-to-face casework and the rise of actuarialism in social work. Whilst this examines the way social work incrementally comes to resemble an executant and functional role that is accountable in moral and legal terms via the social handling of risk, the next chapter charts the emergence of 'technologies of care' that are developed to supplement and harden this shift towards actuarial social work.

'Technologies of care' are examined in Chapter 5 as core methods of intervention that are drawn from rational and efficiency-derived schemas for organising social work as well as rule-bound procedures for how it is carried out and delivered. In policy terms effective social work interventions are increasingly expected to mimic a technological panacea of codified categories, goal orientation and feedback loops. Examples of technologies of care such as care management; risk assessment and evaluation; evidence-based practice; decision pathway practice; networked information and communication technologies are examined.

Chapter 6 explores the relationship between risk and the management and organisation of social work. It shows how the managerialist imagination feeds on the idea of continuous improvement through quality assurance measures, audit and performance indicators. British policy directives in care management and social work organisations are outlined to show how risk regulation and neo-liberal market economics are inter-dependent elements in shaping management culture. Recent initiatives which herald the so-called learning organisation and knowledge management for social work are shown to fit this neo-liberal agenda of managed care. The crucial link between the effective management of risk and care mangement is made with the differing emphases on regulation, performance, audit and accountability. The arenas of health, criminal justice, education and social care are shown to be ones of constestation, with agencies inevitably pulling apart as much as pulling together.

The seventh and final chapter, 'The Practice of Value', draws together the preceding analysis in a conclusion that stresses the defining and distinctive strengths of social work. To the extent that social work has creditable aspects, as it plainly does, it is susceptible to being re-constructed. Social work is not ethically indifferent even against the tide of authoritarian politics and self-interest. It refuses to drop the notion that society can be a vehicle for the translation of private troubles into public concerns and the democratically generated search for community, solidarity and the good life. To set a new ethical course for social work based on core values we need to acknowledge that the tradition in which they arose has importantly gone astray. Social workers are shown to be committed to a particular form of ethical life based on 'strong evaluations'.

The new liberal state pragmatics of a post-9/11 world has encouraged a severing of value from practice in seeking to secure compliance with whatever 'security' policies any Western government sees fit to implement. Similarly, efficiency and reasonableness are shown to be too insubstantial, as normative standards and as ideals, to propel a robustly ethical vision of social work forward. A recognition of this increasing enervation of value where the world and ethical relations could otherwise meet, should be a call to engage with serious 'critical' theory in the sanctum of ethical practice, namely social work. In some very important respects social work can turn the neo-liberal economic doctrine on its head by emphasising care, compassion, solidarity and shared values. To this end the concluding chapter reflects on how values and social work may be brought together to take social work beyond itself and more importantly beyond its ever present possibility of slipping into a pragmatic yet unnecessary acquiescence in neo-liberal political rule.

Glossary of Key Concepts

There are a number of important concepts introduced in this book
that may be unfamiliar to some readers. This glossary helps define
some key terms and gives a sense of the orientation of the book.

actuarialism

A systematic method of risk assessment and profiling derived from
the financial insurance sector. It identifies who and which environments in society pose the greatest risk, such that they are targeted in
advance and the risk acted against. Actuarialism uses methods of
profiling which involve identifying clusters of risk in given environments or populations in the light of current technical knowledge. In
social work, actuarialism increasingly shapes interventions in work
with dangerous, challenging and unmotivated clients in fields such
as mental health, child protection and criminal justice.

anomie

The breakdown of the influence of social norms on individuals
within modern society. The weakening of community bonds, forms
of mutual reciprocity and shared values, such that individuals no
longer feel integrated into society.

blame culture

A culture in which, according to sociologist Frank Furedi, people are
increasingly pointing the finger of blame at each other and are no
longer prepared to accept risks. The 'no win [in litigation], no fee'
slogan perpetuated by television adverts, encouraging people to
make personal injury claims, reflects this culture. Furedi thinks this
produces a society of low moral expectations and narrowly defined
social norms, forcing people to constantly look over their shoulder.
It is ironic that whilst we are supposed to increasingly take responsibility for our own actions, there is plenty of evidence suggesting we
wish to point the finger of blame elsewhere. For some the blame for
obesity, for example, lies with the global fast-food industry rather
than with individual choices in eating habits. The number of
complaints received by social services has increased exponentially
over the past decade.

calculative reasoning

This concept has figured centrally in philosophical texts over the past century. Calculative reasoning is purposeful and practical and based on attempts to predict, estimate or count up definite results that are routinised in the social world. For example, the estimation of someone's final degree classification is based on calculative reasoning. Martin Heidegger, Friedrich Nietzsche and Max Weber used the term as a way of developing a critique of the modern age, pointing to the futility of relying on this way of thinking. Some Marxist writers, such as Antonio Gramsci and Georg Lukacs, used the term to describe the alienating effects of capitalism on everyday life and to describe the way we seek to 'reify' or dominate nature. We no longer see a mountain as a mountain but as something to be overcome. Heidegger distinguished between calculative and essential thinking to show how modern societies develop a 'world view' that is dominated by calculation, losing the creative vitality that life offers. In contemporary societies scientific methods and technology are wholly dependent on calculative reason, as are economic, organisational and strategic planning.

complexity

In complex societies our everyday experiences are formed by vast arrangements embedded in an immensely complicated array of dimensions, flows, relations, networks and information. Our modern societies are described as complex because of the speed of change, wider scope of possible choices, greater amounts of information to take into account, limited attention span and predictability problems with unstable environments. There are links with complexity and chaos theory.

decision analysis

An approach to decision making derived from formal mathematical methods, typically based on Bayesian probability theory, used to examine decisions under conditions of uncertainty. Used in medicine, for example, to evaluate clinical decision making.

ethics

The reflective inquiry into the way that people feel, think and behave with a view to formulating norms of conduct and the evaluation of character. Ethics is to be contrasted with morality, which concerns beliefs about what is good or bad, right or wrong. Applied ethics is the study of what kinds of standards can be applied in concrete situations and relationships. Ethical meanings are historical. We know, for example, that the concept of 'good' did not originate out of an altruistic concern for those to whom goodness is shown, but as something that is noble and independent of doing things for others.

empiricism

A doctrine in philosophy and applied science which affirms that all knowledge is based on observable experience, and denies the possibility of spontaneous ideas or a priori thought. It is the opposite of idealism, which claims that behaviour is shaped primarily by the active ideas that exist as mind-dependent categories.

epistemology

A branch of philosophy dealing with problems surrounding the theory of knowledge. Epistemology is concerned with the definition of knowledge and related concepts; the sources and criteria of knowledge; the kinds of knowledge which are possible and the degree to which each is certain; and the exact relation between the one who knows and the object known. Epistemology also investigates the justification, legitimation and validity of various knowledge claims.

evidence-based practice

A methodology borrowed from medicine and health care, introduced into social work in the late 1990s. There are different enclaves within the evidence-based movement in social work which to a greater or lesser extent appeal to the strictures of positivist science (see *positivism*). It is argued that interventions can be systematised, objectivised and rationally planned in an incremental way such that decision making is rendered more effective and practitioners made more accountable. Whilst the concept caught the imagination of managers and policy makers it hasn't really taken off in practice, and due to limited resources its implementation has been very patchy. Some social care organisations have shied away from using the term, preferring the more open-ended concepts of research-minded practice, evidence-informed decision making or more vaguely evidence-influenced practice.

fateful moments

These are critical moments at which consequential decisions have to be taken or courses of action initiated by people that may leave them feeling helpless, resulting in the need for support.

governmentality

A concept introduced by the French historian and philosopher Michel Foucault in his later writings. Governmentality is linked to concepts of political regulation and social control. It refers to the way we think about governing others and ourselves in the most minute detail and across a range of contexts. Typically it entails principles that lead to population management and control, involving ways of accounting for people. For Foucault this is a historically specific programme in which the exercise of power changes from being primarily concerned with institutional control to the regulation of everyday life. Governmentality is a more active form of power than institutional control because it concentrates on regulating individuals from the 'inside'. Power is de-centered, with individuals playing an active role in their own self-governance. Dieting and fitness regimes are good examples. Forms of knowledge and expertise are developed to facilitate governmentality. In highlighting these new techniques of power, French philosopher Gilles Deleuze has described our contemporary situation as one of 'societies of control'.

heuristics

Heuristics uses past experience to make educated guesses about the present. These are simple, economic rules of thumb which have been proposed to explain how people make decisions, come to judgments and solve problems, typically when facing complex issues or having incomplete information. These rules work well under most circumstances, but in certain cases lead to systematic cognitive biases. Much of the work of discovering heuristics in human decision makers was developed by the cognitive scientists Amos Tversky and Daniel Kahneman.

ideology

A constellation of ideas, values and beliefs that reflect the interests of dominant groups in society. Ideology is used to manipulate the way people think and to legitimate positions of power and privilege amongst dominant groups.

individualism

A political philosophy derived from libertarianism that promotes the rights, responsibilities and choices of the individual. It opposes state intervention for social well-being and collective struggle. Individualism counsels us to be opportunistic, acquisitive and selfish. This term is sometimes used interchangeably with that of 'individualistic relations'.

late modernity

The current phase of development of modern institutions in Western societies, marked by the radicalising and globalising of basic traits of modernity. Rather than seeing society as having progressed to become a new type (for example, post-modern), it is argued that we are simply living in a more mature state of modernity. In this book the term is often used interchangeably with those of 'reflexive modernity' and 'advanced capitalism'. Sociologists have suggested that the phase of late modernity began in the 1960s in Western societies.

life planning

This term, derived from the work of sociologist Anthony Giddens, refers to the strategic adoption of lifestyle options, organised in terms of the individual's projected lifespan, and normally focused through the notion of risk. In some important respects social work is primarily an activity concerned with life planning for individuals, families or groups during fateful moments (q.v.), times when they feel most vulnerable and when support is most needed.

neo-liberalism

Neo-liberalism is a set of political programmes and economic policies that have become widespread during the last 25 years in modern societies. The neo-liberal programme has been globally imposed by powerful financial institutions like the International Monetary Fund (IMF), the World Bank and the Inter-American Development Bank. The main ideological strands of neo-liberalism can be defined as: the rule of the market; cutting public expenditure on social services and reducing the safety net for the poor; de-regulating systems that diminish profit; privatising public enterprises; and eliminating the concepts of the public good and of community, replacing them with those of individual responsibility and choice (see *individualism*).

ontology

A branch of philosophy dealing with problems of the nature of being and kinds of human existence. It specifies the most fundamental substances and structures out of which the human world is made and the foundational categories of existence. If epistemology asks questions about 'how do we know?', ontology asks questions about 'what is it to be?'.

ontological security

A sense of continuity and order as regards people and events, including those not directly within the perceptual environment of the individual. Habits and daily routines help give us a sense of ontological security and well-being.

phenomenology

A mainstream perspective in philosophy that emphasises the importance of lived experience. This lived character, as a constituting process, consists not simply in what is felt or undergone by people across the passage of time but also of how these passing moments are meaningfully accentuated and preserved. Meaning does not simply lie in the experience, but in those moments which are grasped reflectively. Phenomenology highlights the significance of creativity, imagination and art (see Bachelard's *Poetics of Space*, 1969). Important thinkers in this tradition are Gaston Bachelard, Edmund Husserl, Martin Heidegger, Emmanuel Levinas, Paul Ricoeur, Jean-Paul Sartre and Maurice Merleau-Ponty. To date there has been no comprehensive modelling applying phenomenology to social work.

positivism

The epistemological doctrine that physical and social reality are independent of those who observe them, and that observations of these realities, if unbiased, constitute scientific knowledge.

practice of value

An approach to social work practice that attempts to re-orientate it by emphasising the centrality of values in guiding intervention and social ethics in the cultivation of professional practitioners. This perspective maintains there is a strong link between how practitioners reach professional judgements, the ethics they adhere to and the way that social work can multiply power enhancing 'good encounters'. The practice of value stresses the importance of caring, virtue and recognition as antidotes to extreme individualism (q.v.). It militates against such professionalised moral codes and obligations of duty as those laid down in British Association of Social Workers and General Social Care Council literature.

privatisation of risk

A current trend taking place involving the breakdown of the public sphere and the dismantling of civic safety nets, whereby individuals are increasingly expected to take responsibility for risks. Bauman (1999) thinks that the global neo-liberal agenda (see *neo-liberalism*), with its unchecked liberalisation of trade, privatisation of public services, 'flexible' short-term labour contracts and monopoly on new capital markets, renders people in a state of constant insecurity about the future.

reflexive self

The process in which self-identity is constituted by the reflexive ordering of self-narratives, or 'self talk'. It literally means a referring back to oneself. The reflexive self comes into prominence during late modern times (see *late modernity*). It mirrors the developmental phase of society because it involves a 'turning inwards' that entails tense confrontation. It is important to recognise that the human subject in possession of a self, free will and conscience is not a natural given, but is a result of historical and social evolution. 'The self' is a relatively recent invention. The *reflexive* self is quite different from the *reflective* self that is commonly referred to in the social work literature.

risk assessment

The identification of risk, the measurement of risk, and the process of prioritising risks. Its methods are based on strong notions of predictability and calculation that a future event is likely to occur (see *calculative reasoning*). These partly rely on existing scientific knowledge, which is often provided by experts. In social work the assessment of risk often lacks scientific rigour and may or may not be modelled in a satisfactory way. Some uncertainties can be reduced by further research while others remain irreducible. Risk assessment is pervaded by value-laden assumptions and is often used as a rationing device that excludes some from service provision.

risk governance

This refers to the sum of political, economic, legal, scientific and technical components that allow the operation of hazardous activities and uncertain conditions. Increasingly risk assessment and management take place in the context of a global governance system where specific organisations or people are entrusted with the task of assessing and managing the risks.

risk management

A systematic approach to reducing loss of life, of financial resources, of staff availability, of safety, or of reputation. It involves a structured process for analysing social care organisations' exposure to risk and determining how best to handle such exposure.

risk society

Ulrich Beck coined this concept in his celebrated book *Risk Society* (1992). It refers to a particular phase in modern society in which new risks or hazards emerge as by-products of science, technology and industry. Beck divides modern civilisation into three epochs: pre-industrial society, industrial society, and global risk society. In risk society we are preoccupied with regulating the future, normalising things and bringing them under our control. According to Anthony Giddens, in the Middle Ages and in traditional cultures there was no concept of risk. In contemporary societies, 'mad cow disease' (BSE) and global warming are good examples of manufactured risk. The failure of experts to deal with risk leads to a paradoxical situation whereby new and ever more scientific methods are developed to control and counter the risks that society itself has manufactured. Following September 11th with the so-called 'War on Terror' we have seen how the language of risk and security is mobilised to play a dominant role in goverment policy and in the media. Risk society theorists claim that contemporary life is saturated with considerations of risk, resulting in increased anxiety, uncertainty and even emotional breakdown.

short-termism

This term was introduced by American sociologist Richard Sennett to show how we are entering a new phase of capitalism. Work which was once considered stable and predictable becomes increasingly contingent, and as people change jobs more frequently employees are told there is 'no long term'. Short-termism pervades many aspects of social life, from how long people stay together in intimate relationships to how long they reside in a particular community. Speed dating and tactical voting are emblematic of short-termism in modern societies.

social capital

This concept is linked to notions of trust and reciprocity. Social capital refers to those stocks of social trust, norms and networks that people can draw upon in local contexts to solve common problems. It is an informal, normative resource that promotes co-operation and reciprocity between two or more individuals. Social work makes a positive contribution by increasing or diversifying the stock of social capital held by clients.

solidarity

This term was introduced into English when the French Chartist Convention was translated in 1848. It was popularised in the social science literature by the French sociologist Emile Durkheim, who distinguished between 'organic' and 'mechanical' forms of solidarity, to highlight differences between modern and traditional societies. For radical thinkers, solidarity is regarded as a fundamental ethical value of social resistance which obliges people to support the struggles of others.

state, the

The state is a specialised type of political organisation in which a government has sovereign power. It is characterised by a full-time, professional workforce (police, army, judges, social workers) that exercises authority over a defined territory. The first known states were created in ancient times in Egypt, Mesopotamia, India and China, but it is only in modern times that states have almost completely displaced alternative, 'stateless' forms of political organisation. For centuries political theorists have debated the role of the state, its monopoly on political violence and the legitimacy of its political rule. Critical theorists claim the advanced capitalist state is a parasitical agency that seeks to capture, exploit and control its citizenry.

technical rationality

This term is often used interchangeably with 'instrumental rationality' and linked to the concept of calculative reason (q.v.). According to the historian and sociologist Max Weber, modern societies have developed a new system of rationalisation in which the practical application of knowledge is used to achieve specific desired ends. Weber was concerned that technical rationality was becoming more dominant in Western society than other types of rationality, extending to many fields, including science, military training, the law, sport and even choices about suitable partners. This is sometimes referred to as an 'outcome mentality' whereby rules, regulations and procedures prioritise the ends to be achieved rather than the means used to obtain them. In policy documents you will see how the language of efficiency, effectiveness and 'what works' often constitutes the central categories. Assessment of risk or need in social work is governed by functional forms of technical rationality.

technologies of care

A term used to describe an emerging constellation of techniques, methods and apparatus in social work that combine to de-skill practitioners and reduce their professional autonomy. Technologies of care typically entail processes whereby local skills are expropriated into abstract systems and re-organised in light of technical methods and knowledge. As top-down instruments they impose on social work the character of a function, with practitioners as low-level administrators dealing largely with assessment.

trust

Trust is confidence in the reliability of another person or organisation. It involves the vesting of confidence made on the basis either of reputation over time, or of a 'leap of faith' which lacks or ignores information. Given that reliance on someone or something thus develops, it is a source of risk. eBay, the internet technology for buying or selling things, is a good example that demonstrates the interplay of trust and risk.

virtue ethics

A normative theory according to which all moral value is derived from the character of moral agents. In emphasising a person's character and the way they reach judgements, it is often seen as running contrary to rule-bound, duty-bound or guiding conceptions of moral principles. Derived from the classical writings of Aristotle, virtues are admirable human characteristics or dispositions that can be learned, and which distinguish good people from bad. Virtue ethicists emphasise an aesthetics of existence by stressing the importance of achieving a meaningful life.

1

Social Work, Risk Society and Modernity

Introduction

The concept of risk is one of the most significant in modern times. We live in a world saturated with and preoccupied by risk. Despite unparalleled degrees of social stability and affluence, we are living through a period of acute personal insecurity, anxiety and change. The speed of change, pace of life, choices available and vast flows of information undercut solid foundations in our risk-dominated lives. Many people find it increasingly difficult to trust others or even themselves. Our decisions are often fraught with perceived threats and we wonder what will turn out for the best. We are constantly reflecting on what to do next in our ceaseless chase after success and recognition. In a world of lifestyle consumerism the practical organisation of our daily and future activities has become a preoccupation. Mass society has resulted in an enormous pluralisation of needs, desires, choices and identities. Constructing personal life-plans or having other people help us has become central to our way of coping with life. They help us satisfy our need for fulfilment, map the kind of relations we seek and provide our personal identity with an anchor. This prepares us for decisions and choices during what Giddens calls 'fateful moments'. Life-plans also help us shape a chosen life as a meaningful and authentic one based on our own intrinsic potentials within a vast range of potential. Life planning is multi-layered and complex and may focus on work, career, family, children, parenting, love, holidays, leisure and investment. There are so many decisions to make, choices to be had and information to absorb that modern life has become very complex. Sometimes we need help because we don't know which way to turn, with things threatening to overwhelm us.

The uncertainties of risk in modern society have reached all levels. In *Culture of Fear* Frank Furedi (1997) documents the 'explosion of risks' with which society is increasingly preoccupied. We fear man-made or manufactured as well as natural risks, like tsunamis and earthquakes. Since September 11th, security has become a key term by which politicians justify all kinds of authoritarian legislation in their 'fight against terror'. Risks of terrorism to Westerners and Western assets in Arab countries, and in Chechnya, Kosovo, Bosnia, Northern Ireland and the Basque region, to name a few, as well as fears of increases in al-Qaeda activity as a result of the Iraq war continue to create panic and fear. Fears of biological and germ warfare and 'dirty bombs' are at an all time high level, with 'global terrorism risk maps' now available to help people identify key risk locations of potential terrorist activity. Global warming represents a major risk to our planet, way of life and environment, with scientific data confirming that the Earth's climate is rapidly changing as an effect of carbon dioxide pollution caused by power plants and automobiles that traps heat in the atmosphere. It's projected that flooding will affect coastal areas, sea levels will rise, droughts and wild-fires will occur more frequently, heat waves will be common and more intense and some species will be pushed into extinction. Tony Blair, the British Prime Minister, admitted that he was 'scared' by briefings from the government's chief scientists about the likely effects of climate change and global warning. The Kyoto Agreement appears to be woefully inadequate in preventing the risks of global warming. Pesiticide residues, low-level radiation, electro-magnetic fields and nuclear waste continue to cause anxiety. In Britain 'super bugs' that are resistant to common antibiotics are a major risk for patients in hospitals and nursing homes. People are scared of contracting the MRSA super bug and families are being warned about the risks of staying in hospitals. 'Mad cow disease' or BSE is not confined to cattle and the recent crisis in Britain showed that humans can get a similiar disease called Variant CJD from eating cattle products that affects the brain, neural tissues and spinal cord ulimately leading to death. Calculating and trying to manage risk, which often people have little knowledge of, has become one of our main preoccupations in modern societies.

A central theme of this book is to locate social work within the contours of a complex system called modern risk society. Here I start from the proposition that any explanation of the nature of social work is dependent on a close reading of risk as a significant feature of modern societies. Instead of separating social work from modernity, whether deliberately or by default, the importance of the relationship between welfare expertise and socio-political forms makes it essential to insist on them being read together. Given the inseparability of reflection on social work and on modernity it is helpful to pursue an exposition of the transformations of modernity as its contents are animated by social work. We must try to understand social work within the preconstituted frame of modernity at the moment at which social work constitutes and renews itself. This view avoids reducing social work to a passive set of predispositions that are imposed from outside by discourses, constructions, structures etc. – in short, a general realist history. This reductive social constructivism which is prevalent in theorising social work regards it as a subject that is obligated by the 'something' of discourse without ever having given its consent and without being consulted in the matter. It's my contention that social work actively shapes itself and the propositions, relations and things around it. This book tries to make sense of both how social work is formed within the context of contemporary society and how it reinforces or refutes dimensions within late modernity. If within social work lies the possibility of a re-constructed ethics that stands against dominant political rule, as is argued in the final chapter, then we need to conceive of social work as *creatively animating and not merely being determined by dominant modern discourses.*

Modernity and its institutions, including social work, are represented by a relational process that differentiates and unifies opposites in a continuous movement. Thus social work is analysed as a process that continuously recreates itself and embodies itself in differentiating and constraining structures of modernity. The process of differentiation also occupies a central place in the way social work plans, orders and organises the life of clients. Here key elements of modernity are transmitted into the way social work develops *methods of social regulation, calculating and planning*, as well as in providing security for people. This modernity, or what I call late modernity, in seeking to reflect itself through the lens of social work cannot be apprehended in a straightforward way. Instead part of the argument of this book suggests that we are dealing with a thoroughly ambivalent modernity. Throughout the book this notion of ambivalence as a complex, open, chaotic and dynamic structure in modern risk society is contrasted with the mechanical perspective, with a deterministic, ordered and rational structure that is governed by predictive laws and regularities.

What Is Modernity?

Over the past decade a plethora of books have been devoted to the topic of 'modernity'. It's important to account for this complex cultural system before discussing what I've called the reflexive ordering of human experience as it relates to risk society. This is because it is within the larger story of modernity and its unfolding that risk society is formed and properly understood.

It's my contention that it's difficult to understand social work in risk society unless some general principles that define modernity are agreed upon. Furthermore, it's impossible to understand social work and the likely changes it will undergo without discussing its relation to modernity. Social work is a modern activity. Considerations of social work and modernity are therefore intimately bound together. Not surprisingly, therefore, I've argued elsewhere that the development of modernity is closely tied to the emergence of social work in late Victorian England (Webb, 2007). This relation will be a key consideration in what follows; for now though, I want to start with a basic but difficult question. What is this idea of modernity that has been so central to our way of life over the past three hundred years or more?

Broadly modernity refers to forms of social life and organisation which developed in Europe from about the late seventeenth century onwards and which over time became global in their impact (Giddens, 1990). The time-scale in the formation of modernity has been slow and uneven. It is difficult to establish an exact starting point for the onset of modernity because it is not the outcome of a single process. Thus the precise date when modernity occurred is debatable. Some writers argue that the seeds of modernity were set in the Italian Renaissance, whilst others pin its origins more closely to the early eighteenth century Enlightenment period of thought (Adorno & Horkheimer, 1979). Until this time what passed as authoritative knowledge was dominated by the Christian churches. Enlightenment philosophers challenged the dominant religious view of the world and began to redefine cultural, ethical and politically important ideas.

Theorising Modernity

Let's begin by laying out a few more broad markers about the nature of modernity. Modernist thinking is preoccupied with ideas of progress. Futher on we shall see how preoccupations with progress infect our thinking about and practice of social work. Generally, this preoccupation derives from the idea that technical reason and scientific knowledge can be used to make human life more fulfilling, free from injustice and the constraints of nature. Modernity is a period of rapid change, especially social, political, cultural and economic transformations. Few would deny the links between capitalism and modernity. But modernity isn't a simple one-track development. Instead it includes massive changes in urban life, industrialisation, wealth, democratisation, science and technology. Modernity also signalled the rise in a secular individualistic culture. It is a time marked by increased differentiation between people, which results in the emergence of social class as an indicator of wealth, status, and prestige. New mechanisms of regulation and discipline were imposed on people who resisted social inequities. But modernity is also a time where questions of liberty, freedom and democracy abound in the political arena. Democratisation is a central aspect in the development of modernity. Transformations of modernity involve people attempting to redefine their social position and struggle to obtain greater freedoms, liberties and rights. The Women's Movement and the Black Consciousness Movement in America are examples of this progressive modern trend. The American sociologist Edward Shils describes what he calls the virtues of modernity as follows:

> There is merit in the 'modernity' of society, apart from any other virtues it may have. Being modern is being 'advanced' and being advanced means being rich, free of the encumbrances of familial authority, religious authority and deferentiality. It means being rational and 'rationalized'. (1981, p. 288)

These different evaluations of modernity begin to capture what I have called *the ambivalence of modernity* that is contrasted with earlier types of society. By ambivalence I mean that the contemporary world is sprinkled with natural and cultural locations that have the power to both 'enchant' and 'disenchant' (Elliot, 1996). Ambivalence is not to be understood logically as a tautology or contradiction but as a dramatic tension. It is in this sense that social work's equivocal identity is addressed later on in the book.

According to Giddens the best way to understand modernity is to distinguish it from more traditional societies:

> Modernity destroys tradition. Collaboration between modernity and tradition was crucial in the earlier phases of modern social development, but this phase was ended by the emergence of reflexive modernization or high modernity. The reflexivity of modern life consists of the fact that social practices are constantly examined and reformed in the light of incoming information about those very practices, thus altering their character.
> (www.lse.ac.uk/Giddens/FAQs.htm#ReflexQ1)

Two phases of modernity are identified in the sociological literature. Giddens refers to the early stage as classical modernity and the later stage as late or reflexive modernity. Before going on to examine the specific nature of reflexive modernity there are important features of classical modernity that need to be unpicked. In *Critique of Modernity* (1995) Alain Touraine offers an account that emphasises the importance of reason, order and rationality. 'What could provide a basis for this correspondence between a scientific culture, an ordered society and free individuals, if not the triumph of *reason*. Reason alone could establish a correspondence between human action and the ordered world' (1995, p. 1). This account owes a great deal to Max Weber's theory of modernity. Here the emphasis is on the technical rationalisation of the life-world in the development of modernity. This is chiefly driven by scientific and technical progress through the steady accumulation of knowledge or what I referred to in 'Setting the Scene' as the search for absolute knowledge. The dominance of technology is implied in Max Weber's pessimistic conception of an 'iron cage' of rationalisation, although he did not specifically connect it to technology. Jacques Ellul, another major substantive theorist, makes that link explicit, arguing that 'technical phenomena' have become the defining characteristic of all modern societies regardless of political ideology. 'Technique', he asserts, 'has become autonomous' (1967, p. 6). Or, in Marshall McLuhan's more dramatic phrase, technology has reduced us to being the 'sex organs of the machine world' (1964, p. 46).

Other writers prefer to stress a combination of structural dimensions in the formation of modernity. The influential political theorist Agnes Heller, for example, identifies multiple sources that make up modernity and nominates three fundamental logics – capitalism, industrialisation and democracy. For Heller these logics form a constellation that is complex and conflictual in nature. Similarly,

Touraine suggests modernity is exemplified by a tense relationship between *rationalisation* and *subjectivation* (1995, p. 5). The tension can be characterised as a boundary between, on the one hand, society's bid for self-completion through rationalisation, and on the other hand, the individual's drive for actualisation through the trajectory of self-identity. This tension is crucial in forming the remit of social work. For Touraine it appears that the tension, between objective and subjective rationality, is insoluble. As we shall see throughout this book social work is often caught between the insoluble tensions of these types of rationality. There is, however, a crucial piece missing from Touraine's characterisation of modernity that is referred to in the literature as the *formation of modern experience*.

Modernity as a Way of Life

To understand modernity we need to account for the experience of modernity as a 'whole way of life' which is distinctive from premodern times. Whereas the traditional fabric of experience was governed by principles of continuity, order and repetition, the shocks and uncertainties of modern life disrupt familiar patterns of experience. Modernity can thus be conceived as a particular type of lived experience in modern societies. So whilst modernity refers to industrialisation and urbanisation it also refers to the recognition of consciousness – or what I call below reflexivity – as a force in its own right. It was perhaps Georg Simmel and Walter Benjamin who above all others initiated a concern with the relation between subjectivity and modern life. In the opening passage of 'The metropolis and mental life' (1971/1903), Simmel provides a definition of modernity that contrasts sharply with Weber's:

> The essence of modernity as such is psychologism, the experiencing and interpretation of the world in terms of the reactions of inner life and indeed as an inner world, the dissolution of fixed contents in the fluid element of the soul, from which all that is substantive is filtered and whose forms are merely forms of motion. (cited in Frisby, 1985b, p. 46)

Here Simmel illustrates the rise of reflexive individualism in modern societies. As Frisby explains, 'The external world becomes part of our inner world. In turn, the substantive elements of the external world are reduced to a ceaseless flux and its fleeting, fragmentary and contradictory moments are all incorporated into our inner life' (1985b, p. 45). So the self becomes an inter-subjectively rooted reality that is continuously reproduced in the transactions of modern social life. The experience of modernity means that social practices are endlessly made and unmade through the flows of social exchange and the rich tapestry of fleeting transactions. Thus whilst individuals still face the more traditional contingencies of time and place they also cope with a radical openness that is no longer decreed by a given station in life. The accompanying uncertainties can lead to a profound sense of emptiness and despair as well as new possibilities of freedom. This is why the concept of trust, examined in Chapter 3, is so important to Anthony Giddens' theory of self-identity. In a world dominated by risk and uncertainty trust helps people stave off the insecurities of life and gives them a sense of continuity through the routinisation of intimate relations. Marshall Berman captures the essence of this ambivalent experience of modernity:

> To be modern is to find ourselves in an environment that promises us adventure, power, joy, growth, transformation of ourselves and the world – and at the same time, that threatens to destroy everything we have, everything we know, every-thing we are. Modern experiences cut across all boundaries of geography and ethnicity, of class and nationality, of religion and ideology. (1983, p. 15)

For Simmel the metropolis as the site of cultural crisis is summarised as 'the atrophy of individual culture through the hyper-trophy of objective culture' (1971/1903, p. 338). The experience of modernity is thus reflected in the increasing differentiation of specialised activities and the highly individualised culture of experi-ence.

In one crucial respect the experience of modernity, analysed by writers such as Simmel, is a reaction against structuralism in the social sciences. For Simmel what mattered most in social analysis was an understanding of the way that contingent lived experiences constitute social structure. As we shall see below, this shift is consistent with the reflexive modernity perspective in sociology. E.P. Thompson's classic *The Making of the English Working Class* (1968) is a good example of such a reaction, whereby Thompson refuses to regard social class as a 'thing' but instead conceives of this key concept as part of social and cultural formations (see pp. 12–13). In Thompson's conception the working class is to be conceived not by the existence of deterministic structural relations of production and rationalisation but by the particular experience of class-consciousness and particular forms of organisation. Of these structuralist explanations of working class history Thompson says, 'they tend to obscure the agency of working people and the degree to which they contributed by conscious efforts, to the making of history' (p. 13). Thompson derives his meaning of class in cultural and political elements rather than purely economic or structural relations of class. He's not denying the importance of capitalism as it contributes to the changing experience of modernity but highlights a materialist theory of cultural formations. Raymond Williams concurs with Thompson in arguing that the experience of modernity is distinct from industrialisation. Williams claims that culture makes the crucial difference: 'Where culture meant a habit or state of mind, or the body of intellectual and moral activities it means a whole way of life' (1966, p. 18). The experience of modernity reveals a distinctive orientation and purpose towards the social world. This orientation, however, is permanently undercut by the contingencies of the modern world. As Claude Lefort notes:

> Modern society and the modern individual are constituted by the experience of the dissolution of the ultimate markers of certainty . . . their dissolution inaugurates an adventure – and it is constantly threatened by the resistance it provokes – in which the foundations of power, the foundations of rights and the foundations of knowledge are all called into question. (1988, p. 179)

The experience of modernity signals an ever increasing openness and contingency in social life. This led Karl Marx to recognise that 'All that is solid melts into air.' If nothing can be taken for granted modern society is thus able to confront itself through critical reason. In catching this spirit of modernity Marx recognised that its roller coaster changes and obsession with progress reveal a tense ambivalence.

In summary, the experience of modernity is suspect and fragile, and subject to endless interpretations, changes and challenges. We'll see why this results in *practices of ordering, calculating, planning and regulating* becoming increasingly necessary in modern life and how these are translated into social work practice. Analysing how elements of the experience of modernity are translated into social work will provide a better understanding of its contemporary nature. It will also give us a deeper appreciation of the changes that have helped formed social work at different times. A rough periodisation of transformations in social work through the lens of modernity can be characterised as follows:

Period		Type of social activity	Focus
Classical modernity	(1850–1935)	Charity and philanthropic work	Improvement
Modernity	(1945–1979)	Universal state-sponsored social work	Need
Late modernity	(1979–present)	Neo-liberal social work	Risk

The discussion that follows concentrates on the elements involved in this transformation from modernity to late modernity and the major reconceptualisations of knowledge, practices and values it entails for social work. The book concentrates on the social handling of risk and identifies social work's pivotal role in risk management and life planning in risk society. It confirms Hazel Kemshall's (2002) view that the role of social work has shifted from a preoccupation with need to one with risk. In fact risk and need are often conflated in assessing and determining eligibility criteria for service users. We'll see that this blending of risk and need criteria is partly a reflection of a new hybridised form of risk as social governance in late modernity (Hannah-Moffat, 2002). This is sometimes referred to as the risk-dependency model of social work whereby resources are rationed according to the prioritisation given to clients for eligibility for service resources (see Means, 2000).

In mapping these transformations social work is best conceived as a politically mediated territory. According to Deleuze & Guattari's (1987) concept of territory, it is understood as the environment of a group that cannot itself be objectively located, but is constituted by the patterns of interaction through which the group secures a certain stability, sense of place and location. I'm not suggesting any clean lines or definite breaks between one period and the next in social work. The processes of change are often minuscule, resembling small dislocations, fractures and ruptures. Elements of a previous stage are abstracted, included or subsumed in the next via a process of recodification (see Deleuze & Guattari, 1987). Here social work is conceived in terms of spatial and temporal flux whereby contractions and attenuations disperse near points of practice and bring far distant points of practice into proximity with one another. Such a model confirms Abbott's description of social work as a 'profession of interstitiality' whereby various territorial boundaries are constantly evolving and competing with other professional knowledge claims. As a refigured territory he argues that 'the function of social work, like those of other professions, emerged from a continuous conflict and change' (1995, p. 552).

Abbott (1995) gives examples of such aspects of territorial conflicts in which social work gained or lost ground in 'sub-fields' to neighbouring professions, such as health and education.

Morality and Modernity

Modernity not only involves fragmentary and fleeting experiences, often induced by information overload, but also signals the prospect of moral impoverishment. It is logical to think that if the foundations of modernity are derived from new ways of moral thinking then the demise of modernity is likely to be based on the overcoming of that morality. This was Durkheim's major theme in analysing changes from organic to mechanical forms of solidarity which led to the functional differentation of labour in modern society. Peter Wagner (1994) summarises the Durkheimian position as follows:

> The development of modern society entailed the risk of moral impoverishment, mainly due to two phenomena. The inevitable decline of unquestioned faith eroded a source which could provide foundations for moral behaviour. And it is true that recurring face-to-face interaction is the basis for the solidarity supporting insight to the human likeness of the other, such interactions would be decreasingly relevant in mass societies integrated on the scale of a nation. (p. 65)

Here a central question is how modern societies manage to sustain ethical relations if society lacks solidarity. Indeed, this is a central issue in the concluding chapter of this book where the difference between 'strong' and 'weak' evaluators is discussed. As Wagner argues, modernity allows for the 'self-cancellation' of imposed moral standards and responsibilities. The threat of self-cancellation means that values have to be reflexively reshaped in the face of uncertainty. We'll see how in some key respects social work can be regarded as strategic response to the decline in face-to-face solidarity as well issues of moral uncertainty. It is claimed that adherence to an ethical stance in social work is far more radical than it seems in a society that is permeated with calculative reason, material self-interest and mass consumption. Indeed, the legitimacy of social work is shown to rest on exhortations that betray an ethical intent rather than a set of political or empirical possibilities. I refer to this as the 'practice of value' and identify distinctive elements that legitimate and validate social work.

Reflexive Modernity and Risk Society

Risk society, according to the sociologists Ulrich Beck and Anthony
Giddens, is the society we live in today. But what is risk? A loose
definition is that risk is the recognition and assessment of the uncertainty as to what to do, with risk judgement being the degree of
distance a course of action may be at from certain success. The
concept of risk thus provides the basis for understanding the relation
between judgement and uncertainty. Placed within the context of
society, risk captures the idea that unexpectability conditions the
very structure of events and circumstance. For the individual this
means being faced with choices, courses of action and knowledge
that often lack supporting norms, conditions and expectations. We
are forced to reflect, use our own judgement and make decisions
where reflection wasn't previously required. In their seminal work
Giddens and Beck refer to this condition as reflexive modernity.

Let's try and unpack this knotty concept of reflexive modernity. For
Beck and Giddens reflexive modernity is an advanced stage of modernity or what is sometimes called late modernity. According to Beck in
his influential book *Risk Society* (1992) reflexive modernity is different from modern industrial societies. He outlines the basic argument
as follows: 'Just as modernization dissolved the structure of feudal
society in the nineteenth century and produced the industrial society,
modernization today is dissolving industrial society and another
modernity is coming into being' (p. 10). The other 'new' modernity is
called 'reflexive' and is distinguished from classical or industrial
modernity. In industrial society, according to Beck, the production of
risk is subordinate to the production of wealth, to the extent, as Dean
(1999) says, 'that risks are taken to be predictable and limited but
necessary side-effects of technical and economic progress. Risks are a
matter for the experts and thus for scientific legitimation' (p. 181).

Risk is not a new phenomenon. What has changed significantly is
the reconfiguration of risk with the emergence of reflexive modernity. For Beck reflexive modernity means the self-confrontation with
the effects of risk society. Modernity, as a reflexive social order,
'manufactures' its own (i.e. internally referential) risks and uncertainties in a different way to previous times. The reflexive monitoring of risk is intrinsic to personal and institutionalised risk processes.
Delanty (1999) summarises the key differences between reflexive
and classical modernity in terms of risk. In reflexive modernity or
risk society, risks are abstract and de-personalised and are therefore

not immediately observable; risks are global as opposed to being territorially specific; risks are contrasted to dangers and natural hazards in that they are made by society; risks cannot be limited and are therefore not insurable or compensatable. Let's now turn to a closer inspection of the concept of reflexivity.

Reflexive Selves and Social Systems

Beck constructs a developmental model of modern societies in which the tensions of classical modernity pave the way for reflexive modernity. It's important to recognise that reflexivity is as much a part of social systems as it is of individual cognition. Thus in our understanding of social work we need to acknowledge that we are dealing with a reflexive culture or systems of reflexivity and not just individual reflexivity. A reflexive system, in general, generates an output as a function of an input. The establishment of reflexive systems in late modernity is best considered as an acculturation process that requires a new discipline among the carrying subjects. The reflexivity has to be developed into a communicative competence by controlling emotional and affective layers as well as confronting risk as a matter of personal responsibility.

Let us tarry with this notion of reflexive selves a little because it's a difficult and obscure concept. There's nothing new about the concept of reflexivity. Adam Smith's *The Theory of Moral Sentiments*, first published in 1759, was dealing with something very similar in his considerations of ethical character. He wrote, 'We must imagine ourselves not the actors but the spectators of our own character and conduct and consider how these would affect us when viewed from this station' (1974, p. 109). We'll see below that this is why it's important to connect reflexivity to aspects of risk to properly understand social work in modern societies. The reflexive self calls itself into question. In the process of self-confrontation individuals critically suspend their own certainty in questioning their identities and life-existence. Scolding oneself over poor judgement is a simple example of reflexive processes at work. Giddens summarises reflexivity of the self as follows:

> The reflexive project of self, which consists in the sustaining of coherent, yet continuously revised, biographical narratives, takes places in the context of multiple choice as filtered through abstract systems. In modern social life, the notion of lifestyle takes on a particular significance. (1991b, p. 5)

Reflexivity conjures up an image of an incessant contest with self and others. The reflexive process is inter-subjective in the sense that individuals monitor their own and others' behaviour, not as isolated acts but as instances of shared understanding of how to make sense of a complex life. Their monitoring is not just a passive check but is strategic, allowing them to order the rules of interaction and challenge them in doing so. For Anthony Elliot (1996) this process is referred to as 'reflexive scanning'. Risk society obliges us to be reflexive and this in turn requires individuals to face choice, freedom and responsibility. For those who fail new forms of technical planning, calculation and expert mediation, such as social work, are introduced to structure identity and develop systems of competence and efficiency.

Reflexivity is the ability of the individuals of a social system to reflect on and evaluate both their conception of the system and their role in it and to choose activities according to their own reflexive evaluation. Reflexivity is a turning back on oneself and a form of self-evaluation within the contingencies and uncertainties of risk society (Lawson, 1985). As Dean (1999) usefully notes, 'To speak of reflexivity is not to say that society has become more reflective or thoughtful or necessarily better informed about decision-making. Rather it is to say that modernity finds itself in a reflexive state of "self confrontation" ' (p. 181). For the purposes of this exposition it's important to understand the difference between reflexivity and reflectivity. We are not dealing with what Schon calls the 'reflective practitioner' in this sense. Reflexivity means a confrontation with self-identity. In social work terms if a reflective practitioner is one who thinks carefully and critically about her or his own practice, a reflexive practitioner is engaged in radical confrontation with the very ethical basis and legitimation of practice and self-involvement. In other words, as we shall see, reflexive practice introduces an important moral dimension into social work that is lacking in the reflective practitioner literature.

It is within the context of the reflexive project of self as part of the logic of late modernity that Giddens develops the significance of what he calls the 'pure relationship'. Face-work or intimacy based on recurring social proximity and recognition, such as friendship, become key sites for the establishment of trust and security. We no longer rely on kinship, religion or even family because with late modernity the nature of inter-personal intimacy has changed. Pure relationships occur largely within the domains of sexuality, romance, friendship and marriage. Opening ourselves intimately to others, such as lovers, friends and partners is a key defining moment of life in reflexive modernity.

With the democratisation of the private sphere, lifestyle and choice increasingly link intimacy with trusting relationships as providing a sanctuary for the self. However, this opening to others in order to establish trust and security becomes a distinctive burden of responsibility in modern societies. The pure or intimate relationship, according to Giddens, is something akin to a refuge against the stresses and strains of everyday life in risk society:

> Pure relationships . . . offer the opportunity for the development of trust based on voluntary commitments and an intensified intimacy . . . The pure relationship is a key environment for building the reflexive project of the self, since it both allows for and demands organized and continuous self-understanding – the means of securing a durable tie to the other. (1991b, p. 96)

The rise of expert mediation such as social work, psychotherapy, counselling, mediation services and marriage guidance are closely linked to the emergence of the pure relationship as an evaluative measure of inter-personal value. As Giddens explains, 'The centrality of therapy expresses the fact that the more that pure relationships become dominant, the more crucial becomes an in-depth understanding which allows one to feel "all right" with oneself. For self-mastery is the condition of that opening-out process through which hope (commitment) and trust is generated in the pure relationship' (1991b, p. 96). Self-help and improvement manuals offer endless amounts of advice on how to maintain the pure relationship, ranging from developing listening skills, being self-aware and open to change, to avoiding defensive attitudes. The domain of the pure relationship has become central to the way people organise their intimate lives and also to the way that experts such as social workers attempt to maintain or reconstruct them. Increasingly expert interventions are less concerned with fathoming the great riddles of unconscious life than with a modest sense of problem solving in the face of risk. Experts are particularly concerned with life planning and risk regulation during what Giddens calls 'fateful moments'. Fateful moments, such as bouts of depression, marriage breakdown and loneliness, are all by-products of a reflexive culture with its emphasis on self-governance and responsibility. If individuals are unable to undertake the responsibility for their own self-governance then experts are required to do it for them. Indeed it's during fateful moments and crises that experts like social workers are involved. As we'll see social work often acts as a safety net, which buffers the vulnerable from uncertainties, crises and insecurities.

Neo-liberalism – the Politics of Risk Society

In risk society political rule and power are less concerned with maintaining material provision and wealth than with regulation and compliance. Throughout the book it will be seen how risk society and neo-liberalism in late modernity are intimately linked in shaping social work. Many writers have argued that the modern state is best understood in terms of the politics of governance that constitute its organisation and purpose. In this respect the contemporary state formation has been described in terms of advanced or neo-liberalism (see Dean, 1999; Rose, 1999). Arguably neo-liberalism is *the* political programme of risk society. As Culpitt argues, 'neo liberalism creates the climate of risk in order to justify its overall politic' (1998, p. 117). As we shall see neo-liberalism – as the political programme of risk society – monitors social welfare as a fundamental datum from which to enforce public policy and systems of management on the basis of economic market rationality. We'll also see how the state increasingly comes to endorse a politics of individual recognition over a politics of collective redistribution through this form of political rule. Whilst regulation becomes a significant role for the modern state all individual conduct is increasingly seen as entailing choice, life planning and purposeful paths. Thus individuals are increasingly expected to bear the responsibility associated with risk decision making. This is described in the next chapter as the 'privatisation of risk'. In its attempt to rationalise excess and deficiency in individual behaviour, the neo-liberal state comes into conflict with subjective attempts to pursue chains of democratic freedom that are potentially excessive or deficient, such as alcohol or drug misuse.

In the chapters that follow the relation between social work, risk society and neo-liberalism is analysed in detail. For now it is relevant to comment that the welfare state as an ethos of government has been severely undermined by the onset of the advanced liberal politics. We'll see how the paternalistic welfare state and its universal social services have gradually withered away to be replaced by much more individualistic rationalities of governance. In line with this, a market rationality, in all spheres of human action relating to individual choice, responsibility and freedom, is valorised. Active citizenship is encouraged with individuals being increasingly held responsible for managing and calculating their own risk. In social work we can understand the increasing emphasis on the involvement of 'service users' in this respect. For those groups who are unable to manage their own risk expert intervention is required. This leads to what Dean calls a division between active citizens capable of managing their own risk and 'targeted populations' who require assistance and protection (1999, p. 167). Under such circumstances, as Dean comments, 'it might be argued that the self-determining or free subject has replaced society as the principle of self-limitation of government' (p. 164). In short, risk society is linked to advanced liberal rule and in particular the mobilisation of individualised risk and the retraction of socialised forms of governance associated with the post-war welfare state.

In modern societies the neo-liberal state imposes rules directly by 'command-and-control' legislation or encourages internal control systems within organisations and groups. There's been a vast expansion of the administrative regulatory mechanisms of the state over the past few decades. The co-ordination of information is an important development within the administrative steering carried out by the state. The administrative mechanisms link to the power exercised by the neo-liberal state. As Giddens points out, 'the generation of state power presumes reflexively monitored systems involving the regularized gathering, storage, and control of information applied to administrative ends' (1985, p. 178). Regulation and security are key features of reflexive institutions and are ultimately concerned with planning, calculation and protection. The resultant effect is the development of what Michael Power (1997) describes as an 'audit society' in which performance, accountability and transparency become key elements of regulation. In the chapters that follow we see how anti-welfare tactics of neo-liberalism refuse to acknowledge the ambivalence of modernity and have a blind faith in technical rationality, calculation and planning in installing regulatory regimes to provide security and system rationality.

Regulation and Security in Social Work

There are two important dimensions of risk that are relevant for our understanding of social work in neo-liberal risk society. These are referred to as the *logic of regulation* and the *logic of security* and will provide a framework for understanding contemporary social work. Broadly, these two logics in risk society mirror Max Weber's distinction between instrumental rationality and substantive rationality; the former is means-ends-driven, self-interested, calculating, controlling and predicting, with the latter focusing on broader expressive values, affects and meanings. Instrumental rationality consists in simply calculating the most efficient means to whatever ends are assumed. Calculative thinking or reasoning are the intellectual corollaries of dominant technological systems that fundamentally characterise the modern 'world picture' (Heidegger, 1977). Substantive rationality is governed by the idea that a certain form of behaviour is of absolute value in itself, regardless of its consequences. This is a form of moral-practical rationality whereby an action is orientated towards reaching an understanding (see Habermas, 1990). It is shown how social work is mediated on the one hand by its instrumental rationality, as complicit with calculating and regulatory practices, and on the other hand, by its substantive rationality, in securing identity through dialogic and expressive face-work.

As formulated by institutions the logics of regulation and security are systems responses to modern contingency and complexity. They mediate experience and life planning along lines of certainty, calculation and trust. Regulation and security may complement each other in the social handling of risk or at other times may be in tension with one another. For the purpose of this study these two logics are understood in terms of the way they combine to shape important aspects of social work. We'll see how in social work aspects of security and regulation inter-penetrate each other sometimes in tension and at other times as complementary.

Risk society develops the logic of regulation in relation to organisations, groups and individuals. For example, it deploys legal coercive power and tends towards a monopoly control of the supply of regulation. This has led some writers, such as Malone (1994) to describe the modern state as a 'regulatory state'. Regulation by the state is frequently achieved by legal rules that are likely to be backed by criminal or behavioural sanctions. As we shall see regulation is a regime of risk management carried out by expert mediating systems on behalf of the state or some other institution. According to the influential analysis of Christopher Hood (2001) a successful regulatory system must possess three linked components: information gathering; standard setting; and behaviour modification. In Chapter

2 it will be shown how a new politically driven programme of economic individualism comes to dominate the logic of regulation in modern societies. Furthermore we shall see how in risk society both regulatory expertise and reflexive action are intimately connected within the neo-liberal political programme. As Culpitt points out, 'Neo liberalism represents a political expression about the need to maintain an individual responsibility for certain risks' (1998, p. 105).

The Rationality of Regulation

Regulation penetrates all aspects of organisational life in late modern societies. Informal aspects of the organisation, for example, are increasingly recognised as a 'regulatory space' to be controlled, monitored and audited. Some regulation is anticipative and precautionary, such as the assessment of foster and adoptive parents for the potential of their committing abuse to children. Another example of precautionary regulation involves the installation of virus checkers or firewalls to prevent hackers getting access to computers. Other types of regulation are punitive and criminalise activities. Legislation on stalkers, drink-drivers and calls for paedophiles to be prosecuted if they apply for jobs that involve working with children are examples of punitive regulation. In many respects these may be characterised as risk avoidance situations. State-mediated regulation can take many forms, positive as well as negative. State regulation through the use of the law – often referred to as command-and-control regulation – is perhaps the best known method, but this is just one form of regulation and there are many others. Systems of self-regulation, such as those carried out in universities to assess the quality of teaching and research, are a further example. These systems amount to enforced regulation that increasingly focuses on the technical features of internal control systems, such as those for financial, environmental and occupational health. In Britain the development of the Social Services Inspectorate and its monitoring of residential services is a good example of an enforced system of self-regulation initiated by the mediating state. Based on experience and training, the regulator makes assessments of the quality of various social service provisions – their commitment to regulatory objectives, their record of compliance, the quality of their management and their capacity to comply. Regulation need not always be externally imposed. Self-regulation is achieved in attending self-help groups and our daily activities are permeated by such practices, especially in relation to health and bodily exercises. Working-out and personal hygiene are good examples of this reflexive kind of self-regulation (see Monaghan et al., 2000). How then do systems of regulation operate in the face of risk? And furthermore what core principles underpin the idea of regulation? These are important questions that have often been overlooked in the literature on risk and social work. We can begin by noting that *regulation is an action* or *set of actions*, that in late modern societies are increasingly constructed through individualised ways and methods. To regulate is to govern and control through a set of rule-bound actions or procedures, thereby bringing or reducing a body of phenomena to some given state. In doing so regulation adjusts conditions in respect of time or quantity to some prescribed standard. The key concerns of regulation are order, standards, conduct, calculation and rule following. *Regulation against risk* is its modus operandi. As a form of determinate judgement the logic of regulation monitors specific targets and tries to adjust their behaviour. For regulation to work successfully it requires rules to be standardised and repeatable in achieving the same results. In this sense regulation is a rational response to the intrinsic uncertainties and disorder of late modern life. Given its an avoidance of some supposed threat, or a response to threat, regulation is not a pre-condition for how things are. If there were no risks, hazards or threats then regulation would be unnecessary. To quote Bauman, 'One does not conceive regularity unless one is buffeted by the unexpected' (1992, pp. xi–xii). The relation between risk and regulation is significant for a number of reasons. Regulation is one way in which risks are managed and risk management can be seen as a form of self-regulation. As we'll see demand on governments and the public sector to regulate risks is increasing and this directly impacts on the social work role and its processes (Stalker, 2003).

The Rationality of Security

A further important dimension of modern societies involves what I've called the *logic of security* which is shown to be crucial in understanding social work within late modern society. This important concept is partly derived from the French sociologist François

Ewald's (1991) notion of the role of the providential state in the provision of safety nets for its citizens. As Beck (1999) explains:

Ewald's theory marks a significant shift in the interpretation of the welfare state. While the majority of social scientists have sought to explain the origins and construction of the welfare state in terms of class interests, the maintenance of social order or the enhancement of national productivity and military power, Ewald's argument underlines the provision of services, the creation of insurance schemes as well as the regulation of the economy and the environment in terms of the *creation of security* . . . experts play a central role in answering the question 'how safe is safe enough?'. (p. 226)

How safe is safe enough is a crucial question for social workers, especially in mental health and child protection or work with elderly clients with dementia. Beck acknowledges that Ewald's perspective on the welfare state is an important move away from the overly negative readings of expert mediation as social control. Social welfare is compelled to respond positively to the contingencies of late modernity and to provide security for its citizens. Thus expert welfare systems emerge, such as social work, which are both limiting and enabling. This represents a move away from hagiographic readings of Foucault's theory of power towards a more critical account. Against the narrow readings of Foucault that reduce his later writings on power to disciplinary practice, Gordon argues that 'We live today, not so much in a disciplinary society, as in a society of security' (1991, p. 20). Contrary to certain misleading sociological accounts, Foucault doesn't think that contemporary societies are disciplinary in nature but that they are distinguished by a more complex form of neo-liberal governmentality. Governmentality is a reflexive concern with the rationality of security, which in Foucault's analysis is an inherently open-ended one. The focus is not on closed circuits of control and discipline, but on calculations of the possible and the probable. In its simplest form governmenality is a programme of calculated practices to direct categories of people in a particular manner for particular ends. Foucault's last series of lectures at the Collège de France in 1978 were entitled 'Security, Territory and Population'. They were concerned with the emergence of distinct forms of liberal actuarial security in eighteenth century Europe which were not solely confined to the apparatus of the state. Gordon summarises this often overlooked aspect of Foucault's concern with liberal mechanisms of security in advanced societies:

Foucault characterizes the method of security through three general traits. It deals in a series of possible and probable events; it evaluates through calculations of comparative costs; it prescribes not by absolute binary demarcation between the permitted and the forbidden, but by the specification of an optimal mean within a tolerable bandwidth of variation . . . Security addresses itself distinctively to 'the ensemble of a population'. (1991, p. 20)

For Ewald this preoccupation with systems of security results in the emergence of social insurance and statistical calculations in which each segment of society is a collective risk group of insurers partly protected through the provident state. Ewald argues that risk is thus a collective enterprise whilst accidents are largely personal. As will be seen social work is a decisive element of risk regulation within this emerging apparatus of expert security. The relationship between risk and expert systems as characterised by Alaszewski et al. draws attention to new forms of intervention:

> The role of experts in creating, identifying and managing risks is central to risk society. In situations of uncertainty where risks are high and it is difficult to measure risk, the task of risk assessment and risk management is taken on by experts in risk, usually professionals, whom lay people trust to protect them from hazards. (1998, pp. 19–20)

Technical expertise and the politics of risk form a strategic alliance in neo-liberal society. A normative system of safety-net planning emerges in which attempts to calculate risk are built into the rationality of neo-liberal risk economics. It aims to make risk accountable and calculable as well as compensating for damage in the face of a vulnerable and uncertain future.

The logic of security is often mobilised at the point where our trust in organisations, groups or individuals may well break down. Modern institutions increasingly attempt to insure against the breakdown of trust and certainty. For Ewald the development of a technology of insurance to counter risk is crucial in this respect:

> As a technology of risk, insurance is first and foremost a schema of rationality, a way of breaking down, rearranging and ordering certain elements of reality . . . It is the practice of a certain type of rationality, one formalized by the calculus of probabilities. This is why one never insures oneself except against risks, and why the latter can include such different things as death, accident, hailstorms, a disease, a birth, military conscription, bankruptcy and litigation. (1991, p. 199)

Ewald locates the emergence of the logic of security with its techniques of insurance in various developments at the end of the nineteenth century (perhaps it's no coincidence that this is the period when early social work emerged). Indeed he suggests, 'every type of benefit organization, whatever its nominal structure, becomes an insurance institution *de facto*. Insurance now really signifies . . . an organizing schema of management and rationality capable of being realized in any and every kind of provident institution' (1991, p. 209). Providence against specifically defined risk becomes an essential feature of social existence in the late nineteenth century. This is why charitable organisations were so keen to encourage the poor to open savings accounts, so that they could stave off the hazards of fluctuating labouring opportunities and seasonal variations. Each person is increasingly held accountable for her or his own fate. Personal savings, pensions, trusts and life assurance are matters of self-accountability and providence. This is why Ewald refers to the technique of insurance against insecurity as a moral phenomenon. 'To calculate a risk is to master time, to discipline the future. To conduct one's life in a manner of enterprise begins to be a definition of morality whose cardinal virtue is providence' (ibid., p. 207). People become anxious about whether their personal pension plan is sufficient to take care of them in old age. A constant vigilance is required to guard against the insecurities of risk and hazard. The morality invoked by insecurity can work to provoke communities of anxiety based on sentiments such as 'we're all in this together' during seasonal floods, nationalist movements or warfare, moral crusades against paedophiles, child murderers and 'muggers'.

There is a further important dimension involved with the rationality of security that is overlooked by Ewald and Beck. The concrete experience of security in the daily lives of people is crucial. Therefore the logic of security should be stretched to include safety, vulnerability, coping strategies, social support and protection. Giddens addresses this important inter-subjective dimension in his discussion of 'ontological security'. In this respect the inclusion of Giddens's contribution helps make the important connection between the micro and macro strands of security. It also helps draw out the significance of mechanisms of trust between experts and lay persons. Giddens (1991) emphasises the importance of taken-for-granted routines and continuity in providing a sense of personal security:

The development of relatively secure environments of day-to-day life is of central importance to the maintenance of feelings of ontological security.

Ontological security, in other words, is sustained primarily through routine itself . . . The protective cocoon depends more and more on the coherence of routines themselves, as they are ordered within the reflexive project of the self. (p. 167)

Expert mediating systems, such as social work, are crucially caught within this logic of security. Trust is established through confidence in transactions and taken-for-granted assumptions of reliability that underlie social relations. However, this is a precarious state of affairs because trust is fragile and once the security of the relationship has been violated or abused it is difficult to re-establish. Trust and security are permanently open to challenge and breakdown. In social work we'll see how this results in the necessity for trust relations to be constantly reworked. We live in a security-conscious society in which boundaries between ourselves and other people are constantly redrawn often by self-help groups or mediating experts. A chief consideration is that of trust, confidence and anxiety reduction. To live in a climate of risk it's necessary to establish trust as a protective cocoon that can screen out daily insecurities. From childhood to adolescence and through to adulthood crisis management plans are developed to provide a secure basis for self-identity (see Burkitt, 1992). Social work performs an important role in this task of providing ontological security for vulnerable people in late modernity.

In summary the logic of security is a significant dimension that constructs various dimensions of social work in risk society. Security as a set of social conditions means that *security is the condition of being secure*. To be secure is to be free from fear, apprehension, doubt or alarm. However, security is not just about a present state of affairs but also about the threshold of probable and future events. Individuals and organisations adopt diverse methods for calculating future horizons, ranging from consulting astrologers and reading their stars, to complex risk management techniques. To be secure means to be confident in expectation and having the safe prospect of some future event. This is why Ewald refers to social welfare as providential. It is a guardian-like system that is forward looking, protecting against potential risk, hazard and uncertainty through risk management calculations. It tries to avoid exposing its citizens to risk and danger. We can see that safety and trust are not given but always things to be gained. Under the neo-liberal agenda the dynamics of the logic of security are legitimated in terms which try to guarantee certainty and freedom from risk. *Security against risk and uncertainty* becomes an essential modus operandi for individuals, organisations and communities in late modernity.

Conclusion

The remaining chapters show how regulation and security in neo-liberal risk society combine to reconfigure key aspects of social work. They show how risk regulation comes to dominate social work, and the way in which the handling of risk is increasingly displacing need as the focal point and justification for intervention. Whilst expert knowledges, such as social work, continue to play a significant role in life planning and responding to fateful moments this is changing dramatically as a consequence of risk. The implications of this shift are addressed as risk regulation systems tighten their grip on the construction of social work policy and front-line practice. It's projected that technical expertise and actuarial science come to play a dominant role in defining social work, especially within the neo-liberal political context. The importance of and increased sensitivity to security, as trust and intimacy, in late modernity are attributed to the widespread view that existing forms of social solidarity, co-operation and reciprocity are being increasingly eroded. From a political viewpoint, *risk is understood as a form of governmentality that undermines traditional practices of value and relationship building*.

Neo-liberal governance depends on the reflexive ordering of social life and privatised risk within the context of the market. As Beck argues this kind of individualisation means 'the disintegration of the certainties of industrial society as well as the compulsion to find and invent new certainties for oneself and others without them' (1992, p. 14). For those who struggle or are unable to find these certainties or take responsibility, expert interventions, such as social work, are justified through categories of risk. Risk governance increasingly regulates populations and individuals who fall outside the safety net of normalised society. In this sense social work is increasingly involved in the regulation, normalisation and monitoring of what sociologists have called 'the underclass', that is the dispossessed and excluded sections of society, who exhibit multiple social problems, such as unemployment, poverty, substance misuse, mental health issues and domestic violence. However, trust presupposes risk, with experts offering protection and security in the face of contingency, uncertainty and complexity (see Hudson, 2000). In contradistinction to the regulating and normalising tendencies of neo-liberal risk systems it's argued that social work exhibits a mix of security, trust and recognition or what is called in the final chapter the practice of value. It is argued that this can offset the regulatory logic of social work as embodied in neo-liberal political rule. The practice of value can be deliberately cultivated through the unfolding of ethical and evaluative face-to-face relations, proximal sociability and trust that amount to a new ethics of social connectedness in social work.

2

Risk, Regulation and Neo-liberalism

Introduction

This chapter focuses on contemporary aspects of risk regulation in social work as indicative of changes taking place in politics in late modernity. In doing so it contends that social work is situated between the rationality of risk and neo-liberal regulatory politics. The chapter examines how the regulation of risk reflects broader economic and political change in the advancement of neo-liberal welfarism. Whilst the analysis concentrates on changes in the UK the findings are generalisable, showing how principles of welfare shift from concerns with social solidarity in the post-war period to preoccupations with economic individualism from the early 1980s onwards. This exposition of the social handling of risk in advanced liberalism draws on the writings of Nikolas Rose who demonstrates how neo-liberal political rule is the dominant ideology of public policy in risk society. Not only do advanced liberal democracies construct new forms of freedom, security and autonomy for individuals but also deploy complex means of regulation, authoritarianism, exclusion and normalisation of social life. We'll see how neo-liberalism engages with social work as a fundamental datum from which to enforce public policy on the basis of economic market rationality.

The analysis undertaken here leads to the conclusion that social work is increasingly framed within neo-liberal strategies. The neo-liberal programme, politically hostile to Keynesian economics, makes its entry on the welfare stage by initiating and extending a market rationality of individualism, competition and efficiency which have a decisive impact on social work. The chapter identifies key affinities between neo-liberal welfarism and the technologies of risk regulation. Neo-liberal welfare society concerns itself with an emerging division between active citizens, capable of managing their own risk, and targeted marginal 'underclass' populations, who are high-risk and dependent on expert safety-net intervention to conduct their lives. It will be argued that social work cannot be properly understood outside of these political formations in risk society.

Before the analysis of social work and risk regulation takes place it's necessary to examine the changing context of social welfare from the post-war period onwards. This will help complete the picture of how social work develops regulatory mechanisms involving the management of risk. It also contextualises British social work within the political arena of neo-liberal welfare endorsed by successive Conservative and Blairite New Labour governments. This section traces a crucial shift in Britain occurring roughly between 1950 and 1980 and also in other advanced liberal societies. This shift represents a change from a Keynesian liberal to a neo-liberal welfare strategy.

Mapping the Social: Social Work and State Welfare

Modern welfare states have their roots in the first decade of the twentieth century when the integration of capitalist economies reached a high plateau. Richards (2001) summarises this development of the Keynesian paradigm of welfare provision:

> This paradigm had its peak in the war-time and postwar creation of a welfare state providing planned security from cradle to grave, with a protected economy to maintain full employment, and powerful professionals to ration resources according to their judgements about need. (p. 62)

After the Second World War the British state became over-stretched with its operations becoming increasingly bureaucratic. Thus expert mediating systems such as social work and educational welfare came to play a significant role in the Keynesian 'planned economy'. For Parton, the resultant effects of this intermediary safety-net positioning of social work simply confirm modernity's ambivalence. Whilst my argument is that social work is ambivalent precisely *because of* modernity, Parton argues that the ambivalence occurs due to its positioning within a hybrid space. He says, 'the ambiguity arises from social work's sphere of operation: between civil society with its allegiances to individuals and families; and the state, in the guise of the courts and their "statutory responsibilities" ' (1998, p. 11). However, Parton fails to acknowledge that organised modernity abstractly models these system differentations between the state and civil society; public and private spheres; and families and community in new ways. It does so whilst simultaneously initiating the possibility for its own critique through political processes of developmental democracy. Parton restricts the notion of the hybrid positioning of social work to the practices of the social, that is, to that which occurs within institutions of social welfare, not to that which created them, which in my terms is the complex systems of differentation in modernity.

Social insurance against risk and the promotion of social solidarity sat at the centre of early welfare reform in Britain. As Parton points out:

> Post-war welfarism was symbolized by the idea, following William Beveridge, of social insurance. Social insurance fundamentally transformed the mechanisms that integrated the citizen into the social order. Not only were individuals to be protected from the evils of 'Want, Disease, Idleness, Ignorance and Squalor' but they would be constituted as citizens bound into a system of solidarity and mutual dependence. (1998, p. 12)

The legitimation of social work rested on a double alliance. On the one hand, its mediating role meant it attempted to break down social differences and promote solidarity, whilst on the other hand, it satisfied the demands of the state through social networks of regulation. Social work mediated the mutuality of social risk through regulatory practices and normalising processes which attempted to construct individuals, families and communities to some ideal-type. These practices often focused on 'high-risk' marginal populations such as criminals and the mentally ill. We can see how this fits with Foucault's thesis on governance and the relation between state welfare and expert power (see Chambon et al., 1999; Walters, 2000). According to Foucault, extension of the state's capacity for governance was dependent on professional expertise and on the development of expert techniques of calculation, notation, documentation, evaluation, and assessment. Foucault (1979) reckons that the expert mediating professions were intimately involved in processes of normalisation of the citizen-subject in enabling the modern nation-state to govern.

The Crisis of the Keynesian Welfare State

Few anticipated the crisis of the Keynesian welfare state that occurred in Britain towards the end of the 1970s and through the 1980s. It's generally agreed that the global breakdown of fixed exchange rates, high inflation, oil-price crises, high unemployment and interest rates all contributed to this breakdown. This decisive change of fortune had significant implications for social work and welfarism. It led to a crisis of the welfare state. Taylor-Gooby summarises this crisis:

> The half-century experiment of the British welfare state is everywhere in retreat
> . . . The Beveridge settlement promised universal care, from cradle to grave . . .
> Modern politicians are more modest and rely on market solutions wherever practical, offering 'work for those who can' and restricting security only 'to those who cannot' in an efficient system 'where costs are manageable'. (2000, p. 2)

Most writers agree that the golden age of the Keynesian welfare state is over (Esping-Andersen, 1996). In Britain from the 1970s a type of market-place liberalism came to dominate considerations of social welfare. The central planks of Keynesian policy, of central planning, engineering and universal provision were rejected as economically untenable. Progressive ideas of people acting together collectively and out of social solidarity were also rejected. As we'll see this had profound effects on social work as it increasingly entered the neo-liberal era of welfarism. The mediating space that social work occupied in what Donzelot calls 'the social' has been largely dismantled. It's been replaced by the onslaught of economic individualism and a refashioned social contract based on the idea that each person is a completely free, responsible, independent, choosing individual (see Mary Midgley's critique, 1996).

The end of the Keynesian programme means that a providential state gradually comes to replace the universal welfare state. The former is governed by an ethos of prudentialism that is dependent upon the segregation of populations within ever finer future-oriented risk categories (Ewald, 1991). Risk society transforms social welfarism beyond recognition. Woollacott (1998) makes the telling point that:

> . . . the old welfare state was mainly about retrospective help for those who had fallen on hard times. The risk society is about identifying dangers before they happen, including dangers arising from the effects of welfare measures. The

political point is that future risk can only be scientifically measured and managed collectively. The provisions government must make are not only to protect citizens against some risks they take as individuals, but about managing the whole body of risk. (pp. 121–2)

The neo-liberal welfare programme for the management of risk is identical to all political persuasions. Taylor-Gooby argues that New Labour simply extended earlier Thatcherite Conservative welfare policies. Under New Labour the citizen's rights are conditional on individual responsibility and moral judgement about future risks. The politics of competitive individualism comes to replace that of collective solidarity. Increasingly, the average working family is abandoned to the pressures of the market. The British government's policy to introduce 'baby bonds' is an example of neo-liberal anti-welfare strategies aimed at creating 'prudential children'. The government puts down an initial state dowry, worth £300–500, for all new-born children which is topped up by sums of £50–100 three times as the child grows up. The move, billed as a drive against child poverty, provides incentives to save as a form of social insurance. It aims to produce entrepreneurial children who invest in the future. This represents a double strategy of risk management with social insurance against welfare dependency. Its strong message is that people have to 'stand on their own two feet' and cannot depend on welfare. The burden of individual responsibility can of course weigh down heavily on people, especially if it includes responsibility for others such as children. To illustrate the negative side of responsibility, in Britain a single-parent mother from Oxfordshire was jailed for 60 days because her two daughters were persistent truants from school.

The Rise of Neo-liberal Welfare

Social welfare is radically revised with the onset of a powerful neo-liberal programme preoccupied with regulating risk and consumer-driven markets. Giddens claims that neo-liberalism is the programmatic political response to risk society. Increasingly the key strategic role of the state is seen as dealing with contingency rather than providing universal solutions via centralised planning. As Giddens argues, 'The welfare state is a system which is designed to protect you against risk and contingency in life: the risk of illness, the risk of disablement, the risk of becoming unemployed, the risk

of becoming divorced' (1999, p. 2). This push towards greater individualisation helped in the creation of a residual safety-net model of
social welfare. With this development welfare provision comes to be
based almost entirely on a 'minimal safety net'. The 1950s push for
social solidarity is vastly weakened and replaced by the free market
individualism of the 1980s. In Culpitt's view anti-welfarism is rife;
social welfare is cast in pejorative terms with 'risk being one of the
underlying themes of this new rhetoric' (1999, p. 13). Post-
Keynesian welfarism loosens the link between shared responsibility
and social solidarity. This helps explain why voters rail against
government tax increases to fund public sector services. Risk is
allied with individualism and random fate and not a shared sense of
public duty and civic responsibility. For neo-liberalism the principle
of the 'common good' which provided a justification for early social
work can no longer be tied with 'the social'. The advanced liberal
programme of governance constructs politics not through normative
appeals to the greater good of society, but through the rational ordering of the calculating, private choices of entrepreneurial individuals
(Culpitt, 1999, p. 72). Risk and neo-liberalism are at odds in this
respect. As the sociologist Richard Sennett has put it, where politicians speak the language of individual responsibility and entrepre-
neurialism, they suppose 'a confidence that ordinary people often do
not feel' (*New Statesman*, 17 December 2001).

Rose contends that neo-liberalism marks the advent of the 'entrepreneurial self' interspersed in all walks of life. In Britain direct
payments made to adults in need of care are one very spectacular
example of this mentality of the entrepreneurial self at work. The
Community Care (Direct Payments) Act 1996 enables local authorities to make cash payments to service users with physical and
sensory impairments and learning difficulties under the age of 65.
They are encouraged to design their own care packages and advert-
ise, interview and agree contract terms with potential service
providers. This gives users control over money spent on meeting
their community care needs, rather than receiving services arranged
for them by the local authority. They select and recruit 'personal
assistants' who are issued with job specifications, see to their day-to-
day management (e.g. time sheets, rotas and supervision) and make
payments to them. Prior to this service users are assessed to determine how many hours can be allocated to their care. Social work
thus acts as an independent regulator in the assessment of the
amount and quality of care provided (Pearson, 2000). This move

towards the entrepreneurial client speaks for itself. It brandishes capitalist business as the role model of the good life. Here social work cedes to market operators, with social workers as the servants of an entrepreneurial ethos.

Taken together the above points have led many theorists to argue that the 'death of the social' is no longer just a proposition but an established fact in the world of possessive individualism (Reddy, 1996; Rose, 1996a; Hindess, 1997). In the push towards neo-liberalism state-led welfarism comes to be seen as a liability as well as an economic luxury. One key theme running through the writings of Beck and Giddens is that the welfare state is vulnerable to loss of authority and deference in late modernity. There is mistrust and loss of faith in welfare professions on the part of governments and service users alike. Expert decisions by professionals, such as social workers and medical doctors, are increasingly challenged by more sophisticated but sceptical service users. In becoming more reflexive, consumers increasingly reject expert opinion and openly challenge its knowledge claims. The gap between lay persons and experts is significantly narrowed as consumer-oriented service users access their own expert technologies such as the internet. Policy statements are littered with recommendations about involving stakeholders and service users in social work. Not only does this point to the link between public sector service provision, consumer culture and the democratisation of ordinary life, but to an interesting tension. Some may be sceptical about the genuineness of these moves to involve stakeholders. It's clear that the professionalisation of everyday life from the 1950s onwards rested on the assumption of the incompetence of ordinary people in coping on their own or managing their lives (Furedi, 1997, p. 136). Herein lies the contradiction. The push for greater involvement of service users inevitably rests on an entirely different assumption: that they are now socially and psychologically competent to make significant, knowledgeable and presumably fair-minded contributions to care planning. Of course, some will be more capable than others, but perhaps all we are seeing in this new trend of proto-professional inclusivity is the recognition that consumer-oriented service users are far more reflexive within a blame-dominated culture.

The increased reflexivity of service users results in tighter systems of accountability governing social work intervention. Rather paradoxically, this means that expert systems have to develop additional layers of expertise to help them maintain professional–lay boundaries. O'Malley (2000) extends these arguments to risk in his critique of neo-liberalism. He says that we've entered an era of neo-liberalism in which risk management becomes the dominant strategy for the regulatory governance of welfare; or better still a programme of calculated practices to direct categories of people in a particular manner for particular ends. This strategy becomes circular because the increasing accumulative effect of 'manufactured uncertainties' results in risk management being continuously undermined and then having to be renewed under new expert guises. Expert systems crack under the weight of their own internal inconsistencies and the pressures of reflexive consumerism and the demands of service users.

On the neo-liberal bandwagon the quest for greater and greater choice becomes the pinnacle of 'value added' for the public sector. The old Labour Party stalwart Roy Hattersley commented, 'The idea of promoting choice has become so fashionable that it appeared high on the agenda of a Third Way Conference at Hartwell House' (*Guardian*, 10 June). In fact neo-liberal political ideology is rather straightforward. It amounts to the affirmation of economic desire as the sole authority for cultural practice. The resultant effect leads to what O'Malley (1996) calls an 'enterprising prudentialism' in which stakeholders, service users and consumers are sovereign. An individualised focus of service provision becomes the central plank for measuring the quality of social care. Typically, the UK Minister of State at the time, Frank Dobson, in the introduction to *Modernizing Social Services* (1998) stated, 'our Third Way for social care moves the focus away from the providers of the care and places it firmly on the quality of services experienced by individuals.' Here we can recognise the neo-liberal mantra of a consumerist culture as applied to the provision of social care. As Rose points out, individuals are 'not merely free to choose, but *obliged to be free*, to understand and enact their lives in terms of choice' (1999, p. 87) We know however that the idea of choice, incessantly peddled by government departments, is often hollow and differentiated along social class lines. There are reflexive winners and losers in this neo-liberal game (see Williams, 1999). We also know very well that the inevitable consequence of this choice-promoting ideology is that the self-assured middle class colonise the best schools and hospitals and the timid poor are left to pick up the scraps in a divisive rationing system. Enterprising prudentialism means that certain groups in society milk the system for themselves – and the devil take the rest. Neo-liberal welfare thus emphasises enterprise culture, mixed-economy service and most significantly, prudent service users who through individual choice and responsibility maintain their liberty. (See 'The Code of Social and Family Responsibility' policy developed in New Zealand as an example of neo-liberal moral welfare ambitions; Department of Social Welfare, 1998; and Patterson, 2002.)

To conclude this section it's important to briefly note that the dominance of neo-liberalism is a global phenomenon, which was arguably launched as a social and economic experiment in New Zealand in the early 1980s (Peters, 2001; Peters & Marshall, 2001). Not only have Western democracies endorsed this perspective but as Kwong-Leung (2000) shows Hong Kong, South Korea and other Asian tiger economies have also adopted neo-liberal programmes. Olsen (1996) discusses the effects of neo-liberalism on Norwegian social care and how it undermined the universalist state responses to the public sector; whilst Sunesson et al. (1998) discuss the impact of neo-liberalism on Swedish health and social governance.

Neo-liberalism and Empowerment

Neo-liberal conceptions of self-governance dovetail nicely into notions of empowerment in the caring professions. In reflecting the neo-liberal agenda Braye and Preston-Shoot (1995) define empowerment as enabling individuals or groups to gain control of their own circumstances, achieve their own goals and increase their ability to take effective decisions. This 'individualistic' perspective on empowerment has political implications. As Cruikshank (1995) ironically points out in her criticism of the self-esteem movement, we mustn't confuse the 'empowered' with the powerful. Empowerment in social care is effectively the activation of the consumer service user under the thin veneer of leftist rights language. Ultimately empowerment is caught between neo-liberal strategies of individual autonomy and choice and an ethical socialism that emphasises the need for shared responsibility in being able to make choices. Similarly, the purchase–provider split developed in British social services in the 1980s reinforces neo-liberalism by restructuring social care along market lines (Allen, 1992). The new public sector management, which has increasingly influenced social services organisations, is likewise an attempt to consolidate this neo-liberal shift. The emphasis is on individual units of performance, outcome-based targets, and auditing the quality of provision whilst making it transparent and accountable to consumerist service users. We now live in an era of neo-liberal social work with recent moves towards a stakeholder culture being merely a hardening of this ideology. The shift towards a dominant neo-liberalism complements Giddens's reflexive modernisation thesis. Reflexive life planning that focuses on empowerment, self-reliance, stakeholder involvement fits neatly with neo-liberal identities. Only the fittest, the most calculating and enterprising survive in this harsh Darwinian landscape. Indeed, one of the advantages of living in a risk society is said to be the explosion of choice, which is differentially distributed, in reflexive patterns of consumption (Giddens, 1998, p. 30). The flipside is that if service users are unable to cope with the reflexive repairs required under neo-liberalism they must be regulated, normalised and exposed. A primary objective of social work is to provide a safety net for the vulnerable and the 'dispossessed underclass' with its multiple problems of poverty, ill health, mental illness, drugs, violent relations, poor education, racism and crime. We can detect the manner in which risk management increasingly becomes a key technology in regulating the residual underclass as those most at risk to themselves or others in this entrepreneurial culture (Byrne, 1995). Those members of society who cannot be accommodated through programmes of social inclusion, such as Sure Start in Britain, are kept outside the entrepreneurial game. They become what Beck calls the indolent players or the 'waste-product of the game' (1997, p. 41).

Neo-liberal Regulatory Regimes

We've seen how neo-liberal welfare differs significantly from its Keynesian predecessor. A crucial difference thus far neglected is the regulatory role of the neo-liberal state. Malone (1994) points out the neo-liberal state is increasingly concerned with regulation rather than central planning and social engineering. The regulatory state focuses on preventive strategies of governance and risk reduction. Braithwaite (2000) notes the influence of Thatcherite privatisation policies on the formation of the regulatory state:

> . . . when British telecommunications was deregulated in 1984, Oftel was created to regulate it, Ofgas with the regulation of a privatized gas industry in 1986, OFFER with electricity in 1989 . . . When the Thatcher government radically shifted the provision of nursing home beds from the public to the private

sector, 200 little nursing home inspectorates were set up in district health authorities to upgrade the previously cursory regulatory oversight of the industry. This led Day and Klein (1987) as early as the mid-80s to be speaking of the rise of a new regulatory state in the health and welfare sector, replacing the Keynesian welfare state. (p. 224)

Braithwaite argues that regulation increasingly substitutes for the direct command-and-control methods of the Keynesian welfare state. This political strategy is operationalised in moves toward devolved or decentralised government. Here governments attempt to rid themselves of the responsibility for managing risk by pushing it onto individuals or 'third party' agencies in the statutory, voluntary and independent sectors.

One has to be careful here because this dialectic of regulation and deregulation was perhaps more a politically expedient strategy of achieving a neo-liberal outcome by stealth than it was in itself an outcome of neo-liberal ideology, which would of course demand complete deregulation in a robust competitive market. This is clearly what has been happening under European Union directives such as the telecommunications convergence green paper (1997) and the earlier 'TV without frontiers' (1989 et seq.) directive inspired by the conclusions of the Bangemann Report 1984. There is no real oversight body that 'regulates' in this case, just reviews of how the liberalisation policy is working. In other words, we might more accurately describes the de-/re-regulation strategy in itself as part of a fairly traditional conservative policy approach in its combination of allowing individual enterprise to flourish within a structure of due process.

Privatised Risk, Social Exclusion and the Urban Underclass

Regulatory welfare governance is increasingly dependent on expert life planning to ward off or divert risk. As Taylor-Gooby explains, 'the welfare state is often seen as a solution to the problem of meeting the risks encountered in a typical life course' (1999, p. 177). Under neo-liberalism, however, the state increasingly takes a back-seat and circumscribed role. The use of safety-net and regulatory techniques focuses on the entrepreneurial service user and individualised factors of risk, rather than community or social networks (Levitas, 1998). What will be referred to as 'privatised risk' rather than community risk and social solidarity is at stake. As Mary

Douglas argues, 'the dialogue about risk plays the role equivalent to taboo or sin, but the slope is tilted in the reverse direction, away from protecting the community and in favor of protecting the individual' (1990, p. 7). When government welfare policy does invoke the role of communities it's usually about communities taking responsibility for their own problems or being in partnership with government. They should fight street crime through neigbourhood watch schemes, pay for private community wardens, or co-opt charity organisations to increase community volunteering (Stenson & Sullivan, 2001).

This shift can be usefully described as the 'privatisation of risk'. Here individuals increasingly bear the responsibility associated with risk decision making. This process of individualisation has effects on definitions of citizenship. The rights enjoyed by citizens under universal welfare regimes are attacked because they create a culture of dependency and a 'client mentality' (Rose, 1999, p. 256). The marketisation of pensions in Britain with its emphasis on private schemes is a good example of the rolling back of the dependency culture of welfare. With private pensions risks and costs are regarded as part of individual consumers' responsibility (Peggs, 2000). A further example is the preventive strategies around HIV infection as one of a portfolio of 'lifestyle' risks for which individuals are expected to take responsibility (Rhodes & Cusick, 2000). In social work the privatisation of risk explains the language shift from talk about 'fellow citizens' to talk about clients and presently service users. It leads to what Rose describes as 'a regime of self where competent personhood is thought to depend upon the continual exercise of freedom, and where one is encouraged to understand one's life, actually or potentially, not in terms of fate or social status, but in terms of one's success or failure acquiring the skills and making the choices to actualize oneself' (1999, p. 87).

Social work is preoccupied with future risk either as individualised factors or categories of risk populations. It targets marginal groups, such as asylum seekers, the homeless, sex workers and street-crime offenders, through strategies of risk regulation (see Garland, 2001). Presently, we'll see how risk management becomes the defining feature of neo-liberal welfarism. Parton observes:

> Increasingly, social workers and social welfare agencies are concerned in their day-to-day policies and practices with the issue of risk. Risk assessment, risk management, the monitoring of risk and risk-taking itself have become common activities for both practitioners and managers. Similarly, estimations about risk

have become key in identifying priorities and making judgements about the quality of performance and what should be the focus of professional activities. (1996, p. 98)

As we'll see safety nets and risk regulation combine to dominate the remit of social work. First, let's look at the links between neo-liberal risk society and social exclusion policies. Important sections of the population are excluded from the neo-liberal politics of choice, entrepreneurial responsibility and self-management of risk. Social exclusion remains a fundamental problem for many individuals, groups and communities in risk society. As a result social work is increasingly mobilised to intervene with residual populations occupying the margins of society. This explains why recent British social policy focuses on targeting select groups, such as with the Sure Start and Connexions programmes, rather than implementing forms of universal welfare. Targeted assistance splits and antagonises people: it sets 'people who give' against those who 'take'. As Garrett (2003c) points out, the Connexions programme, run at the street level by 'personal advisors', couples tactics of electronic surveillance with behaviour modification techniques to regulate young people who are vulnerable and at risk of dropping out of school, offending or drug misuse. He notes 'the sheer prominence given to risk in the *Connexions* literature' (p. 132). Rose (1999) describes the relation between what is referred to as the new 'urban underclass' and expert mediation as follows:

> Upon this territory of the marginalized, expertise is integrated in an ambivalent manner into technologies of government that are increasingly punitive. The marginalized, excluded from the regime of choice, no longer embraced within the social politics of solidarity, are allocated a new range of para-government agencies – charities, voluntary organizations supported by grants and foundations. A new territory opens up 'on the margins' – advice bureaux, groups of experts offering services to specific problematic groups, day centres and drop-in centres, concept houses and voluntary homes. (p. 89)

According to policy makers the dispossessed underclass is thought to be comprised of those who live in the very worst social and economic conditions (Lister, 1998a, b). William Julius Wilson's *The Truly Disadvantaged* (1987) powerfully describes the processes of social dislocation and exclusion of an American black underclass concentrated in the urban centres of the US by the attraction of work in the factories of Los Angeles, New York, Chicago and Detroit. The urban underclass includes drug addicts and hustlers; the unemployed;

lone parents; illegal immigrants; the homeless; prostitutes; community-based psychiatric patients; child molesters; street criminals; tramps; and teenage 'yobs'. These are the contemporary equivalent to the pauper and mendicant of late Victorian society and the post-war 'problem family' and 'delinquent'. Social welfare mobilises vast amounts of financial and human capital in dealing with these multiple problem groups. Indeed, some writers have gone so far as to argue that the urban underclass is an effect of post-war welfare dependency with its culture that is antithetical to the work ethic of wider society (Mead, 1989; Murray, 1990; Katz, 1993). The risk management of the urban underclass, who are further disadvantaged by spatial segregation, by experts on social exclusion is tightly bound to the safety-net ideology of neo-liberalism. As we've seen, with Sure Start, New Deal for Communities, Safer Communities Initiative, Youth Inclusion Programme, Children's Fund and Connexions exclusion and safety-net strategies become key organising terms for interventions with the excluded underclass in Britain. From the perspective of Giddens social exclusion policies form part of a generative politics in which citizens are encouraged to be actively involved in combatting risk. He says, 'generative politics is a politics which seeks to allow individuals and groups to make things happen, rather than having things happen to them, in the context of overall social concerns and goals' (1994, p. 15). It can be observed in this respect that Giddens's notion of generative politics mirrors the advanced liberal agenda of individualised choice and self-responsibility.

A deep contradiction is at work in New Labour's social exclusion strategy. Hills et al., in *Understanding Social Exclusion* (2002), maintain that programmes of social exclusion attempt to divert attention away from insufficient wages in employment and the inability to raise people's living standards above the poverty line. The real issue of income inequality means that families and communities are afflicted with a huge burden of responsibility in having to sort out their own problems with a little push from the experts. Economic and structural disadvantage is ignored. In fact it is the privileged 'over-class' that is socially excluded and untouched by New Labour's policies, and thereby able to maintain a privileged position and oppose any collective benefits such as tax increases. Hills et al. doubt whether social exclusion actually exists if this means the poor living apart from the rest of society. Households on low income, the authors maintain, are not excluded from basic activities; they work, have friends, participate in community life, share in local knowledge, indulge in media entertainment and leisure activities and participate in elections. In their book *Empire* (2000) Hardt and Negri argue that these kinds of social exclusion programmes construct ethnic minorities, the poor and other disadvantaged groups as 'Other' and exterior to the rest of society. Drawing on the work of Gilles Deleuze, they claim that racism, for example, has never operated by exclusion, or by the designation of someone as Other, but instead by 'the determination of degrees of deviance in relation to the White-Man face' (p. 193). This challenges social work to conceive of racist or sexist practice not in terms of binary divisions of excluded and included, but as 'a strategy of differential inclusion. No identity is designated as Other, no one is excluded from the domain, there is no outside' (p. 194). Thus social work may well profit from understanding power relations in terms of subordinating differences according to degrees of deviance from normative and dominant designations.

The social exclusion strategy is divisive and undermines shared solidarity and collective responsibility. Social problems derived from a combination of material and personal insecurities are dispersed through the selective targeting of exclusion programmes (Pierson, 2002). In this climate clients are dispersed through selective expert intervention, but reunified through the harsh morality of abjection and rejection. For Rose (1999) social exclusion is regarded as a cynical expression of initiatives functioning at the rhetorical level with a surface appeal to notions of community in the traditional social sense while at the same time employing community in other implicit and morally constructed ways. The cornerstone of Rose's argument is that the socially excluded are no longer seen as a single group with common characteristics who are provided for by unified social services through generic social work, identifying common roots of social inequalities and problems. In the process of specification of excluded groups a plethora of interventions emerge for adolescent support, rough sleepers, family support, neighbourhood crime, school exclusion, literacy schemes, homestart, lone parents, welfare to work, parenting, breakfast clubs, neighbourhood capacity building, loan schemes, credit unions and faith-based work. We can see why the slogan 'clients are our fellow citizens' has little political value with the present de-differentiation strategy based on individual moral responsibility. For Rose the dispersion process means that 'The excluded have no unity amongst themselves . . . the excluded are fragmented and divided, comprising all those who are unable or unwilling to manage themselves and capitalize on their own existence. Their particular difficulties thus need to be addressed through a variety of expert specialists' (op. cit., pp. 258–9). New Labour's social exclusion policy is a strongly individualistic strategy. It expects individuals to bear the responsibility for participation and risk taking. According to Colley & Hodkinson (2001) the Social Exclusion Unit's report *Bridging the Gap* locates the causes of non-participation primarily within individuals and their personal deficits. 'Yet it denies individuality and diversity by representing the socially excluded as stereotyped categories' (p. 335).

Within this individualising strategy Rose explains how the socially excluded are reunified morally and spatially. He explains, 'they are re-unified ethically in that they are accorded a new and active relation to their status in terms of their strategies and capacities for the management of themselves: they have either refused the bonds of civility and self-responsibility, or they aspire to them but have not been given the skills, capacities and means' (1999, p. 259). The second spatial pole of the reunification of the socially excluded means that they are 'reconfigured in marginalized spaces: in the decaying council estate, in the chaotic lone parent family, in the shop doorways of inner city streets' (ibid.). For Rose front-line social workers are complicit in peddling double standards in these urban margins of deprivation in advanced liberal society:

> Equipped with counselling skills and psychotherapeutic ethics, a radical politics of rights and empowerment or a commitment arising from personal experience, 'volunteers' come to play a key role in the proliferating agencies operating on the margins, establishing relations with those in distress that are no longer mediated through the complex bureaucracy of care. It is no critique to note that these workers in the twilight world of the marginalized so often deploy the logics of normalization, social skills, self esteem and so forth in order to 'empower' their clients at the same time as they contest the politics which has made these the organizing principles of 'social' policy. (1999, p. 260)

Jock Young (1999b) concurs with Rose that New Labour's is a phoney policy of social inclusionism based on what Garland (1996) calls a 'responsibilisation strategy' to bring back duty-bound notions of moral responsibility. He says that 'To include a person within a community in a just and integrative fashion demands that jobs are available which are fairly paid, secure and which provide some measure of a career structure. The forcible coercion of people into the most transient and humiliating work below the poverty levels, for the families involved, is simply inclusion of people into the labour market not into a society of full citizens' (p. 146). Young goes on to argue that the New Deal and social exclusion policies confuse the market-place with society and the commodification of labour with community, which leads to a process that is 'experienced not as social inclusion but the creation of an underclass of servants and second-class citizens. It is seen not as inclusion but as exclusion' (ibid.). Choice, empowerment and individual responsibility sit at the centre of the social exclusion rhetoric even though the groups themselves have little opportunity to attain such socially distributed values. Moreover, the socially excluded are offered choice and self-determination, whilst their conduct and patterns of life are simultaneously regulated and normalised. In this respect Rose describes social workers and probation officers as 'petty engineers of human conduct' who think and act 'a bit like experts' (1999, p. 92). Similarly, Margolin (1997) reverses of the idea of a benevolent helper and argues that social workers control clients through the rationality of expert intervention. Accordingly the techniques of social workers bring the regulation of subjectivity into line with the new rationalities for the governance of fateful moments and transitory vulnerability.

Life-conduct is often normalised by delineating 'high' and 'low' risk categories in order to determine eligibility criteria and rehabilitate lifestyle. Risk assessment schedules in mental health, for example, require summary statements of 'low', 'medium' and 'high' risk in relation to categories of suicide, violence and neglect. In a variety of highly individualised settings levels of risk, signs of risk, indicators of risk, risks of exclusion and risk hazards are identified and translated into care rehabilitation plans.

Risk Regulation and Social Governance

We've seen how risk and regulation are increasingly inter-dependent concepts in social work. This is evident in the plethora of literature focusing on implementing regulation and risk management strategies in social work. In 1997, for example, the Labour government 'Best Value' policy was considered at an Association of Directors of Social Services and Policy Studies Institute seminar called 'Best Value: Regulation and Risk'. Prior to this, however, according to Kemshall (2002) the 'Risk Initiative' by the Social Services

Inspectorate in 1995 was a significant watershed in defining risk as a standard setting preoccupation for local authority social services departments (p. 82). Protection from risk is a key consideration for social governance in late modernity. The influential World Bank Group, for example, has recently developed a major funding programme based on a framework for social protection grounded in social risk management (www.worldbank.org).

Neo-liberalism required a shift away from the allocation of public sector provision as discrete service silos, preferring instead 'joined-up practice' between statutory, voluntary and private agencies in the management of risk. In public policy parlance risk management is increasingly regarded as a type of investment in 'social capital' generation (see the discussion in the final chapter). Poverty, for example, is understood as exclusion from the resources and benefits necessary to fully participate as a citizen in community life. Risk and poverty are reconceptualised in terms of vulnerability. With this kind of market-oriented discourse the poor lack both social and economic capital. They are typically the most vulnerable in a society because they are often the most exposed to a range of risks and have the least access to appropriate risk management strategies.

We can summarise this section by identifying three strategies for the social governance of risk that predominate in social work. Firstly, there are prevention strategies aiming to reduce the probability of a risky occurrence. These strategies are introduced before a risky occurrence happens and include practices such as providing visual aids for blind service users. In the present climate the preventive work is largely carried out by the voluntary sector. Secondly, there are mitigation strategies that also come in before the risky occurrence happens but whereas prevention strategies aim to reduce the probability of it happening, mitigation strategies aim to reduce the potential impact if it were to happen. Good examples of mitigation strategies are the various respite care regimes that social workers make use of. Finally there is a coping strategy aimed at relieving the impact of a risky occurrence once it has happened.

Front-line workers often contend that their job is nothing more than 'the management of risk', having to 'make risk judgements' and 'take risky decisions' (Alaszewski et al., 1998). A few examples will suffice at this stage of the discussion. In adoption assessments potential adoptees are carefully filtered by social workers prior to formal adoption panels, by subtle processes of risk judgement. Youth offender teams increasingly play an important role in the early identification of those at risk of becoming pimps or sex workers, many of whom have previously lived in local authority care homes (May et al., 2000). In sex offender work two research assessment instruments predominate: the Rapid Risk Assessment for Sex Offence Recidivism (RRASOR) and the Structured Anchored Clinical Judgement (SACJ) scale (Grubin, 1998). Safety, vulnerability and protection are key elements of these risk assessment activities.

With the risk management strategies the logic of prediction increasingly comes to replace that of diagnosis in social work. As Rose points out, 'the problem is to deploy actuarial classifications of risk to identify and control risky individuals to ascertain who can, and who cannot, be managed within the open circuits of community control' (1991, p. 261). This rationality of regulation through prediction and calculation of targeted populations increasingly dominates front-line practice. We've observed that regulation is constructed in terms of a 'foreseeability' of an anticipated state within an actuarial domain of factors of probability. In general regulation need not be always characterised as reactive, as with the coping strategy, but can also be preventive as in the first and second risk strategies identified above.

Social Work as Regulated

There are two distinctive ways of understanding regulation in relation to social work. Firstly, there is the regulation *of* social work; and secondly, there is social work *as* regulation. Let's examine each of these dimensions in turn. Hood and Scott (2000) summarise the three general characteristics of regulation of public sector services. Firstly, one organisation or office attempts to shape the behaviour of another; secondly, there is some type of arm's length separation between the target organisation and the unit carrying out the regulation; and thirdly, the overseeing organisation has some formal authority or mandate to scrutinise the unit being overseen and seeks to influence or change it. Typical of this kind of regulatory body in social work is the General Social Care Council (GSCC) that regulates and standardises the workforce. It is charged with producing protocols for best practice, assessing effectiveness and with its sister organisation the Social Care Institute of Excellence (SCIE) demonstrating 'what works' in social work. The former is also expected to enforce national standards to tackle inconsistencies in the quality of social care provision. Presently, the new Commission for Social Care Inspection (CSCI) will monitor social services. This commission will combine the functions of the Social Services Inspectorate and the National Care Standards Commission in Britain. As we'll see in a later chapter these forms of re-regulation of the public sector are increasingly outcomes-based, performance and results-driven, rather than concerned with reflexive processes of practice.

In Britain in some key respects the caring professions have been afforded autonomy to undertake their own self-regulation. Through professional training and registration systems social work has limited access to professional practice. Social work agencies have conducted their own disciplinary procedures against recalcitrant professionals and in some cases their own hearings in disputes between professionals and clients. They undertake their own in-house monitoring of the assessment and care management process. And they have assessed and accredited education and training courses giving their stamp of approval only to those deemed to meet the old Central Council for Education and Training in Social Work (CCETSW) requirements. Social work has been self-regulating and up until recently enjoyed a complete, state-sanctioned monopoly over the supply and provision of professional services. This enabled qualified social workers to enjoy some professional autonomy, security and rewards unavailable to their non-professional social care counterparts. The justifications for these arrangements were that social workers were motivated primarily by an ethic of concern for their clients; that their knowledge and expertise were such that only fellow professionals were able to give reasoned assessments and intervention in areas of professional concern with service users; and that only the community of fellow professionals could determine levels (and costs) of services in the best interests of clients. For neo-liberals these justifications sounded increasingly hollow following the variety of child abuse scandals, poor quality residential care and the 1980s challenges to the professions from ideologically motivated neo-liberal governments using notions of the market, increased competition and service users' rights.

Historically, the NHS and Community Care Act 1990 was crucial in extending the regulatory logic *of* social care. This represented a shift from service-led to needs-driven welfare provision. It allowed for the development of 'arm's length' inspection units for all local authority social services departments. The Care Standards Act 2000 some ten years later tightened the regulatory grip on social work and social care. Its key provisions allowed for establishing an independent National Care Standards Commission to undertake the regulation of care and nursing homes, children's homes and other agencies accommodating children; the setting up of the regulatory councils, such as the General Social Care Council in England, for the social care workforce and for preparing codes of conduct; establishing local authority responsibility for regulating child minding and day care for children; creating registers of individuals deemed unsuitable for working with vulnerable adults and laying down the requirement of small children's homes to register with Regional Children's Directors.

Inspection plays a pivotal role in the regulation of social care. The task of monitoring the inspection units and their operational framework was given to the Department of Health's Social Services Inspectorate (SSI). Inspection should be understood as part of the broader process of regulation taking place in social work. It should also be seen as an element in extending the logic of expert systems in relation to risk. Indeed, as Parton (1996) suggests, the development of the 'Risk Initiative' by the Social Services Inspectorate in 1995 started with the assumption that social work is primarily concerned with 'risks to service users, carers and care workers, and the impact on this of the policies and actions of assessors, care managers, care workers, managers and agencies' (p. 103). Such regulatory regimes are often based on the idea of 'tolerable risk' which is an attempt to anticipate what kind of public or political response is acceptable or otherwise.

To a large extent the increased regulation of social work over the past decade derives from the recognition that self-regulation has not produced consistent high standards of professional practice. As Challis (1999) claims the regulation of social work through inspection units is to a large extent a result of the gross abuse that has occurred in residential homes over the past decades in Britain. The main focus of inspection is on regulating quality control as a continuous process of organisational improvement. Clough (1994) argues that the regulation of social care actually makes people less trustworthy because the service providers adopt the habit of relying on regulators to impose standards, thus diminishing their own sense of responsibility. Standardisation is a key tool in the regulation of residential homes for older people. Regulation is designed to produce uniformity. It aims to scrutinise and monitor various fields of expert planning in order to ensure adherence to minimum standards.

Sanctions and the implied threat of their use, such as deregistration of residential homes, are also significant elements in the regulatory armoury of inspection of social work (see Wing, 1992). Ironically perhaps, some authors view inspection as a core principle in the protection of service users from experts and front-line workers. 'Inspectors have to deploy an increasingly wide range of skills to deliver the level of protection that is now expected for vulnerable children and adults living in settings as diverse as boarding schools and homes for older people' (School, 2001, p. 167).

One very obvious point stemming from these organisational changes is that front-line workers often perceive regulatory audit and inspection in negative terms. They deepen the suspicion and anxiety within an already vociferous blame culture. They also shift the priority from meeting the needs of service users or forming genuine partnerships with stakeholders, other professionals and organisations (Parton, 1996). Within blame culture, risk avoidance becomes a key priority for care managers and front-line practitioners. Ever tighter mechanisms of accountability and transparency are introduced. This in turn hardens the defensive tactics of front-line workers, resulting in secrecy and mistrust. People become scared. In local authority social services departments elaborate complaint systems are put in place the purpose of which is to make definitions of responsibility specific, narrow, and precise, rather than to nourish a sense of shared responsibility. In line with neo-liberal practice they put the question of responsibility into the context of a contest, not the context of common values. Cynics argue that rather than making professionals more accountable these blame systems put a very high premium on avoiding responsibility and deflecting possible blame or legal liability onto someone else.

Social Work as Regulating

The second axis, that of social work *as* regulatory is more complex. Here social work relies on normalising and standardising practices that are primarily future-oriented. It regulates against the potential of something happening or attempts to ensure that something will happen. 'At Risk Registers' in child care are good examples of this type of regulatory practice. They attempt to estimate uncertainty based on the distribution of risk within a defined population. Here the probability of a type of action occurring within that population is regulated. To be at risk, however, is not just a matter of what kinds of things someone does but it is also about what kind of person they are. Assigning people to risk registers therefore regulates factors of individuality. As Furedi (1997) points out, ' "being at risk" becomes a fixed attribute of the individual, like the size of the person's feet or hands. Consequently, experts in different professions draw up profiles of who is at risk' (p. 19). Similarly, in assessments of looked-after children and reported child abuse there's an increasing tendency to categorise children as belonging to 'high' or 'low' risk abuse categories. Types of intervention and resources are often determined by whether the child is categorised within the high or low-risk group. This trend is evident in the Department of Health's recent *Safeguarding Children Involved in Prostitution* whereby the 'problem' of youth prostitution is simply transposed into a 'problem' of risk of child sexual abuse (Phoenix, 2002). Of course, such categorisation doesn't take account of the fact that children and families can easily move between low-risk and high-risk groups (Garrett, 2003b; Williams, 2004). Nevertheless we can see how regulation standardises behaviour through risk calculations of the possible. In their ethnographic study Scourfield and Welsh (2003) give examples of this, arguing that risk regulation in child protection represents a shift away from family support and child welfare to one of social control through the increasing use of forensic techniques and regulatory powers. Regulation consists of reducing degrees of freedom for individuals or groups through the self-selection of future risk events. It is concerned with possible loss reduction. Therefore we can see how risk prevention and mitigation explicitly calculate the possibility of breakdown, disruption and permanent damage.

Risk Management and Risk Assessment

We've seen how the management and assessment of risk come to dominate social work. Taken together these calculating rationalities attempt to predict future risk and regulate some individual or organisational reality (see Filer, 2000). Whereas risk assessment is largely concerned with individual risk, risk management focuses on categories of people. The assessment of risk is commonly defined as a process that assesses the likelihood of harm occurring in the future and tries to predict its eventuality. It often takes place to prevent the recurrence of harm and protect vulnerable service users (Sargent,

1999). A practice setting example will suffice to show the centrality of risk in health and social care. The Queen's Medical Centre in Nottingham has developed an inter-professional risk framework to address issues of safety in a busy children's unit. Large clinical areas on two floors of a busy teaching hospital are compartmentalised in subunits each having a named health, safety and risk management link person. This person, who may be a social worker, nurse or doctor, attends regular meetings to discuss risk-based issues. These link people target 'risk zones' on the two floors of the hospital and use risk inspections to identify hazards and potential hazards. They then numerically calculate the hazard as a risk score. The hazard is then risk-assessed and all risk indicators are prioritised for the children's services directorate team (Stower, 1998).

A detailed analysis of risk assessment is provided in Chapter 5. For now a broad-brush overview of this risk methodology is given. Risk management is a relatively underdeveloped area compared to risk assessment in social work. Typically the risk management process has four major components: risk identification; risk analysis; risk reducing measures and risk monitoring. Risk management can involve, for instance, the screening of whole populations of parents of newborn children to identify those likely to commit abuse or neglect (Browne & Saqi, 1988; Downing et al., 1990). Attempts to regulate risk are conducted via assessment formats based on a technical rational model of human behaviour. Risk factors, such as teachers discovering multiple bruises on a child at school, set off an automated child protection response, which brings the assessment process into play. In the field of mental health targeting scarce resources is organised around three areas: treating severe mental illness; reducing suicide; and obviating risk to the wider community. High-priority clients are those who either present with psychotic symptoms, or who are perceived to be a high risk to themselves or others.

A plethora of training manuals and guidelines has been developed to draw attention to risk issues in social work (Aust, 1996). The publication of the book *Dangerous Families* (Dale & Morrison, 1986) by the Rochdale NSPCC team was pioneering in this respect. This book on the assessment of child abuse was the precursor of much of the current work on risk assessment in social work. It very much captured the spirit of the time and reinforced the shift away from 'problem families' to 'dangerous families' as well introducing the idea of 'dangerous social workers' that maintained the dynamics of abusing families (1986, pp. 34–8).

Assessment is an essential component in determining eligibility for services in social work. It occupies a dominant role in social work, particularly in adult services, where meaningful aspects of direct casework have given way to low-level functional tasks. As far back as 1983, Black claimed that assessment and investigative work forms roughly 65 per cent of all client referrals and long-term work. Social workers' responsibility for assessing referrals is a primary role undertaken to make decisions on behalf of service users or fulfill statutory obligations. Assessments are sometimes called evaluations that identify the sort of intervention needed through care plans. As Coulshed (1988) noted, 'they are essentially speculations' based on a variety of subjective and objectives sources (p. 12). Obtaining as much information as possible about the client allows for a planned intervention that can be carried out efficiently whilst trying to avoid risky situations. Davies (1994) confirms that assessment involves drawing up a balance sheet along the three dimensions of *risk*, *need* and *resources*. He suggests that front-line workers need to ask, for example, whether 'the risk of keeping a client in the community will be too great' (p. 151). Similarly probation work is increasingly dominated by assessment tasks. In the Home Office guidelines *Evidence Based Practice: A Guide to Effective Practice* (1998) probation officers are advised that 'Assessment is a continuous, dynamic process which involves gathering and analysing information in order to ascertain the level and type of risk posed by, and the criminogenic needs of, an individual offender.' These kinds of emphasis confirm Rose's earlier question about whether service users can be managed in the open circuits of community control, or whether social care is becoming little more than a safety-net operation for marginal populations.

In summary we can see that risk assessment aspires to prediction and determining probable outcomes. In its regulatory ambitions it's a way of breaking down, rearranging and sorting out specific factors relating to targeted individuals and populations. We can see how care assessment has a dual ordering function: (1) it attempts to establish the regularity of certain risks; (2) it is based on a calculus of probability, attempting to deduce the chances of an incident actually occurring. Assessments try to determine, for instance, how often a frail elderly woman wanders around outside the house after dark. A follow-up consideration might be what the likelihood is of her being attacked or injured in such a situation. Various physical and psychosocial variables are then identified to determine the probability of adverse effects.

Risk assessment has the effect of sealing the destiny of service users by determining whether or not an intervention or resource is required. In this sense it is a normalising process in that the risk assessment decides issues about resource entitlement. It may be decided on the basis of a rationing system that a lonely elderly man is not entitled to receive home help, meals-on-wheels or a place in a local day centre. Individual care provision, particularly in adult services, is often compromised by the emphasis on risk assessment. Rummery and Glendinning (2000) capture the effects of this in the following:

> Assessments have increasingly been used as mechanisms for prioritizing needs and restricting services for all but those deemed most at risk. Indeed, many social services departments now ration access to assessment itself, through a range of managerial and bureaucratic procedures which effectively delay or circumvent the assessment and care management process for all but those considered to be at the greatest risk of harm. (p. 51)

Those social workers who work with elderly people with dementia are very aware of the divisiveness and inequity of this rationing system of which risk assessments form a legitimating part.

A number of flawed assumptions underlie risk assessment. In attempting to objectively determine the distribution of risk in a given target population or environment, risk assessment depends on a rational-linear model of reality. It will be argued that social life does not work the way that the rationalist programmers and planners think it does, such that assessment tools are prone to error. They rely on a naïve and static objectification of the current situation. By limiting and filtering the observed empirical reality, the assessment structure enables it to be transcribed into a language of fixed categories (e.g. level of need). Assessment rarely deals with the interactions between variables, because of its dependency on fixed categories. This is why in child protection assessment is often referred to as showing a checklist mentality (Corby, 1996). The naïveté stems from view that the descriptions of the client's reality, their personality traits, skills or emotions, represent the actual nature of the problem. By means of a structuring process, it is believed that assessment renders a variety of complex and changing relations amenable to a fixed logic of objectification. In fact, assessments mechanically reduce individual experience to a system of variables whose values have already been designated, if not by quantity, at least by a finite set of descriptions already given in assessment manuals (see McBeath & Webb, 1991a).

As Middleton (1999) has argued, 'The routine collection of standardized data has too often become a substitute for intelligent enquiry' (p. 21). It's likely that a small number of open-ended questions would reveal much more about the nature of the client's lifeworld and relations than the closed tick-box method. In his discussion of risk assessment, Parton claims that:

> Risk assessment suggests precision, and even quantification, but by its nature is imperfect. Given the mobile character of the social world and the mutable and controversial nature of abstract systems of knowledge, most forms of assessment contain numerous imponderables. (1996, p. 109)

Risk assessments differ from other methods of social work assessment by focusing exclusively on risk factors. They often exclude the two important dimensions of service user need and resource availability. Brearley's *Risk and Ageing* (1982) was one of the first writings to introduce risk assessment in assisting decisions about resource allocation for work with older people. Kemshall (1996) notes: 'risk assessment and effective risk management are likely to become the main preoccupations of the probation service' (p. 134). Offender-work guidelines on risk management enunciated by the Association of Chief Probation Officers (1997) manual call for a more active response to risk. Recently nationwide computer software called ASSET (Assessment Methods for Offender Services) was introduced to help predict high criminality with young offenders. Similarly, in mental health services, the *Report of the Inquiry into the Care and Treatment of Christopher Clunis* (1994) stated that after-care plans should include 'an assessment as to whether the patient's propensity for violence represents any risk to his own health or safety or to the protection of the public' (1994, para. 45.1.2). In 1994 the Department of Health (DoH) in typical fashion produced another set of formulaic guidelines for assessing risk for service users with mental health problems (Department of Health, 1994b). Risk in child protection work was originally used to identify risky populations. As Craddock (2001) points out:

> Their concern was with the correlation of differential material and social benefits with differential incidences of child abuse. Such studies were solely concerned with identifying risky populations and almost always carried the caveat that they should never be used in the context of particular assessments of particular situations. In other words, risk assessments were seen as a necessary source of data for the policy making field, not guides for the practice of child protection workers. (p. 7)

In Britain this emphasis began to change in the late 1980s as risk assessment strategies came to dominate children's services. The checklist or tick-box mentality as it is often called was consolidated with the publication of the DoH's (1988) *Protecting Children: A Guide for Social Workers Undertaking a Comprehensive Assessment.* Throughout this document a highly mechanical conception of checklist criteria is used. It provides social workers with methods for paring down the uniqueness of individuals so that they fit the checklist profiles (e.g. of 'good parent') (Aust, 1996). Such guides use various value-laden terms like 'over-inhibited', 'immature personalities', 'innate and flat personalities', 'low self-esteem' and 'dangerous families'. Such terms are low-level conceptual borrowings that attempt to create an objective designation of individuals. In fact, they are key elements in distributing norms of regulation in that they form part of what Max Weber called technical means-end rationality. Power relations between care managers, social workers and service users can govern the outcome of risk assessments. Service users are managed through networks of question schedules that subordinate them to the assessment's pre-determined agenda of categories. The validity of a service user's contribution to risk assessment is relevant only insofar as it can be interpreted through the fixed categories of the guidelines (McBeath & Webb, 1991a, pp. 142–3).

Risk assessment is permeated with subjective values and contextual noise. As Douglas and Wildavsky remark:

> Risk analysis was produced as a tool for engineers and statesmen who needed more facts. They asked for objective facts . . . There is the delusion that assigning probabilities is a value-free exercise. Far from being objective, the figures about probabilities that are put into the calculation reflect the assigner's confidence that the events are likely to occur. (1982, p. 71)

Douglas and Wildavsky point to the fact that risk assessments are part of a wider political and cultural domain and are always subject to different perspectives. Risk assessment is coloured by subjective judgements at every stage of the process – from the initial structuring of the risk problem, to the processing of what is considered relevant information, to deciding which configuration of risk factors to include in recommendations and the kinds of outcomes that experts are seeking (Slovic, 1999). The next chapter examines some important aspects of this reflexive dimension as part of care pathway planning in social work and the construction of security and trust for service users.

Conclusion

This chapter has explored risk and social work in relation to expert regulation in the context of neo-liberal political rule. By identifying a crucial shift from universal welfarism to neo-liberal welfarism we've seen how an austere form of social governance increasingly shapes social work. The substance to this shift is further clarified in the discussion on front-line practice that follows. Social work is regulated to fend off risk but also to provide secure moorings and a safety net from which to intervene with targeted marginalised groups. We've seen how social work is regulated and regulating; inhibiting and permissive; and destructive and beneficial. Social work is 'a site of expert-mediated action' which, according to Bauman, is necessary in risk society due to the uncontrollability of its systems and actors (1991, p. 210).

Within the contours of late modernity, social work partakes in projects of calculation and regulation in the face of risk. This, however, signals a potential contradiction for neo-liberal social work. If expert mediation, as part of the logic of regulation, becomes prominent in social work, this will seriously undermine the reflexive potential of individual choice, personal responsibility and risk estimation so keenly advocated in neo-liberal political rule. As we shall see, the move away from intensive direct work undermines personal needs for trust, recognition and intimacy in face-to-face work with people. We've seen that with neo-liberalism the individual is quintessentially a single entity: the individual as consumer who is 'a package, an enterprise with nothing to do but manage his own affairs' (Strathern, 1992, p. 175). The Marxist sociologist Georg Lukacs (1971) warned that the application of the principles of 'rational mechanisation' and 'calculability' to every aspect of life leads to reification, by which he meant relations between people increasingly take on the appearance of relations between things.

Social work is increasingly shaped by this individualising enterprise of privatised risk. Insofar as regulating privatised risk is concerned the next chapter shows how life planning strategies are crucial to social work. Life planning is done for those who by virtue of their lack of competence or capacity for self-management require expert mediation. We've seen how members of the dispossessed underclass are framed as 'waste-products of the game' and subject to the maintenance regulation strategies of 'petty engineers of social conduct'. But we've also noticed how smarter consumer-driven service users increasingly challenge expert systems and their risk knowledge management. We'll see in the chapter on technologies of care (Chapter 5) how under such circumstances expert-mediated action is forced to retreat into ever more abstract system-methods to maintain the gap between professional and service user.

Whilst the need for social work will not diminish, its generic status based on universal service provision will dramatically alter, with the prospect that social workers are replaced by family care workers, personal advisors, coaches, rehabilitation and youth offender workers each combining multi-disciplinary skills with targeted interventions aimed at micro-sections of people on the edge of society. Specialised local agencies will develop to pool knowledge, skills and resources in attempts to provide seamless services. It's likely that risk regulation in social work will lead to a decline in face-to-face work, especially in adult statutory services. In what follows the development of new risk-based technologies of care is shown to be a major factor contributing to this gradual decline.

3

Security, Trust and Care Pathways

Introduction

We've seen how risk regulation and expert mediation are inter-woven because of conditions of uncertainty in neo-liberal risk society. As a net effect security and trust have an increasingly dominant place in our risk-inflated daily lives (Bauman, 2001). This chapter examines how the relationship between security, trust and life planning in risk society impacts on care planning and pathways in social work. It is shown how life planning, as a kind of reflexive ordering, emerges around the need for security and order. This results in the development of expert forms of social protection with social work acting as a safety net. The argument runs that the concept of safety net is *empirically grounded in an understanding of risk and vulnerability and is mobilised for those made transitorily vulnerable by livelihood shocks or fateful moments.* Here social work is characterised as expert mediation that protects targeted populations against risk contingencies. Thus social work provides a kind of planned insurance against risk and undergoes significant transformations as a result of new demands for security, safety and trust within neo-liberal political rule.

Social Work and Ontological Security

The literature on risk and social work has tended to concentrate on discursive and structural dimensions. By focusing on these formal aspects it discerns only a narrow deterministic standpoint. There's an additional level of analysis which concentrates on the experience of late modernity (discussed in Chapter 1) and expressive relations as explored in Giddens's writings on 'ontological security'. He draws attention to the way security is a major consideration of individual choice in choosing a partner, finding a safe neighbourhood to live in, following a personal diet and hygiene, and reducing possible environmental risks. As Buzan points out, 'The individual represents the irreducible basic unit to which the concept of security can be applied' (1991, p. 35) and not the nation-state, discursive regimes or social institutions. Carol Smith (2002) forewarns us, however, that 'ontological security and the (uneasy) comfort of relative certainty are bought at a cost. In the interests of order, the state assumes responsibility for shaping social relations, law governs the dangerous moral proclivities of individuals and socialization ensures the assimilation of moral codes' (p. 44).

In risk society people are increasingly required to develop microskills associated with ensuring security in their lived environment and plan for future hazards. They learn to reflexively scan and monitor the external environment for perceptual indices of risk and hazard. Security is increasingly negotiated at an expressive interpersonal level. Giddens's account pays close attention to the way that security is bound up with aspects of reflexive identity. In the words of Lash & Urry (1994), such an approach requires that we do justice to 'an increasingly significant reflexive subjectivity and the consequences of a subjectivity engaged in a process of reflexive modernization' (p. 3). Social work practice involving trust, personal security, confidence, and life planning is an important dimension that has been overlooked in the literature. The relation between these practices and risk society has only recently begun to be explored. The social work literature of Ferguson (2001), Powell (1998), Christie & Mittler (1999) and Thorpe (1997) has advanced an important Irish social policy perspective on reflexive modernity. In doing so these writers have profitably explored how reflexive sociology relates to social work.

The professional expertise of social work is increasingly challenged in risk societies. As Ferguson (1997, cited in 2001) points out, 'the same individuals who are increasingly subject to, and the subjects of social regulation have simultaneously become increasingly critical and *reflexive* with reference to them'. He's indicating a narrowing of the gap between expert and lay person as a core element of reflexive modernity. This leads to the development of what DeSwann (1990) calls 'proto-professionals'. A new relation between service users and experts is established, based not on welfare bureaucracies but on the economics of desire as manifest in imperatives of self-actualisation. The new proto-professionals, clients or often middle-class carers (such as foster carers) act as 'translators' for service users, often speaking the jargon of profess-ional discourse and keen to work in partnership as part of their life-style choices. We know from research that caring resources are not necessarily given according to need but can be influenced by those proto-professionals who most effectively articulate their needs (Twigg & Adkin, 1994). The resulting effect can lead to a hierarchy of care provision in social work whereby there are reflexive winners and losers among client groups.

Ferguson (2001) detects the prospect for a newly fashioned and revitalised social work derived from what he calls 'life politics'. Life politics differs significantly from structural or emancipatory politics in its emphasis on self-actualisation and the reflexive order-ing of choice, rather than structural and economic transformation. Giddens defines life politics as follows:

> Life politics does not primarily concern the conditions, which liberate us in order to make choices: it is a politics *of* choice. Whilst emancipatory politics is a politics of life change, life politics is a politics of lifestyle. Life politics is the politics of a reflexively mobilized order – the system of late modernity – which, on an individual and collective level, has radically altered the existential para-meters of social activity. It is a politics of self-actualization in a reflexively ordered environment . . . .(1991, p. 214)

In this account life politics concerns political issues that flow from reflexive processes of self-actualisation. Giddens regards the reflexive project of the self as a continuous dialogue, where the goal is to re-establish a cohesive but ever revised biography in a setting of many choices. Ferguson's overall exposition picks up this recast-ing of reflexive politics in late modernity and imaginatively deploys it within the context of social work. He suggests that social work is primarily constituted by the social value of 'life politics', focusing as it does on loss and bereavement, adoption work, relationship counselling and children and family work (2001, p. 50). He tells us that:

> While referral practices and the help seeking of service users reflect crucial aspects of social work and life politics, life planning has a longer-term resonance in post-traditional social work. This relates to processes of self-actualization,

healing and the acquisition of 'mastery'. Enabling a person to (re)gain a sense of mastery over their life needs to be at the centre of social work and life politics. (2001, p. 52)

Ferguson's humanist account is governed partly by a 'rule of optimism' which resembles the politics of economic individualism espoused by neo-liberalism. It avoids the complexities surrounding the ambivalence of expertise in late modernity and fails to take the politics of neo-liberalism seriously. By concentrating on the positive nature of life politics it neglects the tensions between ethics and politics in modern societies and the structuring of inequality (Garret, 2003). Neither does it properly acknowledge the critique of governmentality, as a form of social control, initiated by Rose and Mitchell and in social work by Nigel Parton (see Scourfield & Welsh, 2003). Similiary, it ignores the hardening of an actuarial rationality in social work. Ferguson may be pointing social work in a misleading direction, both morally and politically, by accentuating individual choice and responsibility, albeit within an ethics of care or critical best practice framework. We've seen in the previous chapter how this neo-liberal agenda significantly undermines public ideals of social solidarity and the common good. Life politics are privatised utopias. Ferguson's life politics can have the effect of reinforcing a narrow therapeutic discourse that individualises problems and downplays structural inequalities of wealth and power (see Specht & Courtney, 1994). Indeed, Skehill (1999) criticises Ferguson's former colleague Fred Powell's analysis of reflexive modernity in Ireland for precisely this failing. She shows that Powell fails to acknowledge the contradictory role of social work as regulator and enabler (1999, p. 802). Nevertheless, Ferguson's perspective provides an innovative departure in theorising core interventions in social work. It is suggestive of a radical overturn of some key values and concerns in current practice. Implicitly at least, it requires a shift away from the structuralist emancipatory politics of social work with its attendant concerns with oppression and discrimination. Such a perspective is antipathetic to so-called post-modern and critical social workers who pursue 'practice theories that prioritize structural analyses' (Healy, 2001). In undertaking this critique Ferguson opens the door for a critique of anti-oppressive practice and its concern with an emancipatory politics of structural change.

The Logic of Security in Social Work

In order to develop the idea of social work as a response to security, with its life planning and safety nets, it will help to remind the reader what ontological security means. For Giddens it is a sense of confidence and trust in the life-world and security of personal well-being. He describes ontological security as the confidence that most human beings have in the continuity of their self-identity and with the regularity of routine and habit. Much of the work that goes on in maintaining or restoring a sense of ontological security takes place in intimate relationships and at home. The private realm is a place where people's basic security can be restored, maintained or damaged. This is not to downplay the significance of the work-place but serves to underline the relevance of privatised risk in late modernity. In social work basic security in trusting relations with clients is achieved through dialogic relations of proximity and interaction. Unlike other abstract expert systems in scientific professions of engineering or telecommunications, social work develops trust relations through face-to-face work.

Let's look at some concrete examples of the social handling of security and safety. Social workers and occupational therapists often conduct a 'pre-discharge home visit' before older people leave hospital. Each pre-discharge visit is case-specific and follows a hospital assessment that is carried out prior to the discharge (Gillespie et al., 2002). A key consideration with these visits is the assessment of factors of risk that create insecurity. Social workers thus undertake what are often referred to as 'hazard assessments'. With hazard assessments the experts construct the home as a site of insecurity and risk. Here health and social care experts are primarily concerned with the reduction of fear for service users. They try to allay fears around discharge; these include anything from safety, to strangers gaining access to the home and people's ability to get around the home. Older people often have fears about falling and not being found or able to get help. Getting stuck in the bath is a constant anxiety for some people. Social isolation is another key concern for them so they are encouraged to attend luncheon clubs or day centres. This can help integrate older people into the community and provide them with a sense of social security. The recent death of a spouse can exacerbate insecurities surrounding social isolation. They also feel insecure about attendant risks outside the home, such as poor street lighting, broken paving stones, and rowdy gangs of youths who run from house to house 'door knocking'. Even animals, such as large dogs, in or around the home are considered by the social worker as a potential hazard or danger.

Internal environmental risk is another concern for the social worker in search of hazards. Many older people leaving hospital are 'multiple fallers'. Professionals are expected to closely assess risk involved in the environment such as loose floor-mats, telephone wires trailing over a main walkway, lighting on cellar steps and tinned food stored in high cupboards which might fall on the older person or increase blood pressure as they reach up. Safety on stairs is a key issue with adequate lighting, unworn carpets and grab-rails all coming into consideration. Fire and the accidental starting of fires are a key concern for social workers during their hazard assessment. In some cases, cigarette smoking is considered a significant risk in case an older person falls asleep with a lit cigarette. Tell-tale signs of these 'bad habits' for social workers are burnt chair-arms and holes in nearby carpets.

A further risk considered during the hazard assessment is referred to as 'cognitive risk'. This involves how well an older person can function in the home. Some older people have a disorientation of time, poor memory and tend to wander around both inside and outside at all hours. This can increase their vulnerability by either them getting lost or increasing opportunities for people to take advantage of them. Psychogeriatricians and social workers assess whether older people are a risk to themselves and need to consider how to make home environments safer by providing, for example, visual prompts and memory aids to prevent them harming them-selves. Visual aids are also used to increase their sense of security, for example by reminding them to lock doors and take the key out. When visiting older people's homes one is often confronted with large signs in large print, which are stuck everywhere as memory props. Some older people increase their vulnerability and risk by hoarding money in the home, often forgetting where they've hidden it. Adult protection workers consider these older clients to be at risk of burglary or theft and find it difficult to protect them. They consider putting digital locks on the door using a key-pad system which allows home helps to access the house without the older person having to come to the door (see Mackenzie et al., 2000).

Ritual and habit are important ways of structuring life for older people. Indeed, domestic rituals such as hoarding food or money, concern for locks and keys, as well as regular home visits are all conducive to a sense of security and well-being. Grab-rails and grip-per bars, for example, reduce the attendant risk of climbing stairs or negotiating a tight space. In sum, this apparatus of life planning security undertaken by social workers provides a feeling of insurance against risk. In this example of hazard assessment for older people leaving hospital different forms of mediated action join together to delineate domestic space. The home is cut across by expert risk assessment but also by an emotional investment based on the social proximity between the older person and the social worker. If social work is serious about listening to service users' views it should acknowledge the importance given to the home as a site of emotional security. Research has shown that older people, for example, prefer home visits and individual interviews at home to telephone conferencing and focus groups (see Patmore et al., 2000).

A manifest concern for safety, trusting relations and a sense of feeling secure are at work in these kinds of front-line practice. The overall effect is to produce a 'security of well-being' and safety from risk for older people. This sense of security is an emotional rather than a cognitive phenomenon and closely linked with habit and routine in the home. Thus we can see that much of the expert mediating work that goes on in maintaining or restoring the security of well-being occurs in the private sphere (Dupuis & Thorns, 1998). Similarly, there's been a longstanding concern with the continuity of care of older people. Continuity of care is seen as an important influence on the life-chances of older people with changes in residence being a key consideration (Biggs, 1987).

Security as a Metaphor for Social Work

The security metaphor sits at the centre of social work discourse. In England a good example was the Place of Safety Order in Section 28 of the Children and Young Persons Act 1969. Regulated by law the orders were used to detain a child in a place of safety as defined by the courts. If granted, the orders authorised the detention of the child in such a place of safety for 28 days or specified shorter periods (Dingwall & Eeekelaar, 1982). Largely used in emergency crises these orders did nothing more than allow the authorities to remove the child and detain her or him. For example, medical or behavioural assessments could not take place unless the parents' permission was obtained. The kind of regulated security offered by this legislation was conceived entirely in terms of a sense of place and location. Social workers are quite literally guardians of place in providing security for children. In effect Place of Safety Orders are spatial practices concerned with ensuring security for children. They authorise spatial appropriations by withdrawing children from an unsafe location (the home) and relocating them in a secure place. The place of safety is supposedly enclosed and insulated from risk. But social workers are also concerned with the crisis of place as a temporal insecurity. This begs the question as to whether the regulatory 28 days were arbitrarily conceived. In some respects they were, but crucially, they routinely order the crisis of place within the continuity of fixed time (a month) as a point from which to intervene. The time period is a metaphor for the dialectic of regulation and security. The very fixing of the number of days at 28 conveys that the child is somehow safe for at least the period of time evoked. Here we can see how regulated time aims to restore security. Safety and security are often the key motivating forces for the ordering of space in child care. That crisis intervention is regulated by time is suggestive of the compulsion to re-establish the continuity of place whilst regulating normality. Continuity is considered normal whilst crisis is a displacement of this ideal. This is why the concept of 'placing for permanence' was so warmly received in social care when it emerged in the late 1970s. It invokes both the security of place and continuity as well as a sense of certainty across time. A vast corpus of literature has emerged around permanence in social work (see Wulczyn et al., 2003). Permanence is making something of a comeback as an influential concept in current looked-after children policy in Britain. In 1980 Mary White enthusiastically claimed that permanency planning for children was a 'national goal' in America. The concept was developed to counter the risks associated with 'children adrift in foster care' and according to Maluccio was used to 'describe the instability, uncertainty ... of temporal and remedial programs' and against these wishing to emphasise the 'critical importance of permanence and the child's need for continuity of parental relationships' (1981b, pp. 6–7). Another author in the same collection suggests that placement itself has meaning. Dorothy Hutchinson believes that 'the request frequently involves the parent who can no longer stand the strains pressing on him *from without* and *within*' (my italics) and that placement always involves 'new and old anxieties for parents' (1981, p. 53). Thus anxiety reduction and trust become significant concerns for social workers dealing with looked-after children in attempts to mirror the security of the home.

Social Work, Security and the Home

The home is a key strategic site for social work. Understanding the connections between people, spaces and place will give us a deeper appreciation of the way the logic of security underpins social work. Research on spatial relations such as continuity, neighbourhood, insideness and outsideness, disjunction and connection, have been largely overlooked in social work. As Fischer & Kargel (1997, p. 15) argue, 'Spatial arrangements matter. We tend not to think about such things, especially in social work.' The significance of home visits for social workers in late Victorian England, for example, was that they provided a bridgehead for confidence building and establishing trust relations with the casual poor (see Webb, 2007). Face-work cemented stranger relations, proximity and the felt solidarity of direct involvement. In this respect modern social work is little different from its Victorian predecessor. Whilst meanings associated with home change over time the value attached to the 'comforts of home' in an increasingly privatised world is central. The essence of 'being at home' is based on its sense of orientation and emotional belonging. Its opposite, 'not being at home' or 'homelessness' as a phenomenology of lived space is something quite different. Not only does it concern insecurity and fear, but 'being out of touch', 'not knowing which way to turn' and 'beside oneself'. As R. Cooper points out, many of these common idioms about home are 'strikingly spatial' and that 'being spaced out' is quite distinct from 'being homed in' (1989, p. 43). The spatial-ness of home is not just something that surrounds us, but also a field of openings and depths, which lean towards security or insecurity.

In modern societies the sense of place attached to the home has made it a site where people feel most in control of their lives and a secure base around which self-identity is preserved. Social work, along with midwifery, is one of the few female-dominated professions that has 'legitimate' access to other people's homes. Home visits by a social worker or preparation for people returning home help mediate the active search for 'homefulness' as safety and security. They achieve this by focusing on the well-being of clients within various domestic proximal spaces. At the same time with its pre-occupation with safety and trust, social work attempts to provide 'guarantees' of expectations across time-space. The home increasingly symbolises safety and trust in modern society. Whilst it links together material and physical aspects that provide ontological security, it also reinforces deeply felt meanings related to permanency, belonging and continuity. Expert representations of the home are based on assumptions of relatively centered, permanent identities set against a backdrop of increasingly uncertain external risk environments. We saw this emphasis with permanency planning but it's also evident in social work literature on looked-after children, and the dominant attachment theory on child well-being, attachment disorder and neglect. Whilst the language has shifted from 'children in care' to 'looked-after children' the dominant view remains that the best interests of children are served in preserving relationships with their parents, other kin or carers. The effect of this rhetorical shift has led to an absurd situation whereby some family services outline key policy objectives as 'preventing children from becoming looked after' to avoid the language of reception into care. The latest fashionable term emphasising the security of children's well-being is the American notion of 'kinship care' (see Ainsworth & Maluccio, 1998; Schwartz, 2002). Kinship care is one of the fastest growing forms of foster care in the US and Australia (Wilson et al., 2002). This really amounts to saying that children are best looked after by extended family members, such as grandparents, older siblings and neighbours, rather than being in fostering or residential care. This, of course, is an extremely cheap and cost-effective strategy for coping with ever-increasing numbers of children coming to the attention of social workers following family breakdown and abuse (Testa, 2001). However, the linguistic use of security as found in terms such as 'care', 'vulnerability', 'attachment', 'permanence' and 'trust' often involves appraisive value judgements. This helps us understand how shifts of attribution in professional discourse can create homogeneity of practice and favourable public opinion through the rhetoric of persuasion.

We can see how a sense of belonging, safety and trust as it contributes to ontological security is located deep within social work (Freeman, 1983). Some writers in social work go so far as to claim that the security associated with the thread of continuity of place and time is a 'crucial instinct of survival' (Marris, 1974, p. 17). The crux of my argument is that social work maintains and restores a sense of ontological security for service users within risk society. This is particularly the case in relation to the security and proximity offered within the home. We need to recognise the beneficial nature of social work in attempting to reinforce people's 'centred' sense of security in terms of 'being at home'. So attachment theory might better acknowledge the imporant of place as well as persons in its thinking about childcare relations. Social work positively intervenes and confronts the felt alienation of people in a world increasingly pre-occupied with risk. There are, however, some unfortunate examples of negative intervention in social work. These will be focused on presently in the section on residential care.

Security, Social Proximity and Residential Care

This section focuses on residential secure units for children. These secure or 'closed units' for children have a long and at times tarnished history in social care. In Britain they were originally set up to cater for children who persistently absconded from school. After the implementation of the Children and Young Persons Act 1969 small secure units were developed as a backup to open education. Schedule 4 of the 1989 Act also empowered provision for 'the control and discipline of children in such homes'. In Britain during the 1970s an increasing number of children were in placed in care not for offending or psychopathology but for 'protection' or in the cases of girls for being considered to be promiscuous or running sexual risks of different kinds. These residential secure units were not established on the basis of having punitive or deterrent roles but were instead intended for developing a positive or therapeutic role. In 1971 a discussion paper on *Development of Secure Provision in Community Homes* characterised risk, security and safety in a variety of imaginative manifestations. 'Central secure units' were larger independent units; 'intensive care units' were attached to smaller community homes; padded rooms in residential homes were referred to as 'maximally secure rooms' or also commonly known as 'safe' or 'protected' rooms (Cawson & Martell, 1979, p. 39). This report outlined various perspectives on residential secure unit provision. As Cawson and Martell remark:

> The report adopted an underlying medical model of treatment and healing and suggested that one of the useful functions of closed provision was to enable regressive-acting out behaviour to *take place safely in a process of reliving and growing* through early developmental stages. (1979, p. 35, emphasis added)

In 1979 they were the first researchers to introduce the concept of risk behaviour into residential childcare literature. This was done partly to counter the dominant medical model. Risk behaviour was distinguished from nuisance behaviour to mark out the future-oriented nature of risk. It was defined as follows:

> Risk behaviour incorporated the characteristics which had been used as the justification for the units because they were a potential risk to the child or the community: persistent absconding, offending while on the run; physical violence towards others; and commission of a dangerous offence, such as arson, theft, robbery or rape. (1979, p. 93)

Here risk becomes a unifying set of categorising factors for children in need of residential care. The use of the term 'risk' was initially conceived to offset deviance and pathology models that had previously dominated social work thinking. As Cawson and Martell explain the 1971 report adopted an extreme psychoanalytic perspective and medical model of treatment in which 'security risks' could be taken in the residential setting if this enhanced the child's development. Diagnostic types were developed for treatment of the children. The notion of children 'acting out', reliving experiences and engaging in regressive behaviour in a safe environment comes remarkably close to Simmel's description of the tension of modern individuality. With this tension, society on the one hand, in this case residential social workers, set the limits to excessive or deficient behaviour, whilst on the other hand, individuals, in this case children, are expected to take responsibility for their excessive or deficient actions. In Giddens's terms it was assumed that the security provided by closed residential units for children would lead to a protective environment, underpinned by the coherence of routine structures and trust mechanisms. Within closed institutions this requires a fine balance that can sometimes go horribly wrong. As we've seen in Britain residential homes have themselves at times become risky and insecure places for some children (Colton, 2002).

Pin-down as Insecurity and Social Abuse

The flip side to security, either of a personal or institutional kind, is insecurity. Some writers have argued that neo-liberal policies on the part of a government increase insecurity for its people. Wacquant (1999) argues that the generalised increase of carceral populations in risk society is due to the growing use of the penal system as an instrument for managing social insecurity and containing the social disorders created at the bottom of the class structure by neo-liberal policies of economic deregulation and social welfare retrenchment. In this section I want to trace the way in which some extreme forms of social work intervention in residential homes can contribute to the abuse and insecurity of clients by using individualistic strategies of regulation and social distance.

In England in the mid 1980s the pin-down scandal in children's homes in Staffordshire was an extreme example of regulated 'secure' environments (Levy & Kahan, 1991). Care programmes based on behavioural psychology and 'time out' systems of stimulus reduction provided the theoretical backdrop for the pin-down regime (see Ions, 1977, for a critique of behaviourism). For the badly trained and poorly educated residential staff in the children's homes this amounted to 'the appliance of science'. The children's home log books, control books and 'rules of the establishment' provide good evidence of a secure environment slipping uncontrollably into a brutally regulated regime of containment. Children's clothes were removed, basic privileges such as the use of telephones were denied, communication with other residents was restricted and they were often placed in solitary confinement. The pin-down philosophy aimed to re-establish control of the young people so that they could 'by taking responsibility for their actions earn the privileges previously denied to them . . . and have a say in their future' (Kevy & Kahan, 1991, p. 120). It seems like a perverse utilitarian logic was at stake in which the ends outweighed the means. The children's homes became a law unto themselves. The universal appeal underlying this regime was probably based on the idea that 'this will hurt me more than it will hurt you'. The vexing issue of whether this was simply a sadistic regime of social containment that was 'out of control' remains a pressing concern. It's clear that many of the residential staff where cruel and abusive. However, the residential documentation also refers to children's future prospects, emotional progress, preparing for independence, insecurity in an adult world, signs of hope, working through problems, positive role play, developing life skills. In other words, perverse though it may seem, the residential staff held on to beliefs about individual liberty even in the face of the repressive depersonalising regime they exercised! How can we explain this in light of our considerations of risk society and its attendant insecurities? It seems that the pin-down experience in children's residential homes is indicative of certain *negative effects of the enlargement of expert mediated action* within technologically saturated (behavioural decisionist) environments. The so-called

expert, in this case the residential care worker, stands between individuals and their actions, making it impossible for the children to
experience them directly. In effect, they reinforce ontological insecurity through the mediated imposition of spatial and emotional
(in)difference with stereotyped factors of risk such as needing to re-
establish control and earning privileges. This amounted to regi-
mented life planning for the children through harsh routines and
regulations.

We've seen how ontological security in the home requires integration through social proximity. We discover this at the heart of the
phenomenological writings of Emmanuel Levinas. For Levinas
there is an irreducible ethical proximity of one human being to
another – morality, and through that encounter a relation to all others
– justice. His book *Otherwise than Being or Beyond Essence* (1974)
emphasises the theme of moral commitment within an ethics of
proximity as social interaction (Benso, 2000). The extreme behavioural regime of pin-down led to the development of single-minded
authoritarianism that eradicated social proximity or 'closeness'. The
quality of the moral drive of the residential staff – even when reinforced against a background morality of progress and development
– became increasingly independent of the closed regime that
supplied the behaviourist framework for interaction. The pin-down
'philosophy' allowed for the successive staging of 'social distance'
as regulation by moving children through 'sympathetic pin-down',
'relaxed pin-down', 'basic pin-down' and 'semi-pin-down' to 'heavy
pin-down', 'nasty pin-down' and 'total pin-down'. Following
Bauman, we can assume that the further away the pin-down staging
moved from its original treatment of sympathetic to total pin-down
the more it was guided by purely technical considerations of the
behavioural control treatment. Eventually, the children were placed
in a 'remote control' closed order that lacked any moral prohibitions
of treatment by the residential care staff.

Pin-down led to a gradual silencing of the moral inhibitions of the
residential staff even though they maintained an ideal-typical notion
of progress and development. Principles of social justice and individual liberty were largely set apart from the local conditions experienced by the victimised group of children. The children became a
different category of risk, so that in Hilberg's terms, whatever
applied to that local category did *not* apply universally to all (cited
in Bauman, 1989). A moral conscience is not so easily pricked when
the categories deployed are hardened within stereotypes and abstract

behavioural regimes. The universal benchmark of individual liberty didn't apply to pin-down children because they had already been set apart from its conditions given that they were targeted as in need of special treatment. The slippage of pin-down care workers into the language of rights, justice and liberty was a temporary flight from the local to the universal. Pin-down was more than just a cynical manifestation of extreme forms of social control. Instead it was an evacuation of moral responsibility derived from the abstract technological transformation of the children's identity through mediated expert practice. These practices closed down any trust obtained through proximity and intimacy. The tactics of separation operated through a variety of regulated practices. These included segregated 'time out', forced outdoor physical exercise in underwear, induced inter-personal conflict, constructing a fear of the unknown, removal of clothing, ritualised bathing, solitary confinement and even mild starvation. These appalling tactics of separation eroded the moral responsibility of inter-subjectivity that is entailed in social proximity. As Bauman explains:

> The moral attribute of social distance is lack of moral responsibility, or heterophobia. Responsibility is silenced once proximity is eroded; it may eventually be replaced with resentment once the fellow human subject is transformed into an Other. The process of social transformation is one of social separation. (1989, p. 184)

This deepening phenomenology of resentment initiated through social distancing is observable in references made by residential staff about the children. The Pin-down Inquiry report tells how staff variously referred to the children as 'runts', 'no better than animals', 'disgusting', 'morons', 'gutterish' and coming 'close to death'. This abusive language completes the process of differential distantiation in a closed regime (see Hardt & Negri, 2000, p. 195). Trust between children and social workers no longer obtained in such a brutal environment. Instead relationships were constructed along lines of fear, suspicion, resentment and insecurity. Thus we can see how forms of child abuse in secure residential homes are instances of trust displaced and the deliberate mobilisation of insecurity. It was shown in Chapter 1 that trust is established through confidence in transaction and emotional reliability and closeness. Pin-down helps demonstrate how trust mechanisms are fragile and the way in which once the security of a relationship has been violated it's difficult to reestablish. Indeed, it is rather ironic to note that in the Pin-down

Inquiry evidence given two expert witnesses emphasised the importance of social trust. Perhaps in recognition of the necessity of a tight
relation between expertise and trust, an NHS consultant psychiatrist
observed that cases like pin-down meant that 'a child's trust in social
workers might be dented or further dented' (Levy & Kahan, 1991, p.
125), with another researcher in child psychiatry commenting that
children 'might develop an adversarial relationship with members of
social services' (p. 124).

Life Planning and Reflexive Governance

In late modern society our lives are dominated by forward planning
and calculation. A plethora of self-help publications about life planning and life strategies can be found at high street newsagents. The
guru of the art of self-governance Dr Phillip McGraw has published
his *Self Matters: Creating Your Life from the Inside Out*, following
up his best selling *Life Strategies*. This pop psychology has a strong
market niche in an individualised consumer culture, and while it is
full of recipes for how to succeed, it is largely silent on how to cope
with failure. As we shall see life planning is a central feature of a
reflexive consumer culture.

Life planning also becomes a particularly important activity in
societies that are structured by risk. As Giddens points out, 'reflexively organized life-planning, which normally presumes considerations of risks filtered through contact with expert knowledge,
becomes a central feature of the structuring of self identity' (1991b,
p. 5). The common view we share in modern societies is that life is
something we are to lead and not something that we allow to happen
to us. We suppose that we need to shape our lives, instead of leaving
them to risk, chance or circumstance. This principle rests on the need
for a kind of reflexive ordering of our lives to avoid chaos and uncertainty. The guiding assumption of life planning is that we should take
charge of our lives and bring them under some kind of order as best
we can. Life planning embodies the rationalities of security and regulation. It requires that we assign overarching principles to our daily
activities, in other words, a life is one which we regulate ourselves
according to a plan. Such life planning is thought to offer us the best
security against the failures we are likely to experience in trying to
come to terms with a complex world. Personal security comes about
through foresight, self-control and individual responsibility.

Life-plans are forms of reflexive governance in the face of risk or what Giddens (1994b) calls 'manufactured uncertainty'. Social work intervention is an expert response to this increased emphasis on the subjective calculation of risk. Since many aspects of our lives have suddenly become open, they are organised in terms of 'scenario thinking', and the mandate of social work is to respond to the 'as if' construction of possible future outcomes on behalf of clients. The persuasive power of life planning lies in the prospects of reflexive order, stability and security that it progressively holds out for service users and social workers alike. But life planning in social work is normative in structuring life according to age, education, gender and status and in offering an age-integrated life course for people (see Leisering, 2003). This analysis points to the centrality of social work as an agency of life planning for vulnerable people during long-term or transitory periods.

Some moral philosophers have gone so far as to claim that the rational planning of life determines the 'good life'. John Rawls (1971) said in his theory of the good life that 'The rational plan for a person determines his good' (p. 408). Plans are attempts to domesticate time in order to grant us some security of being able to predict and control future events. In securing ourselves we wish for assurances against surprises, against an open and uncertain future. Simpson (1995) locates our preoccupation with planning alongside the development of technical rationality in modern societies:

> Planning is a forward-looking activity, where interest is fixed upon the future. In planning we have toward the future an enabling and allowing intentionality, a preparing and making way for intentionality. A plan is a recipe for attaining a future goal-state by means of an ordered sequence of actions. Since the timescale of a plan can be arbitrarily long, the future envisioned by us as planners must be indeterminately open. (p. 52)

When we put our plans into action they run the risk of being usurped by contingent forces. On occasion life-plans break down or reach crisis-point and require expert intervention. Social work intervention is often invoked during what Giddens refers to as 'fateful moments'. These fateful moments are times when individuals or families reach a crossroads in terms of their own life planning capacities. Since plans in late modernity are constantly revised due to the contingency of social life, individuals often resort to expert advice to help them. Giddens sees this is a site of potential empowerment for lay people. It allows them to appropriate knowledge and new skills whilst trying to formulate their own life-plans. However, fateful moments are marked by the requirement either to seek help from expert systems or to develop strategies of self-help through planned activities. As Giddens explains:

> They are points at which, no matter how reflexive an individual may be in the shaping of her self-identity, she has to sit up and take notice of new demands as well as new possibilities . . . Fateful moments are transition points which have major implications not just for the circumstances of an individual's future conduct, but for self identity. (1991b, pp. 142–3)

These fateful moments are often the culmination of deficiencies or excesses in people's lives. These may include violence, loneliness, addiction, isolation, bereavement, physical injury, disability, homelessness and mental breakdown. These fateful moments are the very stuff of social work. Thus it is often during transitionary periods, such as leaving or entering care, returning home after periods of hospitalisation, that individuals encounter expert mediating professions who construct proximal events of well-being through life planning. Direct work with children who are separated from birth parents, group work for children who have witnessed domestic violence and respite care for parents of disabled children are all examples of expert mediation following fateful moments in family life. However, social work intervention, during fateful moments or otherwise, is not merely a method of helping individuals to make adjustments to uncertain circumstances. More significantly, it's an attempt to manage and predict risk through rational life planning. Task-centred and solution-focused interventions, as well as notions of 'joined-up' practice typify this kind of life planning. Social work attempts to facilitate strategic options and organise these by rational projections regarding some future state of affairs.

The Growth of Care Planning

Discussion of care planning and management has circulated widely over the past two decades in Britain. Indeed, at policy and practice levels planning has become a veritable obsession in social work and a significant feature of its regulatory practices. Bamford (2001) says that planning is the staple diet of social services. He summarises the plethora of care planning as:

... governed by the ever-increasing number of statutory plans ... the list includes the Children's Services Plan, the review of services to the under eights, the Community Care plan, the Joint Investment Plan required for each care group, the Drug Action Team annual plan, the Youth Offending annual plan, the Community Safety annual plan, the local performance plan and a series of action plans to satisfy the latest government initiative. (p. 21)

Planning in social work is widespread. It covers a continuum of activities from plans with aggregate groups and communities, to plans for meeting specific types of panned user needs, to plans for individual service users. As far back as 1989, however, Thorburn provided a detailed discussion of social care planning in providing secure fostering for children (pp. 45–8). Clearly the development of this kind of practice links closely to the idea of providing social insurance against breakdown, disruption and abuse. Thorburn's appeal for life planning methods in children and family work was legislated for via the Children Act of 1989. Guidelines were produced by the Department of Health (1991) in *Working Together Under the Children Act 1989*, which emphasised the centrality of social care planning. An entire section was devoted to the 'need to develop a written plan' and the requirement to produce a child protection plan was considered to be the major tool for future work. The written plan has to be agreed with carers and parents in light of statutory agency duties but the implementation of the plan is the responsibility of individual agencies and key workers (1991, pp. 32–3). These were modernised through Children in Need Plans introduced as part of the new Department of Health Integrated Children Systems model of service provision. This brings together the Assessment Framework and Looking After Children System under one framework. Here a child's plan is set out at the end of an assessment record specifying areas for behavioural change and support through three sub-plans: care plan; adoption plan and pathway plan. The latter relates to the UK Children (Leaving Care) Act 2000 which endorses life planning strategies with the introduction of 'pathway planning' for those leaving care. Ironically perhaps, the 'fateful moment' for young people occurs as they leave the care of local authority social services. The pathway plan includes assistance with accommodation, education and finance. We can see here how consequential decisions impact on shaping young people's identity. Personal advisors construct pathways plans to ameliorate and manage the uncertainty associated with leaving care. Similarly, in 1990 the methodology of life planning was legislated for in relation to adult community care in Britain. The NHS and Community Care Act 1990 required social services departments to prepare Community Care Plans for all disabled or elderly clients in need of help. The plan outlines the resources that are needed by the client and the proposed method of providing these through various voluntary, statutory or private care agencies. A care manager is nominated for each identified client to undertake an assessment and then construct a care plan. This is sometimes referred to as the Care Programme Approach, which emphasises managed life planning (Davis, 1996). In the field of mental health, Community Psychiatric Assessments (CPAs) combine care plans with risk management plans in identifying the priority of cost-related interventions and levels of risk involved.

Care planning has grown enormously over the past decade. There is even an American nursing profession website which is 'dedicated to address the entire care planning process including assessment, implementation, planning and evaluation as defined in the nursing process' (www.careplans.com/pro/default.asp). Against this backdrop the Department of Health (1991a, b) in Britain outlined seven core tasks to structure the process of what it calls care management. Four of these tasks focus on the development, implementation and monitoring of care plans for work with adult service users. Life planning is considered a fundamental priority for meeting the needs of adult service users. It is deployed as a risk filtering strategy for those adults who are unable to construct their own life-plans or who unnecessarily interfere with other people's.

Social workers are required to be vigilant about the way in which the daily routines of service users can impact on the care plan and potentially undermine it. The following is fairly typical of the kind of considerations given to care planning:

> A needs-led care-planning process must take account of the individual requirements of a person in relation to the service provided. For example, someone needing assistance to wash and dress in the mornings should be helped to identify how and by whom that service should be provided. (Morgan, 1996, p. 116)

As well as offering material resources such as home help services, the care plan may well involve direct work, such as counselling, family work or group work. Care planning as an incremental process and orderly sequencing of events is often juxtaposed against emergency or crisis intervention, which is often a result of risk (Bullock, 1990). It is a way of intentionally breaking down, rearranging and ordering certain elements of a client's reality. Typical of the centrality given care planning in social work is the Care Programme Approach introduced in 1991 and regarded as the cornerstone of the Government's mental health policy in the UK. It is linked to the Care Management Approach practised by local authorities, whereby social services departments assess need and purchase services under the NHS and Community Care Act. This care pathway process has four key stages including (a) a systematic assessment of the service user's personal social care and health needs, and (b) the development of a care plan involving the service user and any informal carers. Here care is organised in a temporal and structured sequence. Its value is not determined according to the instruments that permit its deployment (e.g. the dispositions that social workers bring to bear on the intervention) but according to the conditions which bring it into effect (e.g. the reasons for the referral). Care planning isn't linked to the simultaneous spaces of differences and identities which exist between social worker and client, but instead is a temporal set of successive interventions. Of course, a major problem with care planning is that things change over time. Department of Health guidelines stipulate, 'The care plan should be reviewed at least annually. More frequent reviews may be necessary if either the service user's or carer's health or circumstances change significantly' (1991, p. 10). Care plans assume that a client's life-world can be defined in terms of its finitude and that this definition exists once and for all, except when it is mediated by staged reviews. However, uncertainty confounds the prospect of the determinate outcomes anticipated in care plans. Planning for children in care, for instance, is notoriously difficult and subject to a variety of accidents and contingency (Millham et al., 1986).

The emergence of Family Group Conferences (FGCs) further testifies to the weight given to life planning in social work. Originating in New Zealand, FGCs are convened by independent co-ordinators who arrange meetings for the professionals and families in order to plan for children's care needs (Marsh, 1994; Morris et al., 1998). A National Children's Bureau Highlight (1999) gives a flavour of this preoccupation with life planning. It discusses the aims of FGCs as 'constructing a plan to address identified reparation issues'; the way in which 'plans are monitored and reviewed'; the need to construct 'a plan that is focused on the child'; the need for 'plans to be agreed on' by all parties and crucially how the model is used internationally 'to help people plan in a wide range of situations'. FGCs are planning devices, which attempt to bridge differences between expert and lay people through mediation whilst emphasising the rights of children. They are organised within a projected time-span and are focused through notions of risk and potential harm, whilst straddling the neo-liberal strategy of empowerment discussed above. FGCs are very concrete examples of life planning in social work. Expert mediators in calculating the prospect of family breakdown or disruption produce detailed checklists. This is referred to as the 'tick-box' mentality by social workers. Indeed, the concept of risk is pivotal to FGC work as a whole. Some writers consider FGCs to be an essential component of the practice of empowerment in social work since they rely on service user involvement and aim at family self-reliance (Lupton, 1998). Again, with FGCs we see the rhetoric of the activation of the power of the service user at work issued through notions of trusting partnerships between expert and lay persons.

Giddens suggests that our propensity to reflexive governance is impacted on by social class, gender and age. Anecdotally, a proba-tion officer remarked to the author that the co-ordinator of a staff training cognitive-behavioural group therapy programme observed '70 per cent of professionals were likely to be reflexive' whilst '70 per cent of clients were likely to be activist'. The aim of the programme was to get probation officers to translate activism into reflexivity for offenders. Here a normalisation scenario develops whereby experts are converting their working-class client group from activism to reflexivism. Clearly a mix of reflexivity and diver-sion would be necessary for such a programme to stand any chance of success. Otherwise once the direct work is over offenders simply re-embed themselves in the local culture, which reinforces their criminality. Lifestyle criteria associated with excessive activism – which is presumably linked to criminal opportunism – are expunged in these normalising processes.

Trust and Social Work

Trust is intimately related to risk. As Luhmann (1988) explains, 'Trust is a solution for specific problems of risk' (p. 95). Under condi-tions of neo-liberal rule, 'trust' and 'social capital' have become fash-ionable keywords in policy discourse that seeks to understand how effective social governance is possible under conditions of risk. Trust becomes a concept that bridges individual and organisational responses to risk, and increasingly impacts on the evaluation of good social work practice.

A subjective estimate of risk is involved in trusting relations. Social workers are well aware of the problems of placing trust experienced by clients, which involves making estimations about the future uncertain and uncontrollable actions of others. The increasing call to involve service users in decisions and plans is dependent on strong trust functions. There is always the possibility that our entrusting will be violated, taken advantage of, or that all our efforts to evoke trust, for example by greater involvement of service users, will backfire and produce contempt rather than tighter bonds. Heightened risk can lead to suspicion, blame and secrecy, in turn contributing to the hardening of a culture of mistrust and increased litigious action. As Furedi (1997) has argued, social relations are becoming increasingly impoverished in terms of people's confidence in trusting and this leads to a morality of low expectation of other people. Increasingly people expect to be blamed, deceived and become mistrustful in societies which are dominated by risk perceptions. It's against this very difficult backdrop that social workers are expected to carry out their professional responsibilities. Fear of taking risks and the changing emphasis on trust and safety have transformed the work of social workers. There is a general social backdrop to this. As Furedi points out, 'This worship of safety has influenced attitudes towards all aspects of life. It has fostered an inclination to continually exaggerate the problems facing society, which in turn has encouraged a cautious and anxious outlook' (1997, p. 147).

Trust is integral to the smooth running of modern societies. Indeed social order and harmony is often dependent on the establishment of trust relationships. In order to reinforce and foster trust there is a need in modern societies to create conditions for shared deliberation and opportunities for active involvement and participation by people who are trying to sort out or plan their lives (Misztal, 1996). The social amplification of risk can have serious knock-on effects, for example, loss of confidence in public sector institutions and diversion of resources for regulation or protective action to address risks that would have otherwise received less priority. As we shall see, social work plays a key mediating role in fostering relations of trust, albeit that this sometimes goes badly wrong. In some key respects social work is a mechanism of trust which attempts to persuade people that they are embedded within a society which cares for their needs and wants. Trust is based on a presumed reliability that is socially embedded and supported by a normative structure of social relations. It therefore rests on shared values and meanings, which underlie social transactions.

People deeply feel the need for trust in late modern societies. Mary Douglas has observed, 'everyone is affected directly by the quality of trust around him or her' (1986, p. 1). Seligman (1998) makes an important link between trust and risk. He argues that trust is important for people living in late modernity because these societies are characterised by the lack of predictability and the lack of routine (cited in Anheier & Kendall, 2000). Here we can see how trust is intimately connected with cognitive understandings of risk and the information strategies that people use to try and minimise uncertainty.

The flip-side of trust is mistrust. I've often spoken with social workers who are reluctant to tell people, even friends, about their job because of negative stereotypes it throws up. These stereotypes are essentially bound up with notions of mistrust. As Giddens explains, mistrust can be directed at abstract systems, expert institutions or individuals:

> The term 'mistrust' applies most easily when we are speaking of the relation of an agent to a specific system, individual or type of individual. In respect of abstract systems, mistrust means being skeptical about, or having an actively negative attitude towards the claims of expertise that system incorporates. In the case of persons, it means doubting or disbelieving the claims to integrity their actions embody or display. (1991, p. 99)

Here we can detect how prejudice about social work is caught in the popular imagination. Lay scepticism about social work is based on mistrust.

Coding Trust in Social Work

Trust and confidence figure very highly in the British General Social Care Council (GSCC) Code of Practice. Trust as a construct of moral behaviour figures in two out of six key headings: social workers will be expected to 'strive to maintain the trust and confidence of service users and carers' and 'as a social care worker you must justify public trust and confidence in social care services' (see *Guardian*, 9

January 2002). One should accept that such standards of conduct are always written as declarative sentences that are as unequivocal as possible so as to state clearly what is expected but also acknolwedge that they involve regulation of professional practice in terms of accountability. Here we can observe the enforcement of trustworthiness, or more precisely agencies of accountability such as the GSCC, who monitor and sanction the conduct of the trustee. The Code of Practice issued by the GSCC is based on expectations of benign conduct and independent acts of trusting. What is most disappointing about the GSCC code is its defensive stance. It is a calculated modulation of conduct driven by a defensive culture which mixes accountability with risk management. There is a paradox involved in this coupling of trust to accountability. As Sztompka points out, 'The emphasis on accountability and pre-commitment means that trust in a regime is due precisely to the institutionalization of distrust in its architecture' (1999, p. 140). The Code of Practice fails to recognise, as will be further discussed in the final chapter, the value of social work in deepening trust relations as a feature of various ethical relations that are increasingly under threat in neo-liberal culture (Putnam, 1995). Moreover, as Sztompka notes, such codes are prone to failure because they include a variety of trusting expectations from the most demanding to the least risky bets. He says that trust expectations about moral conduct are more risky than expectations about the reasonableness of individuals, such as timekeeping or working in a dependable manner. According to Sztompka moral expectations of trust are the most difficult to meet because 'the number of biased, unfair, abusive or exploitative actions are quite considerable in every society' (1999, p. 54).

In social care settings a fundamental quality of trust has been understood for some time. Trust is fragile; once it has been violated it is difficult to re-establish (Slovic, 1999). It is typically created in a slow sequential order, but is damaged in an instant by accident or mistake. Thus once lost it takes time before it can be regained. The heavily publicised child abuse scandals as well as the popularist view of social workers as well-intentioned but interfering busybodies contribute to the public's mistrust. When it comes to risk, trust is ever more important when the stakes are high in social work. The not-so-impressive statutory record of residential childcare in combination with the stigma associated with removing children in sexual abuse cases has tended to compromise the credibility of its 'trusting' message. What turns child abuse scandals into something of a real life drama, witnessed by a global audience, is its extensive media coverage. As the production of risk comes to dominate society, social work is extensively mediated by external sources such as television, newspapers, pressure groups and the internet. Even when risk communication is good its effectiveness may be limited because of the lack of trust by the public in the message source. Indeed, Smith & McCloskey (1998) point to the differences between expert and non-expert views of risk as being one of the key issues facing the public in terms of risk communication. They argue that there is a 'prevailing popular view which sees experts as being unable to articulate adequately the uncertainty inherent in predicting outcomes for complex problems' (1998, p. 44). They also contend that there is a lack of faith in institutionally based expertise and that this lies at the heart of many risk debates.

Trust and Confidence in Social Work

We've seen how trust figures strongly in social work and cuts across practice in diverse ways. Alaszewski et al. (1998) draw out the various trust relations at stake with welfare professionals:

> Trust is both the cement of relationships and the lubricant of interaction between the public, the welfare agency and its front-line staff. The public trusts agencies to protect them both as anonymous members of the public and as potential or known users of the agency services. The front-line worker is trusted by both the agency and the user to deliver appropriate care and support. Front-line workers have to trust their organization to protect them from the hazards involved in providing care and support. (p. 148)

Carole Smith (2001) similarly argues that trust is necessary for social work, but that it is best understood in informal and unstructured settings. She convincingly shows that the Government's preoccupation in relation to social work is with confidence, and not trust. The former is based on systematised formal networks of safety and routine – or what Smith calls system confidence. Smith shows that the link between trust and social work hinges on the essentially interpersonal encounter. It is a form of communicative action concerned with achieving and maintaining mutual understanding and trust. Smith's account leads to the conclusion that trust and confidence are potentially in conflict. Drawing on Habermas's distinction, the meaning of the life-world – as an interactive field of possible trust relations – can be limited and reified by the exercise of system power aimed at enforcing public or political confidence in social work (White, 1990). From this perspective social work is a system of actions, in which actions attain a functional value according to their contribution to the maintenance of the system.

Expert mediating systems such as social work rely heavily on supportive judgements of confidence as conveyed by the public, media and government to legitimate their professional conduct. Knowledge and value claims in social work, however, are tested along a trust–mistrust continuum. Institutionalised mechanisms of trust come to dominate the policy agenda. The British Association of Social Workers (BASW) Code of Ethics is one mechanism whereby the trustworthiness of social workers is internally managed. Similarly the establishment of the General Social Care Council under the legal framework of the Care Standards Act 2000, and the Social Care Institute for Excellence (SCIE) might be considered as trust mechanisms aimed at building confidence in the profession as well as standardising and regulating practice. As Smith (2001) points out, the policy and legislative backdrop to these developments is New Labour's reforms and the White Paper *Modernizing Social Services*, which is primarily concerned with regulating local authority departments through new monitoring bodies setting and measuring standards of performance (Department of Health, 1998). Here we see exemplary instances of the way in which risk regulation and trust converge to shape social work practice. Each of these new initiatives is about risk regulation. They aim to regulate social care whilst at the same time mobilising confidence and security for service users. Specifically they aspire to be the guardians of standards for the quality of care provision, increase the protection of service users and tackle inconsistencies of practice. As long ago as 1990, Roy Parker was calling for the establishment of a general council for social work. He captures the key ingredients of regulation, risk and trust. Such a social work council, he argued, 'rested on the conviction that since social workers are entrusted with the exercise of considerable discretion they should be subject to mandatory regulation over and above the control exercised by their employers' (1990, p. 15). The full effects of regulation and trust mechanisms based on 'command-and-control' institutions like the Commission for Social Care Inspection or the General Social Care Council are difficult to gauge. It is clear, however, that social work is fast becoming an arena for intense competition for contracts and tenders.

Internal and external auditors, legal specialists, case managers and quality inspectors are seeking footholds in the neo-liberal market for social care. They are also part of the burgeoning audit culture for defining regulatory compliance of standards, performance and accountability.

Trust and Voluntary Welfare Agencies

Comparative studies of statutory and voluntary welfare agencies in relation to issues of trust have not been fully explored in the social work literature. In Britain over the past three decades the public and media mistrust of social work has largely concerned statutory local authority social services departments. The voluntary and even private sectors have remained largely immune from sceptical and negative public attitudes. Obviously, the reasons for this derive from various child abuse and mental health scandals, which have been well documented in the social work literature. There may, however, be other key elements that account for the mistrust associated with the public sector welfare organisations as compared with the voluntary sector in late modern societies.

Trust is psychologically stabilising when voluntary arrangements are relatively secure and reliable and entered into freely. Trust forms the basis for the voluntary association itself, in contrast to interest-based notions of confidence, which involves contractual relations among participants. Thus trust is essentially non-contractual and therefore should not be confused with the idea of confidence at a systems level. This is one important reason why the voluntary or 'third sector' in particular has fared better than local authority social services who have a statutory duty to work with 'involuntary' clients. As Anheier and Kendall point out:

> Voluntary organizations assume an instrumental feature: they are intentional participatory organizations that facilitate social connections and co-operation, and by virtue of repeated interactions engender trust among members. (2000, p. 11)

Trust is therefore more likely to appear authentic when services are provided by non-profit organisations such as the voluntary sector. Intuitively the symbolism associated with voluntary organisations as being 'caring', 'empathetic' and 'altruistic' is likely to foster perceptions of trust. Holman (1988) reports that an under-fives voluntary worker told him, 'It's a great advantage being voluntary. It's all informal, we're called by our first names. Lots of mums don't like social workers, they worry because they think they are going to take their children away . . . But we are not a statutory body' (p. 171). Moreover, as Anheier and Kendall suggest, voluntarism per se evokes the idea of action that is not undertaken for the purpose of financial or extrinsic reward (2000, p. 17). Perhaps it is for these reasons that the many religious and church-related voluntary organisations have been well-placed to draw upon a priori perceptions of trusting relations, until of course the recent scandals of child abuse by religious perpetrators rocked the traditional foundations. Perhaps this is why these violations by church-based paedophiles triggered such far-reaching reactions with the public and in the media.

Conclusion

This chapter has examined the way in which risk society mobilises new forms of security and trust and the way these are mediated in social work by care planning. Care pathways and trust mechanisms are caught within the logic of security described in Chapter 1. It was shown how people, space and places are intimately connected in establishing trust and security in social work (see Fischer & Kargel, 1998). The logic of security is often deployed at the point were trust in systems, organisations, groups or individuals breaks down. Social work thus performs an important role in attempting to restore and maintain security for people in modern societies, focusing particularly on the transitorily vulnerable who are exposed to livelihood shocks or fateful moments. In doing so it attempts to confirm trust and solidarity for its service users. We have seen how key concerns for the security provided by social work are based on safety, protection and anxiety reduction. We have seen how life planning becomes a crucial feature of front-line practice at precisely those fateful points in people's lives where insecurity, risk and breakdown loom large. The strategy of life planning in social work is an attempt to manage and predict risk whilst alleviating uncertainty. Life planning has two contradictory sides. On the one hand, it holds out the prospect of empowerment for individuals because they can widen their choices, knowledge and skills through expert interventions; on the other hand, it regulates people within normative moral and rationally prescribed frameworks. By examining the logic of security with its methodology of life planning we have seen how unintended consequences are produced. Social work can produce risk and insecurity as well as trying to provide solutions to resilient problems. It's been argued that negative effects can be understood as by-products of modernity's ambivalence and not simply as oppressive state control or disciplinary regimes of power.

4

Direct Work, Knowledge and Intervention

Introduction

In risk society changes to professional knowledge should be understood in cultural as well as structural terms. In his book *The System of Professions* (1988) Abbott describes how professions define themselves by claiming certain bodies of knowledge. He describes how, for example, in America psychiatry lost ground to social work in the 1950s as social workers developed practice approaches to casework which psychiatrists had previously claimed for themselves. Risk society affects the institutional arrangements for providing social work with the legitimacy of certain knowledge claims, their status, relevance and points of application. It also shapes the professional identity of social workers as well as their psychological conceptions of how people are 'made up' (Hacking, 1986). Particular 'reality constructs' associated with risk and uncertainty are seen to affect psychological models used to predict and make sense of human behaviour in social work and their corresponding psycho-social realities. How professional knowledge and intervention change and what form they take depends on the various institutional, economic and social processes that have significance in risk society.

This chapter elucidates the social and cultural embeddedness of important knowledge constructs in social work and locates these within risk society. It shows how when key constructs are employed they set the parameters for front-line practice, opening up some channels and closing down others. However, I try to avoid the idea of uniformity in front-line practice, simply because we must recognise that practice varies widely depending on situational factors, adherence to particular models of practice, the priorities given over to certain policies, resources and the influence of managers. A form of path dependency is involved in the choice of a legitimate knowledge in social work which is made in reference to other sets of concepts, trends and values. Through the professional meanings that social workers attach to the knowledge and value base, the normative basis of a given paradigm is gradually established and helps reproduce its 'professional identity'. There is with any dominant knowledge base, in modern societies, a contestable arena from which it can be challenged. The boundaries of social work are always to some degree unstable, in that their sense/reference is open to challenge, manipulation and transformation. The essence of paradigm change thus lies in the malleable, shifting relationship between its authoritative sources, reference points and other professional contexts across time. Abbott (1995) refers to this as 'boundary work' in social work and points to the increased reliance on technical and forensic expertise in trying to ensure professional purity. This kind of sociological analysis helps illustrate processes of production and construction of knowledge in social work at an institutional as well as a practice level. Abbott, for example, identifies three acts which characterise what he calls 'the cultural logic of professional knowledge', these being assessment, inference, and treatment. Assessment is the process wherein information is taken into the professional knowledge system, and treatment is wherein instruction is brought back out from it (1988, p. 40). During assessment, relevant information about the client is assembled into a picture of the client's needs. This picture is then categorised into a proper assessment category and resources are identified to treat the client's needs. Inference is the process that takes place 'when the connection between diagnosis and treatment is obscure' (p. 49). In what follows we see how this cultural logic fits within social work and contributes to its professional identity.

A core feature of the chapter charts the rise of empiricism in social work and outlines some problems associated with this approach. It illustrates that risk governance is increasingly rendered within an empirical programme of direct work interventions with its emphasis on effectiveness, time limitation and outcome measures. Against this perspective a model of social work based on qualitative reasoning or 'bounded rationality' is offered. Here the discussion focuses on what are called 'heuristics' and bounded rationality as an alternative for understanding social work practice. Attention is drawn to the signifi-cance of understanding and judgement as benchmarks of good prac-tice, as opposed to skills, competence and standards.

Adventures on the Road to Understanding

In the 1950s a quiet revolution was taking place in social work. Little did Tom Ratcliffe realise when he gave his address on 'The Problem Family' to the Institute for the Study and Treatment of Delinquency in 1957 that this kind of perspective represented a watershed in the history of British social work. Unbeknown to Ratcliffe and his contemporaries this period marked the expansion of social casework and supervision methods that were derived from psychoanalytic theory. What later came to be known as direct work emerged in the mid 1950s as psychodynamic casework. Ratcliffe was adamant that the focus of casework should be on building mean-ingful therapeutic relationships through which the psychological and emotional problems of clients could be rigorously diagnosed. The problems would be then be adjusted or modified through in-depth therapeutic casework. This period in social work also signalled a shift that was concerned with the dynamics of the ego and inter-personal conflict. Ratcliffe pulled no punches in maintaining that 'if the problem family's real difficulty is a primary feature of human relationships, then the only way in which we can hope to modify the situation is by providing these people with some form of satisfactory relationship therapy. In other words we must provide for them, in a therapeutic setting, the experience of a relationship which they can come to rely upon, to trust and to use as a foundation for their future relationships with other people' (cited in Yelloly, 1980, p. 108).

Ratcliffe's address was intended to consolidate the position of the casework movement by building on his influential paper 'Relationship therapy and casework' published the previous year in the *British Journal of Psychiatric Social Work*. Helen Perlman (1957a, b) had published her seminal essay 'Freud's contribution to social welfare' in *Social Service Review* and the textbook *Casework, a Problem-Solving Process*. A few years later a young Noel Timms brought these issues full circle when he wrote an article for the same *British Journal* called 'Theorizing about social casework' (1959) which formed the basis for his highly influential classic *Social Casework: Principles and Practice*, published in 1964. In the same year Florence Hollis published her tour de force *Casework: a Psychosocial Therapy* (1964) which has left a permanent mark on the landscape of social work literature. Hollis claimed that social work is characterised by its direct concern for the well-being of the individual and as a response to the 'needs of human beings for protection against social and natural deprivations and catastrophes' (1964, p. 12). For Hollis, social work from its inception has stressed the value of the individual. Intuitive insights and improvisation by the practitioner would facilitate the kind of self-realisation Hollis had in mind for her clients. On the other side of the Atlantic, Eileen Younghusband wrote her influential introduction to Father Biestek's *The Casework Relationship* (1961). In 1967 Phyllida Parsloe reported that many caseworkers had acquired the therapeutic knowledge base which had previously been the staple diet of psychiatric social workers and that social work was well placed to develop intensive direct work with child and families by working in multi-professional therapeutic teams. The cultural context for this profess-ionalisation of everyday life related to the weakening of taken-for-granted trust relations (Furedi, 1997, p. 134). The search for internal meaning through in-depth direct work was consolidated in the early 1970s by the humanistic perspective in social work. Analytical group work was also in ascendancy in social work. It aimed to facilitate group dynamics and the potential for transference (to the social worker as well as individual group members) to reveal neurotic and unconscious conflicts in order to strengthen the individual by enhancing self-understanding and self-development (Foulkes, 1986). Goldstein's (1973) highly individualistic account brings out the link between feelings and reflexive processes of self. As part of the primary task social workers should have 'the capacity for feeling and sensing, for "knowing" in internal ways the inner states of others, at times without the benefit of specific clues' (1973, p. 104). As Cooper (1989) points out, not only were insights about how the client was feeling central to these developments but also the 'conscious use of the relationship between the worker and the client' (p. 178). The humanistic strand connects easily to this Freudian perspective. Shaw's *The Self in Social Work* (1974) was a further attempt to bolster the reflexive project from a therapeutic perspec-tive. Drawing on the work of Maslow and Rogers he argued for a humanistic therapy that emphasised the primacy of 'self-actualisa-tion'. Here we can see once again how social work encapsulates some central tenets of reflexive modernity by pitting the self against the formative processes of individualisation and group dynamics (Webb, 1996).

American social workers were ahead of the field in developing casework. As early as the late 1930s and early 1940s the role of social work was seen predominantly in therapeutic and clinical terms with by far the most important perspective being psychoanalysis. In Britain in the 1950s three important contexts underpinned the developments of the psychoanalytic casework method, or what was subsequently known as in-depth direct work. The institutional context was crucial in fostering a favourable climate for psychoanalytic ideas in social work. The Association of Psychiatric Social Workers (APSW), the child guidance clinics and the Tavistock Institute all played an important role in the dissemination of psychoanalytic therapy in casework methods. In 1956, for instance, the APSW published two path breaking books, *The Essentials of Social Casework* and *The Boundaries of Casework*. By the early 1960s the Tavistock Institute was running courses on advanced casework for probation officers and the powerful child guidance movement was harnessing psychoanalytic perspectives from the 1950s onwards.

The second context for the proliferation of therapeutic casework is best understood in terms of the history of psychoanalytic ideas. In particular, the work of John Bowlby, Donald Winnicot and Melanie Klein had a crucial influence on casework methods in social work. Bowlby published *Maternal Care and Mental Health* in 1951; Klein's *Love, Guilt and Reparation* also came out in 1951; and in 1957 Winnicot wrote his enormously important *The Child, The Family and the Outside World*. Bowlby was perhaps the most influential writer on social work during this period and he became a director at the Tavistock Clinic in the late 1950s. His central idea of maternal deprivation placed a great deal of emphasis on nurturing, intimacy, basic security, continuous relations, warmth and trust. Here Bowlby was underlining the primacy of affective life and its impact on inner psychological processes. He later consolidated the importance of this affective dimension in his influential work on attachment theory. As we have seen in earlier discussions this is the very stuff of self-identity in reflexive modernity. Clearly, social work was experiencing what might be called a reflexive renaissance during this period. As Elizabeth Irving happily remarked, 'It is no longer the validity and relevance of psychoanalytic theory which is in question, but the extent to which it can be assimilated, and the ways in which it can be applied by the general body of caseworkers' (cited in Yelloly, 1980, p. 108). As Yelloly (1980) shows, by the mid 1950s the practical working out of these psychoanalytic ideas was integrated into the new generic social work courses run by Eileen Younghusband at the London School of Economics. Classic contributions though these may be, we might wonder how many psychodynamic references are on primary reading lists for students on social work courses today. These writings feel dated perhaps because of the use of anachronistic terms such as 'problem families', 'juvenile delinquency' and 'mental retard' (Welshman, 1999).

The final and perhaps most important context is the cultural dimension in which this movement formed and crystallised in social work. Here we see the ways in which people experience changing notions of selfhood and inner understanding as part of a changing sociocultural climate. Crucially, intimate relationships and the discovery of the self are increasingly taken up as privileged sites of inter-personal meaning which are regarded as part of the fabric of a changing private sphere of intimate relations. Social work played a leading role in this journey of cultural change. Arguably the late 1950s to mid 1960s were the high point of the professional standing of social work in Britain. The very success of psychodynamic casework models in social work gains further legitimation and power through the popular recognition of the importance of social work as an arm of personal social services. This was consolidated in various legislative acts, such as the Children and Young Persons Act 1963 and attendant reforms to the structure of the profession. Here success breeds success. Social work was riding high on the legitimation of specialised casework models and professional status was gained from its close relation with medicine and psychiatry. However, a broadly sympathetic cultural climate also paved the way for its success. That is, a general climate emerged which was sympathetic towards therapeutic models of personal and familial relationships and new child rearing practices during this period. This created a kind of sensibility favourable to psycho-'logical' considerations by the informed intelligent public eye and middle classes. The general public tended to lump psychology, psychoanalysis, psychotherapy and dynamic psychology all together. Thus an unarticulated climate of sympathy for 'psycho'-related literature emerged in the late 1950s and 1960s that found a place in the training of teachers and social workers.

What kind of common explanatory framework can be found that underpins all the relationships between the caring professions and society and more generally in individual and familial relationships? A loose cultural skin derived from diverse factors increasingly constellates and deepens the therapeutic mode and the success of social work during this period. The key to this was found in a set of elective affinities which ranged from psychoanalysis and other therapeutic strategies such as existentialism and transactional analysis. These interests proliferated even further in the 1960s with people increasingly looking to make their lives meaningful. Psychotherapy and counselling gain ground in the popular imagination and new interpretive professions mushroom across the cultural landscape. Highly acclaimed academic books were increasingly watered down into middle-range and popular accounts. The bestseller *I'm OK, You're OK*, Eric Berne's *Games People Play*, Eric Fromm's *The Art of Loving* and Colin Wilson's runaway success *The Outsider* are exemplary of the popularisation of this search for an understanding of the inner self, intimacy in relations and self-exploration. From the 1960s onwards self-improvement and actualisation became popular hobbies with the advent of 'Do-it-Yourself' lifestyles. These popularist manifestations of self-help and therapy grew out of the dissemination and mixing of psychoanalysis and existentialism. As we have seen they were also assimilated by social caseworkers. The psychoanalytic accounts of cultural phenomena exemplify how social workers used their commonly shared 'knowledge preserve' to make sense of events and simultaneously to maintain their own professional reality, drawing on wider cultural resources as well as implicitly legitimating the social reality of depth psychology.

The growth of the casework movement in social work during the 1950s and 1960s tells us something important about processes of social and cultural change. It reveals how modernity's market economy emerged along with the arrival of such 'individualising forms of knowledge' as psychoanalysis. This requires people to regard themselves as autonomous, self-determining and desiring individuals in order to consume and advance themselves economically. Psychoanalysis provided the theoretical paradigm through which the promotion of individualisation under late capitalism came to flourish (Leuenberger, 2002). Psychosocial well-being, instead of, say, 'social qualities' under state socialism, defines people's individual characteristics and desires. We can detect the dynamic way in which social work contributed to the formulation of key aspects of reflexive modernity. The casework model signalled a shift in approach from passive to active engagement with clients. It also emphasised the importance of everyday life and its stresses and strains. Again Tom Ratcliffe was at the forefront of this approach when he argued for the worker needing to become more active in the casework relationship and present herself more as a real person, revealing her feelings, thoughts and attitudes and ensuring that sympathy, sensitivity and concern were important in gaining insight into the client's inner world (Ratcliffe & Jones, 1956). Here again we see the elevation of the affective dimension, not to mention the role of unconscious motivations at work in galvanising the call for a psychoanalytically informed social casework. It is here perhaps that we see in some significant respect the consolidation of reflexivity as the basis of social identity in modern societies. The casework approach however did not come cheaply. It required intensive long-term work with clients. Psychodynamic social work demanded a heavy investment of consultant time and its supposed effectiveness was gradual and not readily apparent in the early stages (Skynner, 1967). As Younghusband pointed out, the Seebohm Report was sold on 'this line of thought' and particularly the consultation model (1978, p. 186).

Issues of supply and demand in social work became even more pressing during the 1970s in Britain. There was an enormous increase in demand for social services during this period. This made it impossible for qualified social workers to cope with casework and administrative requirements. This was in part a result of social work's huge success in the 1960s. As Cooper (1989) notes, 'The social worker of the 1960s, who offered clients casework as a marketable skill, enjoyed a considerable degree of public confidence' (p. 177). The increase in demand, however, was more significantly due to the reorganisation of social services departments in 1974 following the Seebohm Report. As Cooper notes, by the early 1970s casework was under attack. She makes the telling point that 'the notion of reorganizing service delivery in the air, an undeniable tension was developing . . . between the one-to-one relationship as the basis of a therapeutic device, and the direct service givers, project planners and welfare administrators . . . not to mention the task centered and integrative approaches which were rounding the corner in the seventies' (1989, p. 179). The nature of social work was changed by the new organisational structures that emerged at this time, with their emphasis on resource management, bureaucratic efficiency and legislative responsibilities.

There was massive under-recruitment of social workers following their reorganisation into generic area teams in the mid 1970s. However, a Department of Education & Science (DES) circular published in March 1974 reported a serious shortage of qualified staff especially in childcare (DES, 1974). This also led to the employment of unqualified social workers, especially in residential care. In 1973 a CCETSW report in on training and qualifications concluded that with a total of 395,000 people in residential care only 4 per cent of the 65,000 staff who cared for them were qualified. As Younghusband pointed out, 'The proportion of unqualified field-workers had doubled from one-fifth in 1972 to two-fifths by 1975' (1978, p. 243). This impacted directly on workload and casework management. Such institutional and economic mechanisms provided social workers with incentives to give up previous casework and therapeutic practices in favour of currently predominant models discussed below. As a result psychoanalytically driven casework, which by definition required intensive and long-term intervention, came under threat. Therapeutic work, group work and focused direct work increasingly came to be seen as a luxury which social work could not afford. It's relevant to note that much of intensive and long-term work has gradually been transferred from local authority social services to private and voluntary organisations. Just as import-ant in understanding these changes was the element of work-based professional autonomy that adherence to a psychodynamic perspec-tive permitted. The autonomy of the psychodynamic worker from institutional management was achieved by dint of the nature of their model of practice. This tied them more closely to a circular process of introspective work between the client and their own professional involvement. This resulted in a relative autonomy from the adminis-trative responsibilities entailed in the structures of social services departments. It was thus difficult to manage the therapeutic case-workers within a traditional formal bureaucratic system. It was, however, largely economic factors forcing the move away from psychodynamic casework. Therapeutic casework was also thought to encourage dependency on the part of clients who were unable to deal with their 'fateful moments'. As we'll see a quick-fix solution, at least economically, was waiting in the wings and one that could be readily justified on expert scientific and technical grounds.

But what happened by the end of the 1970s to all those social workers that had adhered to a therapeutic casework approach? Clearly there is still a preoccupation with attachment theory in child-ren's services and it tends to dominate child development programmes. However, the rising demand for social work services and the consequent pressures on resources led to a decline in therapeutic work. The emergence of task-centered, crisis intervention and behavioural social work filled this gap nicely as more cost-effective intervention. These behaviourally oriented interventions proposed short-term, conflict-oriented forms of therapy that attempted to alter maladaptive behaviour in a beneficial manner according to learning-theoretical precepts. In Britain the attacks on psychoanalytic casework were less brutal than one might imagine from behaviourally minded thinkers such as Eysenck, Hudson and Sheldon. The proponents of behaviouralism and task-centered casework merely chipped away at the foundations of the 'talking cure' approach of therapeutic social work. Holistic casework gradually came to be replaced by short-term models that emphasised a cause-effect approach to change. Brian Sheldon was happy to announce at the end of the 1970s that the press and other opponents of social work had got hold of figures which proved the ineffectiveness of the dynamic casework approach. Clearly issues of trust and credibility were at stake in the critique undertaken at this time. Sheldon was even moved in his book *Behaviour Modification* (1982) to quote, ironically perhaps, that old casework faithful Noel Timms: 'But you can't solve a problem by talking about it. Something's got to be done!' (p. 10). Adherents of the positivist 'what works' slogan wished to replace psychodynamic casework with a more effective approach (see Jordan, 2000, p. 205). The adventurous search for an understanding of the inner world of the client was coming to an end. In 1978 Olive Stevenson and Phyllida Parsloe, two leading academics, did not help the case by announcing that practitioners in social services departments were fast retreating from holding strong theoretical allegiances. Unfortunately they didn't explain why this was happening. Did the goodies win and the baddies bite the dust? Not quite so.

As a consequence of bottlenecks and changes in welfare provision as well as the restructuring of social services departments psycho-dynamic caseworkers mainly disappeared from the scene. Since those heady times, however, some writers in social work have been highly critical of the emerging orthodoxy of behavioural methods. They were sceptical about the cult of empirical realism with its statistical data, performance components, behaviour modification, problem solving and short-term interventions. It must be remembered that the antagonism towards psychodynamic work came not only from the behaviourists but also from the radical left in social work with publications such as *Case Con!* When *Towards a New Social Work* (Jones, 1975) and *Social Work Practice under Capitalism* (Corrigan & Leonard, 1978) were published by the radical left, they rounded on therapeutic caseworkers with all the viciousness of ultra-left entryists. These Marxists found the well-mannered dynamic-oriented caseworkers thoroughly contemptible. Therapeutic methods, such as Freudian psychodynamic approaches, were attacked as scientifically untenable, ideological, internalist and incompatible with Marxist premises. The latter argued that casework was little more than the exercise of power that manipulated and pathologised working-class clients (Broadie, 1978). Psychoanalytic concepts such as 'the unconscious' and the emphasis on irrational processes were seen as a potential threat to radical social work that was grounded in rational and materialist socialist presuppositions. The main contention was that psychoanalysis did much to undermine the profession's social conscience (Sinfield, 1970, p. 57). The radical left gained confidence from their camp followers in the broad-church community work movement that they had infiltrated (Bulmer, 1987). The war on this front was for a time no more than a war of words. Insults were exchanged but essentially it all took place on paper. The caseworkers were well aware that Marxism had its dark side, its excesses, and they tried to understand its tendency to go off the rails, therapeutically. Little did the Marxists anticipate that they would soon be glad of allies from the ranks of the middle-class caseworkers they had so eagerly attacked. The common foe, of course, was the lower-middle-class shop owner's daughter Margaret Thatcher who in 1979 became Conservative Prime Minister. The conflict in social work seemed like a Sunday-school picnic when compared to the arid and despotic Thatcherite onslaught on the welfare state and its sympathetic intellectual cadre. Community work – the preferred field of social work practice for the left which had been widespread in the seventies almost disappeared in the eighties. Later on the enfeebled Marxists discovered they could find their self-expression in anti-oppressive practice.

Let's return momentarily to the story of the demise of dynamic casework. There were various alarmist and polemical contributions made at the time of its demise. Brewer and Lait opportunistically threw in their two-pennyworth with *Can Social Work Survive?* (1980). This publication resulted in some heated debate. They suggested, at least by implication, that dynamic casework was merely meddling with people's problems and that much higher levels of professionalism were required. This unsophisticated tract received more attention than it deserved. It did, however, to some extent put the cat amongst the pigeons for therapeutically minded caseworkers. Some considered Margaret Yelloly's *Social Work Theory and Psychoanalysis*, published at the peak of the crisis of confidence in 1980, to be a significant counterpoint to the flagrant successes of the empirical realist movement. Alas, today it is more often than not read merely as a good history of psychoanalytically minded social work. More recently, David Howe and some of his colleagues at the University of East Anglia have been developing a viable therapeutic approach for social work. Their vigorous attempts to deepen the psychosocial perspective certainly indicate a loyalty to the casework traditions of the 1950s and 60s. The resultant effect is that attachment theory has come to singularly dominate children's services when thinking about child development and parenting skills. It's interesting though, that Howe (1998) is so keen to discuss the ambivalence of attachment and the relation between security and insecurity without ever locating it in the context of risk society. We have seen in previous chapters how reflexive identities are intimately caught up in late modernity with its attendant risk, insecurity and problems of trust. Giddens's framework of ontological security and the contradictions of intimacy and the pure relationship would certainly provide a deeper and critical social explanation for the psychosocial theory of relationship-based social work and forms of therapeutic casework.

We've seen how notions of the self are constituted in social work and perform as a significant means of professional legitimation. Little did the supporters of behavioural and task-centred social work realise, for example, that their victories in the relatively unimportant field of social work (or so the politicians believe) would play nicely into the hands of neo-liberal welfare reformers and the new public management agenda in the eighties and nineties. Their mantra of individual success, as derived from measurable performance, was foreshadowed by the science of behaviourism. Not only do the differences in approach between the mid 1950s and late 1970s indicate a shift from depth to surface, and from holism to particularism, but more importantly they represent significant shifts in the contours of late modern politics. There is an alternative history of casework, therapeutic interventions and direct work that is explored in the next section. This is a socio-culturally sensitive exposition that places the changing fortunes of direct work firmly within the politics of risk society.

Risk, Short-termism and the Empirical Movement

From the early 1970s onwards empiricism has been increasingly entrenched in practice-based models of intervention in social work. Empirical knowledge, simply meaning knowledge gained through observation, is lauded as the most effective method for bringing about psychosocial change with clients. Increasingly front-line practice is reconstructed and re-evaluated in light of the grip this paradigm holds. It signifies the individualisation of practice interventions based on scientific criteria, with common sense precepts replacing depth interpretation and a preoccupation with unresolved desires. We shall see how the knowledge claims of social work are embedded in, shaped by and informed by a wider scientific community that tends to under-theorise the encumbered self of the service user. This shift also represents a closer link between applied and basic research and front-line practice which attempts to ensure social work's scientific relevance in advanced liberal societies.

I now want to turn briefly to the impact this has on practitioner–client relationships. Today statutorily based front-line practitioners report that intensive direct work is in decline. This gradual demise of face-to-face or relationship-based work has occurred over the past 20 years in statutory social services. In his powerful critique of late modern societies Richard Sennett (1998) points to the erosion of enduring relationships that may help explain some of the changes we are witnessing in social work interventions. Sennett traces the decline of long-term, sustained and deep relationships as an effect of transformations in the organisation of work and asks how people can generate meaning and idenity under conditions of increased risk and flexibility. He argues that the replacement of 'linear time' by punctuated 'serial time' (short-term projects, short-term contracts) leads to a series of losses: a loss of committment to the work at hand, a loss of loyalty to the organisation, and diminishing trust between working colleagues. Wittel (2001) regards 'speed dating' as emblematic of these changes and describes the way they affect skills and experience: 'Skills become more portable and experience loses value. The ability to focus quickly on new tasks counts more than the accumulation of experience. Change becomes a value itself and resistance to change is taken as a sign of failure' (p. 63). In social work we can observe this in the tendency towards ephemeral but intense relations between practitioners and clients, whereby fast, over-loaded and time-pressured contacts become the norm. Perhaps the rise of short-termism in social work is an indicator of the growing number of freelancers and agency-based practitioners in statutory social services as well as their inability to recruit appropriately qualified personnel. It was indicated above that much of what was previously considered intensive direct work is increasingly being carried out by voluntary and independent sector agencies. In current practice this serves to ferment the privatisation of risk under neoliberal rule whereby case workers are replaced by personal advisors who negotiate short-term individual care packages and gather information from stakeholders. It should be noted that whilst pockets of practice excellence continue to exist in the voluntary and independent sectors they are fragmented with no coherent strategy or common purpose (Orme, 2001).

We've identified the backdrop to this as the shift from long to short-term work, from holistic to particularistic and from depth casework to ephemeral interventions in local authority social services. The increasing predominance of what I've called empirical realism in social work – behaviourism, task-centred approach, problem solving, crisis intervention, motivational interviewing, and the now fashionable cognitive behaviourism – helps facilitate the short-termism and the privatisation of risk (see Trotter, 1999 for a defence of problem solving intervention). Historically the resulting effect was that short-term and conflict-oriented risk interventions became dominant by the end of the 1970s. The label is not far off the mark given that one of its key advocates, Reid (1994), refers to it as the 'empirical practice movement'. As Jordan (2000) points out, this movement is 'brisk and businesslike' with the 'best results obtained by breaking down complex problems into small constituent elements and focusing programmes on changing the actions revealed'. As a supporter of this perspective Scriven (1997) makes the plea that 'it is better to build on what might conceivably be so . . . than not to build at all and that it is a waste of time to try to solve the problem of epistemology without getting on with the job' (1997, p. 479, cited in Jordan, op. cit.) There are good sociological reasons why task-centred and solution-focused models are reassuring to front-line practitioners: (1) they offer a semblance of order and certainty in an otherwise complex and messy world; (2) they help in verifying whether their assumptions about service users resemble social reality; (3) they help deal with the gulf of execution – the gap between knowing what they want to have happen and knowing what to do to bring it about; (4) they fulfill the over-riding preoccupation with the life planning methodology in social work. This is most evident in Reid's book *The Task Planner* (2000) in which every conceivable problem is listed alphabetically, and typically includes a description of the problem and a list of tasks and checklists that client and practitioner may select to address the problem. The danger with adhering to this kind of perspective is that it can result in crude unreflective instrumentalism, in the bid to water things down to tasks, to dilute difficulty, to make things so simple that they no longer carry any depth of meaning or value for service users. The supreme values of these empirical perspectives are utility and simplicity. From this perspective social work is essentially done for the sake of doing; it is an instrument – a directive instrument – for altering the behaviour of an environment, gathering informating and collecting data. This perspective fits nicely with the neo-liberal political agenda where the utility maximising individual appears everywhere in the face of risk.

Empirical approaches are likely to be far less resource-intensive than long-term casework with clients. The over-stretched and hectic nature of social workers' jobs leaves little time for theoretical reflection or the incorporation of up-to-date research findings. Social workers often prefer the more empirical approaches because they are more practical and straightforward in nature. The mix of approaches derived from learning theory and the positivist paradigm also facilitates an eclectic approach in which social workers adopt a 'toolkit' mentality. Here they select particular bits and pieces from different low-level models of intervention and apply them to specific cases which they consider the most suitable. Carew's (1979) study confirms this and gives examples of responses from practitioners such as 'I try anything that might work'; 'I use different parts of theories according to what's relevant to a particular case'; and 'I tend to be eclectic'. More worrying perhaps is that these early studies show that few social workers had a comprehensive understanding of theory or even used theory at all in their practice (see Howe, 1980; Loewenberg, 1984). Remember this is a long way from the heady days of the theory-immersed psychodynamic casework of the late 1950s. 'Fit the knowledge base to the case' using 'what works' has become something of an anti-intellectual slogan in social work over the past few decades. It's worth reminding readers that the story behind the 'what works' slogan, currently so fashionable with Department of Health and Home Office officials in the UK, lies with the publication of American sociologist Robert Martinson's (1974) article entitled 'What works?'. The manifesto proportions that this article assumed soon became a sobering reminder of the possibilities of research conclusions taking on an inappropriate life of their own in penal policy and crime rehabilitation. Dogmatic adherence to the approach had disastrous effects once the policy makers realised that its key organising principles were over-simplistic, misleading and had serious unintended consequences. From 1974 in the USA and Australia it led to the subsequent reification of 'Nothing Works' with writers arguing that the 'what works' syndrome is an illustration of the potential for research to fall victim to the dangers of socially constructed realities (Sarre, 2001).

Policy statements, case management and practice guidelines for front-line practitioners were constantly revised as certain approaches came to be seen as more scientifically validated, effective and efficient forms of intervention from the mid 1970s onwards. The above discussion has traced the rise of empiricism in social work which we can summarise by identifying five factors that explain the success of behavioural, crisis, task-centred and short-term interventions:

1. Short-term work is economically more resourceful and cost efficient, whilst mirroring organisational changes in workplace culture.
2. Empiricism accrues legitimacy by its association with hard science.
3. Task and solution-centred models are not too intellectually demanding for practitioners.
4. The 'what works' syndrome is appealing because it makes sense.
5. Outcome-based models feed comfortably into the auditing and performance measurement culture.

The risk society thesis helps explain why social workers tend to be eclectic in their use of knowledge-based interventions and skills, that is, in their preference for 'what works' in employing different models for different types of presenting problem. Rather than accounting for this tactic in terms of the pull of competing perspectives another important explanation stands out, that is, the complexity of generated knowledge, which in part determines the preference for an eclectic approach. Knowledge transference in work relies on the constant differentiation of findings in a hyper-complex environment. Thus, the selective sorting out of what counts as knowledge is a result of information overload and a flood of surplus evidence. As Beck (1992) points out, in risk society 'the recourse to scientific results for the socially binding definition of truth is becoming *more and more necessary,* but at the same time *less and less sufficient* . . . the users of scientific results . . . become more dependent on scientific arguments *in general*, but at the same time more independent of *individual findings* and the judgement of science regarding the truth and reality of its statements' (p. 167, emphasis in original). What Beck means by this is that complex knowledge claims about empirical reality fail to become sufficiently grounded at a subjective level. There is a superfluous production of floating facts whereby experts challenge other experts. They work like television quiz shows, reproducing endless amounts of tiny facts, stored one on top of the other, but never amounting to very much.

Empirical practices complement but also contradict and displace each other as new 'systematic findings' become available. Indeed, the falsifiability thesis, on which empirical science is so dependent, makes a virtue out of the superfluity of contradictory findings. The more science the better – even if it cancels out previous truth claims. One researcher claimed social work is *expected* to apply special scientific knowledge in order to solve social problems (Matthies, 2001). And yet increased institutional reflexivity, resource limitations and the superfluity of knowledge mean that front-line practitioners are virtually forced to make their own decisions about what works best. Imagine the difficulties facing front-line practitioners trying to wade through the latest batch of systematic reviews, evidence-based protocols and research-minded guidelines – the surplus of empirical opinion – as they confront yet another difficult client or performance-minded manager! In these circumstances it's likely that front-line practitioners will harbour a deep-seated distrust of rational systems and policy makers who construct them.

Some social workers inevitably remain nostalgic for the traditional professional status that holistic psychodynamic casework afforded them and there is still an appeal for meaningful therapeutic encounters. Perhaps, paradoxically, there's even a residual security to be found in this kind of work because of its uncertainty. As one polemicist remarked, 'uncertainty makes us free!' (Bernstein, 1998, p. 229). Those professing practice wisdom as the basis for their work may view the burgeoning empiricism sceptically. Unfortunately, the remaining front-line workers belonging to the old guard of casework find it sometimes difficult to make the transition to the 'what works' paradigm. They are forced into a kind of schizoid position, writing reports, for instance, in a manner that doesn't reflect the way in which they actually work. The pressure to conform to fashionable paradigms, such as cognitive behaviourism, and abandon previous practices, becomes almost inescapable. As standard setting is enforced, front-line practice may undergo a slower and more multi-layered process of change. There is no doubt that most social workers will be required to adjust to the new knowledge base driven by the empirical movement. As we'll see in the chapter on technologies of care (Chapter 5) these combine economic and technical factors and exert a strong pull on front-line practitioners to think and act according to precepts about 'what works'.

There is another relevant explanation for the decline of face-to-face work that creates favourable conditions for empirically based interventions. Psychoanalysis is steeped in a tradition of radical doubt encapsulated by notions of resistance, inner conflict and the unknown workings of the unconscious. Empirical realism, however, reassuringly purports to offer certainty, facticity, predictability and stability. Paradigms such as behaviourism and task-centred social work rest on the assumption that the future reproduces the past unless modified. In this sense the problem of foreseeability is crucial to the logic of calculating the effects of intervention. Social workers often work with common sense judgement and reasonable foresight about what shapes and governs the lives of service users. If dynamic caseworkers were trying hard to accommodate essential tensions of human indeterminacy as a complex mechanism of the mind, then the empiricists were resorting to the inevitable tendency to rationally objectify particular behavioural sequences and contain them within tight cause-and-effect models.

If the psychodynamic approach revelled in contingency, empiricism attempts to obliterate it. Calculation cannot deal with the unconscious or the ritual battles waged between super ego and id. As Giddens notes, 'Living in a risk society means living with a calculative attitude' (1991, p. 28). Drawing on Ulrich Beck (1992) the first part of my argument is that the emergence of empirical realism in social work lies in the growing awareness of risk in modern societies. The empirical movement can be regarded as an expert technical response to growing fears of risk. The increased awareness of risk is reconstructed as a struggle among rationality claims in which some compete and some overlap. A plethora of empirical alternatives, which are often simply variations of a recurring theme around outcome-focused work, emerges in the construction of legitimate models of intervention. This leads to my second argument. The more we become aware of risk, the more knowledge is generated about the nature of risk, its causes, structures and dynamics. Scientific and empirical knowledge is forced to respond to risk and by doing so opens up decisions and new contexts for action in social work. Thus the rise of empirical realism in social work can be understood in light of the move towards the preoccupation with the calculability of risk. Calculating behaviour along a certainty–uncertainty continuum sits at the centre of short-term empirical work. Measurement and predictability also figure highly in this discourse. Writers from the social learning perspective, for example, are preoccupied with controlled environments, stimulus-control techniques, intermittent reinforcement schedules, shaping adaptive behaviour and optimum modelling conditions. Epstein's (1980) overview of task-centred practice claims, 'The model is capable of measuring outcomes and strengthening accountability' (p. 1), with Sheldon (1982) claiming that 'sometimes when clients set about measuring the extent of their current problems the situation improves' (p. 115). These writers believe that baseline measures of effects are effective because they help clients focus on the minutiae of their daily lives in a controlled manner. This is empirical realism at its starkest, as an administrative technology attempting to functionally cope with risk contingencies. The 'contract' work complements these kinds of interventions; it is in effect an insurance against risk and an attempt to legislate for predictable outcomes. The preoccupations with baseline measurement, controlled environments, low-level data generation and shaping behaviour rely on a particular conception of normality and pathology. As Rose (1985) argues, this brand of empirical psychology grounds itself 'in the belief that there is a symmetry between three registers of norms – norms of socially desirable conduct, norms of the distribution of psychological characteristics and attributes in the population, and statistical conceptions of the normal distribution of variation in large groups' (p. 227). In the messy social world no such normative distributions exist let alone any symmetry between them.

What You See Is Not What You Get

Given its dominance in social work it may surprise readers to know that empiricism is a dead horse in the philosophy of science. It's long been acknowledged that empiricism is conditioned by two dogmas. One is a belief in some fundamental cleavage between knowledge that is grounded in meanings independently of matters of fact, and knowledge that is grounded in fact. The other dogma is reductionism: the belief that each meaningful statement is equivalent to some logical construct which refers to 'given' or immediate experience (Feyerabend, 1981). Empiricism holds that only sensory knowledge is valid, for it alone securely rests on the impressions of the thinking subject. This is classically referred to as the 'myth of givenness' – the notion that facts are out there to be observed. Feyerabend (1981), for example, argued that in principle experience is necessary at *no* point in the construction, comprehension or testing of empirical scientific theories. His devastating critique of science led him to conclude that 'objectivity' is a fallacy and that there may be nothing to choose between the claims of science and those of astrology, voodoo, and alternative medicine. In *Against Method* (1975) Feyerabend undermined science's privileged position within culture and within Western societies. He argued there is no such thing as a pure objective scientific method and that we can't justify science as the best way of acquiring knowledge. The truth, he suggests, is that:

> science is much closer to myth than a scientific philosophy is prepared to admit. It is one of the many forms of thought that have been developed by man, and not necessarily the best. It is conspicuous, noisy, and impudent, but it is inherently superior only for those who have already decided in favour of a certain ideology, or who have accepted it without ever having examined its advantages and its limits. (1975, p. 295)

As long ago as 1956, Wilfred Sellars in his classic paper 'Empiricism and the philosophy of mind' launched 'a general critique of the entire framework of givenness' as the key methodological principle of empiricism (p. 254). In so doing, he questions the notion that empirical knowledge has its foundation in knowledge of a privileged stratum of particular facts, explicitly pointing out that 'if observation reports are construed as actions, if their correctness is interpreted as the correctness of an action, and if the authority of an observation report is construed as the fact that making it is "following a rule" in the proper sense of this phrase, then we are face-to-face with givenness in its most straightforward form' (p. 296). For, he says, on these stipulations 'one is committed to a stratum of authoritative non-verbal episodes ("awareness") the authority of which accrues to a super-structure of verbal actions, provided that the expressions occurring in these actions are properly used' (p. 296). With respect to knowledge itself, he neatly points out that 'in characterizing an episode or a state as that of *knowing*, we are not giving an empirical description of that episode or state; we are placing it in the logical space of reasons, of justifying and being able to justify what one says' (pp. 298–9, his italics). Empiricism tends to freeze all of history in present findings. It rests on the assumption that social relations are controlled by external and eternal 'laws' of nature made visible by facts and statistics (see Bhaskar, 1986; Moren and Blom, 2003). Such a view minimises the generative role of judgement, intentionality, and human activity in producing social life (see Shiva, 1998). It is perhaps as a consequence of risk society that empiricism is preoccupied with the human interest in prediction, calculation and control. Few if any philosophers or cognitive scientists think any longer that perception is given or a purely passive reception of data. Rather it is seen as an active integration and interpretation by way of complex systems of meanings, symbols and different lived experiences.

Heuristics and Social Work Practice

In *New Foundations for Scientific Social and Behavioral Research: the Heuristic Paradigm* (1995) Katherine Tyson provided a compelling critique of the way in which empiricism and logical positivism came to dominate social work research in America (see Smith, 1987). She developed an alternative approach to social work research and practice based on the fast developing 'heuristic paradigm' in cognitive science (Jackson, 1996). Tyson traced the vicissitudes of research in social work with the dominance of logical positivism and its commitment to stability, perfectibility, certainty and predictability. This model views the practitioner as a rational actor who makes decisions on the basis of the logical accumulation of objective facts or evidence. There is a wider cultural context that explains the dominance of empiricism in social work. Tyson sees this as part of the hidden agenda of modernity that abandoned the humanistic tradition in which the essence of the human condition is perceived in meaningful interpersonal relations and valorised masculine models of reason. She claims that positivistic research is in cahoots with the empirical movement in social work in producing barely relevant narrow research boundaries, over-simplified hypotheses that contradict the interests of front-line practitioners, and poor substitutes for scientific methods. Against this tradition Tyson argues that research in social work is context-dependent and based on complex interpretive strategies or 'heuristics'. Practice research is more a process of inferential discovery based on trial and error rather than a mechanical instrument designed to prove observations. This perspective prioritises the immediate certainty of an intuitive and reflective knowing for social work practitioners (Taylor & White, 2000). For Tyson and collaborative writers such as Martha Heineman Pieper the heuristic paradigm is designed to bridge the gap between research and practice in social work and define best practice for service users.

Practice-based heuristics are based on a model of 'bounded rationality'. One way to understand bounded rationality is derived from Simon's concept of 'satisficing' (Simon, 1975; 1987; 1991). For Simon 'the rational actor seldom if ever actually selects the most efficient means to achieve given ends. Instead, s/he selects those means found satisfactory given her/his cognitive limitations, the availability of information, and the constraints placed on her/his time and resources. The rational actor is engaged not in maximizing but in "satisficing" values, that is to say, in achieving satisfactory rather than optimal results' (1991, p. 12). Thus satisficing is a method for making a choice from a set of alternatives encountered sequentially when one does not know much about the possibilities in advance – typical of much front-line practice. In such situations, there may be no optimal method for stopping searching for further alternatives – there would, for instance, be no optimal way of deciding when a person is at risk of abuse or when family disruption or breakdown may occur. According to Simon, 'satisficing takes the shortcut of setting an aspiration level and ending the search for alternatives as soon as one is found that exceeds the aspiration level' (1991, p. 27). In such cases social workers actively seek out evidence that confirms pre-existing beliefs and consider how they can take the most satisfying course of action in relation to a particular case, taking into account any constraints of the situation. It is precisely the reciprocal movement between the beliefs, local rules of interaction and the properties of organisational and policy context that determines the type of judgements reached. Day-to-day social work is thus 'sense making' by dealing with structured familiarities, readinesses, situational discrimination and know-hows that underlie flexible initiative and response (see Saleebey, 2001).

As Hubert Dreyfus (Dreyfus & Dreyfus, 1991) has argued,

although a person pursues purposes, tasks, and ends when acting non-deliberately (which he thinks we do most of the time), she is neither explicitly aware of them nor are they present as some tangible rational representation. By and large social workers do not solve problems, rather they do what normally works out. In his discussion of the difference between competent and expert learning Dreyfus (1997) says that the latter 'responds to each situation as it comes along in a way which has proven to be appropriate in the past, his [sic] behavior will achieve the past objectives without his having to have these objectives as goals in his conscious or unconscious mind. Thus the expert is moving into the future, and although he does not consciously entertain expectations, he is set to respond to some developments rather than others' (p. 15). If events take a new turn or throw up unexpected things the expert is startled and sometimes falls back on competence. So judgement can be purposive without the social worker having a purpose in mind. This, of course, begs important research questions for social work, especially in relation to professional judgement and decision making, that need futher exploration. The dominant rational choice model assumes that individuals move from point x to y in a causal path of linear decision making. The account given here, however, emphasises that decisions are rooted in intuitions, patterns of situated discrimination and familiar experiences of what works. This in turn begs the important question of how social workers turn from one thing to another in interventions. What in the decision making process is the take-off point from this to that in judgement about a case or client? These are phenomenological movements that practitioners barely notice because they are often 'non-deliberative'. That is, the actions that the social worker performs, whilst oriented towards particular ends, are carried out because they make sense to them as know-hows, familarities, relevances and readinesses that underlie habitual responses. Decision is splitting and passing over from one moment to the next – literally, it is the scision – or cut-off point in a passing event that shows up where we were. In some key respects this is why reflective practice in social work is harnessed as an attempt to break into and justify this naturally occurring phenomenon of non-deliberative professional action.

We can see how this paradigm provides a very different vision of how front-line workers make decisions and deal with uncertainty in the messy world of social work. The image of an omniscient social worker computing intricate probabilities and relaying competences is replaced with bounded cognition and dispersed flows of movement. Here front-line practice is about limited location and situated knowledge, not about objective knowledge of the social context (O'Melia & Miley, 2002). The process of care planning, for example, is always satisficing and situated, in that features emerge in the process of 'getting a foothold' on things and events. The practitioner reaches into an adaptive toolbox filled with the messy accumulation of past experiences, inferences, intuitions and a dispersed set of heuristics. From this perspective front-line practice consists of unwritten rules of thumb that cannot be explicitly defined or written in instructional textbooks. It is a heuristic practice-knowledge, mostly good guesses and good experience and only sometimes deliberately orchestrated in lieu of rules, facts and figures (Tversky & Kahneman, 1986).

Heuristics are designed for particular cognitive tasks rather than being general-purpose strategies. This is why only social workers experienced in similiar jobs can understand other social workers and why managers and researchers find it so difficult to break into the knowledge elicitation process of such practitioners. Heuristics are part of an economically adaptive learning skill whereby jumbled-up, unique one-function devices inform decision making. This can be likened to a hermeneutical process whereby a coherent web of understanding gains in coherence as the process continues (White, 1997). We can see why it is that understanding, rather than competence, is the term that comes to mind when thinking of evaluative judgements in social work. Judgement, rather than mere competence, is what the practically wise social worker possesses.

The main premise advanced here is that much of social work decision making can be modelled by such heuristics in which patchwork-type, economical inferences are made with limited time and knowledge (Gigerenzer & Todd, 1999). From this standpoint information searching in social work is largely external and sequential (and thus more time consuming), looking for 'critical cues' embodied in the surrounding environment. This external search includes filtering information in a socially distributed memory, from colleagues, service users, team gossip and patterns of experience as well as in more formal things like casenotes, assessment forms and databases. Practice heuristics don't involve much computation, and do not calculate quantitative probabilities and outcomes. They don't work at all in the way that risk assessment or evaluation models assume. Instead, heuristics are models of bounded rationality and knowledge elicitation that front-line practitioners optimise under constraints. Under such conditions practice learning in social work is not about rational goal-directed behaviour or for that matter reflective processes based on tacit knowledge, but instead is a *process of understanding based on iteration.* As a practice, iteration is a satisfying, pattern-focused, non-linear process that utilises heuristic understandings. This is a stop-start activity that moves between deliberative and non-deliberative action and is shaped by situations and background contexts. This takes place as social workers attempt to gather, weave and filter information about a particular situation, and results in the revision, improvement or modification of possible solutions.

If we further build organisational noise into our argument we find that linear rational planning and calculative judgement are unattainable in settings where knowledge is limited, resources constrained, time pressing and where practitioners simply don't think that way. It strikes me that social work can learn a great deal from recent research in medical education and the training of expert practitioners in this respect. This research has shown that decision making in professional contexts is dynamic because of the uncertain and shifting work environment. Typically front-line practitioners are faced with action/feedback loops and not one-shot decisions, involving multiple players rather than individual decisions in a complex system with many inter-connected parts. As a result of this when presented with a new case or incident practitioners rapidly home in on a number of 'critical cues', tending to focus on surface issues rather than the underlying problem, fit the new data to pre-existing views of that kind of situation, and suffer from Micawberism by believing that everything will work out OK in the end, despite all the contrary indications (Schmidt et al., 1990). In such risky and uncertain professional contexts, Gaba (1992) argues, for example, that anaesthetists ought to be trained explicitly in crisis management in a way similar to the training given to pilots. That is, the training should explicitly address the way that stress, risk, complexity and lack of time can lead to decision making biases, such as cognitive tunnel vision, *and* should train anaesthetists in strategies to combat these biases. Michael Eraut (1997) has been prominent in wishing to emphasise that professional knowledge, as distinct from the kind of epistemological knowledge taught on university courses, should be categorised by the context and manner of its use, rather than its source or epistemological status. Drawing on naturalistic decision making models, Eraut argues it is that knowledge which professionals bring to their practice that enables them to think and perform on the job. This kind of professional knowledge incorporates not only propositional knowledge (in the form in which it is used) but also procedural and process knowledge, tacit knowledge and experiential knowledge in episodic memory. Skills are treated as part of that knowledge, thus allowing representations of competence, capability or expertise in which the uses of skills and propositional knowledge are closely integrated.

In spite of these kinds of research findings in cognitive science and education the linear models of effective practice remain high on leading policy making agendas in social work. As Sue White (1997) points out, the importance of interpretive sense making activities is undermined by this kind of realist epistemology in social work. New motifs such as 'what works' linked to 'best value' policies are used to legitimate this perspective. This is occurring in spite of the long-standing criticisms in the philosophy of science and the development of 'unbounded models' of heuristics in cognitive science. The partisan evidence-based policies adopt a rational-objective and empirical base in spite of well-established and alternative models of practice reasoning. They adopt this knowledge base because it purports to offer scientific credibility, effectiveness and performance measures and potential escape routes from the scrutiny of proto-professionals and government (Kemshall et al., 1997). Perhaps it is due to the strictures of uncertainty in social work that these attempts to replicate the 'established' procedures of empirical science occur in order to attempt to bring some order to things and firm up weak professional identities.

In summary, we've seen how the social conditions for handling risk shape the knowledge base of experts. The manner in which empiricism tightens its grip on social work, how it attempts to legitimate aspects of professional identity is dependent on sociocultural contexts and political rule in risk society. It's this pretence of endorsing the strictures of empiricism through the development of actuarialism that I turn to in the next section.

The Rise of Actuarialism in Social Work

There's a complementary reading of the handling of risk in social work that charts the convergence of technical performance-based rationality and economic rationality through what I've termed actuarial practice. This significant shift was touched upon in Chapter 2 and we saw how in the push towards neo-liberalism, social work comes to be seen as a liability as well as an economic luxury. One key theme running through the neo-liberal agenda is that the welfare state is vulnerable to loss of authority and deference in advanced liberal societies (Yudice, 1995). There is mistrust and loss of faith in public sector professionals on the part of governments and service users alike. Expert decisions by social workers, nurses, teachers and medical doctors are increasingly challenged by more sophisticated but sceptical service users. The gap between lay persons and experts is narrowed as proto-professional service users access their own expert technologies such as the internet. New measures of accountability, performance and transparency become deeply rooted in the governance of social work. It is, perhaps, in response to the narrowing of the expert–lay gap and the burgeoning blame culture that ever more 'expert' technologies, preferably based on a more credible 'scientific rationality', are advanced to shore up fragile professional identities and public confidence. It's important to recognise that neo-liberalism advances the development of a new relation between expertise and politics especially in the realm of welfare. As we shall see an actuarial rationality and new forms of prudentialism manifest and constitute themselves in the language of 'purchaser–provider', audit, performance, and 'risk management' (see Peters et al., 1999).

Within the neo-liberal context methods of actuarial risk develop from these political and economic trends. Pat O'Malley tells us:

> The prudent subjects of neo-liberalism should practice and sustain their autonomy by assembling information, materials and practices together into a personalized strategy that identifies and minimizes their exposure to harm. Such risk management is increasingly associated with access to statistical or actuarial technologies and expert advice that render measurable the probabilistic calculation of future harms. (2000, p. 465)

This perspective has been profitably explored and developed in criminology (Simon, 1988; Feeley & Simon, 1992). Clearly more research is required but a little crystal ball gazing may help us to anticipate some future directions in social work. In its scientific guise actuarial practice is concerned with the construction of models and solutions for financial, business, and societal problems involving uncertain future events. Actuarial practitioners, also known as actuaries, have been described as financial architects and social mathematicians. Jokingly one might say that an actuary is someone who'd rather be completely wrong than approximately right. Actuaries forecast the cost of future risks and improve financial decision making by developing models to evaluate the current financial implications of uncertain future events. In applied mathematics, for example, the main theories of actuarial science deal with the pricing and hedging of risky contracts. Typically actuarial science relies on mathematical modelling of decision making and collective risk management techniques such as Bayesian analysis for evaluating accident proneness or fatality rates (Webb, 2002).

Within the caring professions actuarialism is an emerging technique of social insurance against risk. As we'll see in the next chapter it's dependent on new technologies of computer-assisted integrated assessment, decision analysis, information management, evidence-based practice and risk evaluation. Actuarialism inevitably involves risk profiling of offenders, drug users, adults with mental health problems and older people. The British police force, for example, currently uses risk profiling for offender profiling systems and crime mapping purposes (Ainsworth, 2001). Depersonalised data are used to calculate the scale, scope and cost of crime reduction interventions. Profiling is also used for sexual crimes such as rape and child abductions (see www.crimereduction.gov.uk). Similarly, risk screening as a gate keeping instrument has been used in child protection for some time (see Downing et al., 1990). Risk screening techniques are increasingly being linked to security management in policies for dealing with violence against social workers, fraud and computer-related crimes and health and safety.

François Ewald links actuarialism to social insurance technologies: 'As a technology of risk, insurance is first and foremost a schema of rationality, a way of breaking down, rearranging, ordering certain elements of reality ... One insures against accident through the probability of loss of some good. Insurance through the category of risk objectifies every event as a potential accident. Insurance's general model is a game of chance' (1991, p. 199). With neo-liberalism all types of social intervention increasingly come to resemble geometries of hazard, accident and risk. As Jock Young has argued:

> A major motif of social control in late modern society is actuarialism ... The actuarial stance is calculative of risk; it is wary and probabilistic; it is not concerned with causes but with probabilities, not with justice but with harm minimization. (1999b, p. 392)

For Young risk minimisation and damage limitation replace any concern with rehabilitation, social justice or making sense of problem behaviour in probation and social work (also see Hannah-Moffat, 1999). Social work interventions as they are increasingly moulded within the remit of actuarial culture recast the nature of individual, family and community problems as well as the purpose of welfare provision. These expert interventions entail an intensification of the government of conduct for the poorest members of society, the underclass and socially excluded. They aim to reshape moral and social responsibility, but do so within the respectable aura of expert objectivity (Feeley & Simon, 1994). This is typical of neoliberal Blairite rhetoric in the UK. For New Labour, in promoting its New Deal or Sure Start policies, those who refuse to become responsible, to govern themselves ethically, or refuse to become active members of some imagined community, are jailed or have their benefits withdrawn. Under such regimes of 'compassionate conservativism' harsh measures are considered entirely appropriate for morally irresponsible individuals. As Rose poignantly (1999) puts it, 'Three strikes and you're out: citizenship becomes conditional upon conduct' (p. 267).

Not only does the blend of risk and need assessment explain changing face-to-face work with service users, but also the amount and quality of work undertaken. As Craddock points out in relation to child protection work it is 'no longer the application of a settled craft-like knowledge by social work professionals, but a site of competing and fragmentary expert and non-expert discourses organized through neo-liberal technologies' (see Craddock, web page). In-depth expressive face or direct work is increasingly redefined along lines of resource or cost units in social work (Blaug, 1995). Front-line practitioners in children's services bemoan the effects of the dominant 'tick-box' culture. Here the use of standardised forms and procedures generates the comfortable illusion of objectivity, whilst reducing the time spent working face-to-face with people. Garrett has effectively traced the consequences of this trend in children and family work in relation to the implementation of the Looked After Children policy (Garrett, 1999a, b). Arguably the amount of direct work with clients declines in the caring professions when actuarial practice tightens its grip on the organisational and technological remit. A visit to the local GP is enough to give a sense of this actuarial rationality at work. On entering the consulting room one discovers the GP glued to the flat-face computer screen interface, offering an occasional sideways glance while narrating your symptoms, as the relevant computerised medical data are inputted. The individualised consultation, in the examination of the patient, comes to take on less significance than compiling the computer-based case record or dossier.

In his essay 'From dangerousness to risk', Robert Castel (1991) makes the following telling observation:

> I would like to put forward a line of reflection on the preventive strategies of social administration which are currently being developed, most notably in the United States and France, and which seem to me to depart in a profoundly innovatory way from the traditions of mental medicine and social work. The innovation is this. The new strategies dissolve the notion of the *subject* or a concrete individual, and put in its place a combinatory of factors, *the factors of risk*. Such a transformation carries important practical implications. The essential component of intervention no longer takes the form of the direct face-to-face relationship between the carer and the cared, the helper and the helped, the professional and the client. It comes instead to reside in the establishing of *flows of populations* based on the collation of a range of abstract factors deemed liable to produce risk. (p. 281, emphasis in original)

Castel goes on to argue that the emerging actuarialism radically modifies the relationship between helping professionals and welfare administrators and managers. He says professionals increasingly find themselves in a more sharply defined subordinate position whilst managerial policy is hardened as an autonomous force. The result is that the front-line practitioner is 'reduced to a mere executant' generating low-level data inputs (1991, p. 281).

Healthcare professionals have endured this actuarialism for some time as it sits comfortably alongside models of forensic science and clinical governance. GiRAffe (Generic Integrated Risk Assessment for Forensic Environments), for example, is a self-funded project developed by Julian Fuller, a consultant clinical psychologist at the Forensic Psychiatric Service at Langdon Hospital, London, which is the original pilot site (see www.giraffeonline.co.uk). This all-singing-all-dancing tool is described as a 'computer aided risk assessment, risk communication and research tool for use with forensic client populations, combining clinical and actuarial approaches'. The aim of GiRAffe is to 'co-ordinate the work of multidisciplinary staff teams in the complex process of appraising clinical risk' (ibid.). The software has been developed for use in residential forensic environments such as medium and low secure NHS psychiatric units, high secure hospitals, prisons and young offender institutions.

From a different angle Adrian James (2002) describes this new trend as the 'McDonaldisation of social work'. He makes the important link between the McDonaldisation of social work, as calculating, predicting and quantifying, on the one hand, and the development during the 1970s and 1980s of short-term, task-centred, contract-based and behavioural interventions on the other. James is concerned about the huge price to be paid by social workers in travelling down the actuarial road. The resultant effect is the loss of scope for creativity and innovation, as well as the deskilling of practice and a narrowing of the research agenda. This dulls the possibility of critical reflection and creative professional skills. As Hugh England noted in *Social Work as Art*, 'good social work rests upon the process of criticism . . . A widespread and critical dialogue is the only means whereby the canons of professional judgement and evaluation can be established in social work' (1986, p. 125).

Conclusion

Direct work, knowledge and the practice of value in social work are likely to change as the residualist neo-liberal agenda hardens. The shift towards actuarial practice is driven by influences from medicine, alongside the dominance of empirical social work and its double alliance with micro-management and evidence-based practice. Writers such as Thyer (2001) equate empiral social work with evidence-based practice; he suggests that 'EBP [evidence-based practice] and EVT [empirically validated treatments] actually are variations of the earlier ECP [empirical clinical practice] model of social work, which mandates not only the selection of treatments based on their level of scientific research support but also the ongoing empirical evaluation of outcomes using single-systems and other research designs' (pp. 6–7). This double alliance assumes that frontline practice can be standardised, made more accountable to service users and managers, effectively maximise flows of information, and involve proto-professional service users in decision making. Inevitably actuarial practice will group together types of service user population, as we've seen above with risk profiling and screening. Sometimes the grouping process is crudely conceived in terms of 'high' or 'low' risk groups, as assessments in mental health, child protection and offender work; at other times it will group them according to eligibility criteria for the provision of care services. As we'll see in the next chapter actuarialism combines an economic with a technical rationality to calculate probabilities of risk. Indeed, Eileen Gambrill (2003) enthusiastically likens evidence-based practice to 'a free market knowledge economy' in which we can gain information about 'the degree of uncertainty about a given decision' and capture knowledge flows in social work. The empirically driven 'what works' evidence-based policy helps legitimise the hardening of actuarial practice in social work. Preoccupied as it is with calculating probability, constructing controlled environments which try to remove chance and measuring potential through evidenced-based outcomes, it transposes the logic of regulation into the methodology of life planning.

The privatisation of risk helps account for changing face-to-face work with clients, but also the type, quality and amount of work undertaken. Long-term care of vulnerable adult service users is an example of the privatisation of risk. Here the commodification of care has shifted from being a public responsibility to a private good with little or no debate (Player & Pollock, 2001). It was noted above that direct work is in decline, especially in adult services and statutory social services. What passes for direct work with service users increasingly takes the form of advice from either a personal assistant or a risk-based evaluator. Actuarial practice gradually builds out of the configuration of empirical practices discussed above. As welfare insurance it attempts to predict change in the lives of service users and populations who are only grouped together under regimes of privatised risk. Preoccupied as it is with the calculus of performance, effectivenes and controlled environments that try to remove risk, unless we are careful social work will be increasingly transposed into a regulatory regime based on actuarial outcomes. We should remind the would-be actuarialist that the kinds of social interactions that social workers face daily are too complex for us to predict, at best they show various internal patterns, sketching the 'rules of the game' and portraying the limits and possibilities of social work intervention.

5

Technologies of Care

Introduction

The last chapter showed how the rationality of risk in social work signals an emerging actuarialism that impacts on the organisation and delivery of social services. The increasing predominance of actuarialism was seen as an effect of the reconfiguration of instrumental and economic rationality in advanced liberal risk society. It was suggested that the requirement to manage, channel and avert risk in social work alters relations between front-line practitioners and service users and between professionals, managers and administrators. Social work practice comes to resemble an executant and functional role that is accountable in moral and legal terms. We saw that a gradual shift from a preoccupation with social need to the handling of social risk occurs in determining eligibility criteria and resource allocation for service users. What I've called 'technologies of care' are, in part, a rational response to the changing nature of social work intervention in a risk-dominated organisational culture. In this chapter examples of technologies of care such as care management, risk assessment and evaluation, evidence-based practice, decision pathway models of practice, and networked communication technologies are examined to illustrate the impact of risk society on social work intervention.

In its preoccupation with rationalising risk advanced liberalism tries to construct and render social work into a technical calculable form. It was argued that actuarialism leads to a decline of intensive direct work and neutralises core social work values. In this chapter the implications of this trend are further developed in the analysis of technologies of care. Authentic and effective knowledge creation in social work is deeply embedded in face-to-face and expressive contexts, whilst technologies of care used to support such encounters rely on the assumption that knowledge can be made mobile outside of these specific inter-personal contexts. This chapter draws attention to a critical conflict between knowledge processes in social work and the technologies built to support them. The conflict centres on the fact that authentic and efficient knowledge creation and sharing are deeply embedded in an inter-personal face-to-face context, but with these supportive technologies assumptions are made that knowledge can be made mobile and lifted out of these embedded contexts. By decontextualising expressive relations, instrumentally oriented technologies may inhibit collaboration and trust, especially when the interaction is not nested in embedded ecological contexts. The chapter illustrates some important technological directions in social work, situating these trends within the emerging inter-professional paradigm of social work, health and education.

Before examining social work practice and its various organisational contexts let's unpack what is meant by technologies of care. Technologies of care are part of an assemblage of methodologies configuring social work within defined remits. They involve a certain unity of purpose with the field of possible objects; coherence of mode of functioning; patterns of procedure and articulation; and regular rules for their operations. It's a small but necessary point to recognise that social workers start using email, assessment schedules over the internet and computerised case files, without exactly understanding how their effects are influencing daily work patterns or routines. The impulse to turn to technical knowledge and methods, as external reference points, may offer a renewed professional expertise. In this sense technologies of care are mobilised to shore up the fragile professional status of social work.

Technologies of care are concerned with the governance of uncertainty – they are rational schemas for organising social work and developing procedures for how it is carried out and delivered. In this sense they are programmatic since they are based on sets of calculating prescriptions through which care-based interventions are organised, arranged and regulated. Crucially they are primarily 'end-oriented practices' derived from what Max Weber called purposive-rational (*zweckrational*) schemes. In other words, practitioners and service users are expected to apprehend the world technologically, that is, to see it either as a resource to be used or a constraint to be overcome (Simpson, 1995, p. 16).

Deskilling Social Work Practice

Technologies of care are comprised of practice networks that reframe objectivity through the accomplishment of dynamic operating systems. The main components of these technologies are not individual organisations, but rather particular systems or processes, including procedural guidelines, case reporting systems, care management, information databanks and so on. To give a flavour we are witnessing, for example, initiatives applying knowledge management (KM) processes to develop virtual electronic social care records, and integrated database and management information reporting tools for family assessment. Such technologies comprise the objectification of knowledge and the rules of what counts as a valid knowledge for practice. As Simpson explains, 'We can think of technology *per se* as embracing at once a distinctive cognitive style or orientation, a distinctive mode of action, and a distinctive way of taking up with the world' (1995, p. 15). In this sense technologies of care are to be understood as constellations of knowledge, processes and skills in social work, involving discrete technical methods that connect together to produce a series of real effects at the level of practice. Care planning, pathways and management typically resemble this kind of end-oriented thinking about the social world. Simpson (1995) summarises the step-by-step process of technical reasoning as follows:

> We can characterize the way that technology addresses its problems in the following way: a need is made explicit, or an opportunity made available, by scientific or perhaps other technological developments; is articulated within the context of the need or opportunity; a clear and determinate goal is specified; the major steps to be taken and the major pieces of work to be done are identified; the plan is constantly made responsive to 'feedback' from the result of the work; and typically, the work is organized so that each major segment is apportioned within a division of labour. This way of putting it highlights the important point that the end technology seeks to realize as efficiently and effectively as possible is one that is specified and determined beforehand. It further highlights the importance of planning, or of the rational orchestration of procedure, to the technological enterprise. (p. 15)

This kind of technical planning and rational problem solving sits at the core of much of current social work practice. Care management, for example, tends to be overly preoccupied with the assessment of need and risk and the matching of available services for service users, rather than relationship building or therapeutic direct work. Broadly speaking it signifies a shift from interpretation and sensibility to problem solving and risk management techniques (Hartley, 1990). Effective interventions are increasingly expected to mimic this technological conception of codified categories, goal orientation, system maintainance and feedback loops.

An increase in technologies of care can lead to the routinisation of social work. While work can be analysed in terms of competences and skill requirements such an approach tends to ignore the complex inter-weaving of skills in social work. For instance, consider a young white female social worker involved with an elderly Afro-Caribbean man who is considered at risk of falling down and seriously injuring himself. She visits the home and no one answers the door. This kind of situation requires critical decision making. Should the social worker try and gain access to the house? To make matters worse the social worker has conflicting information to deal with. One neighbour said that they hadn't seen him for a while and that they were worried whereas another said that he'd had gone away for a few days. The social worker also has a strong time pressure (i.e. preservation of life as they were unsure if the old man was still alive) and potential cultural value conflicts. Eventually after weighing up the pros and cons – which amounts to a kind of hypothesis testing – a decision is taken to gain access to the house. This kind of situation brings out the link between decisions under uncertainty, crisis intervention and qualitative reasoning much of which has been overlooked in the social work research literature. Front-line practice is permeated with such unexpected incidents. This means social workers are constantly required to make knowledge-rich interpretations – involving experience, learning, memory, perception and problem solving – based on domain-specific events (Fox & Cooper, 1996). This is not a matter of competence but a question of good judgement and the ability to cognitively discriminate about what is considered relevant or not. Unfortunately interpretive and analytical skills are downgraded within the dominant purposive-rational (*zweckrational*) schema. As Leidner (1993) argues, the routinisation of service work has a poignant consequence. It tends to undermine shared understandings about individuality and social obligations, whilst sharpening the tension between the belief in personal autonomy and the domination of a powerful organisational elite. High status within the caring profession will be reserved for those handling what are perceived to be the most difficult risks and challenges, while those tasks whose uncertainties have been removed will be handled by lower-status professionals or even delegated to technicians and assistants with lesser credentials (Aronowitz & DiFazio, 1994). At the bottom end of this organisational scale many decisions will be made along the lines of previous decisions – 'When this happens, do that.' Systematic reviews, standardised guidelines, procedural manuals all combine to dictate how to approach a particular problem and how to respond when the same or a similar problem arises in a more or less step-by-step programmatic way.

Increasingly social work is required to specify sets of inputs and outputs within an integrated pathway process that can account for risk factors. This requires social workers to prioritise, time and sequence different elements of intervention. The entire process is permeated with normative presuppositions about what ends are achievable and what behaviours are to be transformed or regulated. 'Pro-social modelling' with parents or offenders is typical of this kind of normalisation process. We'll see how technologies of care are likely to come into play when certain groups, families, individuals become what Mitchell (1999) calls 'targeted populations', that is, populations who exhibit high risk or include individuals deemed at risk. Their objectives, according to Mitchell, are to transform their status into one of active citizenship with the capacity to manage their own risk.

Technologies of care are linked to issues of trust and accountability. They present themselves, as Mitchell points out, as 'techniques of restoring trust (i.e. accountability, transparency and organizational control) in the activities of . . . professionals. As such, they presuppose a culture of mistrust in professions, that they themselves contribute to produce and intensify' (1999, p. 169). Inevitably this leads case managers and front-line workers in social work to err on the side of over-stating as opposed to under-stating risk. Thus risk conservatism is deeply embedded in the organisational culture of social work, with blame avoidance tactics being daily rehearsed by practitioners. However, Ellul (1967) argues that such technological developments are now conditioned by nothing other than their own calculus of efficiency. Health and social care are deeply implicated in this logic of technical rationality, aiming to assign and guide service users within the remit of risk calculations. This can have significant deskilling effects on front-line practitioners. As Castel (1991) remarks, the resultant effect is that the 'operative on the ground now becomes a simple auxiliary to a case manager whom he or she supplies with information derived from the activity of diagnostic expertise. These items of information are then stockpiled, processed and distributed along channels completely disconnected from those of professional practice, using in particular the medium of computerized data handling' (p. 293). In these circumstances the case manager is the effective decision maker with the front-line practitioner the functional administrator who collects relevant data. Castel connects such actuarial practice to the neo-liberal ideology of maximising returns on those populations that are profitable to society and marginalising those unprofitable targeted populations. He paints a bleak picture of a socially engineered future in which it may become technologically feasible to 'programme populations themselves, on the basis of an assessment of their performances, and, especially of their possible deficiencies' (p. 294).

Care Management

In the 1970s care or case management in Britain arose as a means of co-ordinating and networking the care of severely mentally ill people in the community. It was a response to the spatial relocation of risky populations from institutions into the community (Department of Health, 1994b). During this time issues of risk and safety came to feature prominently in work with people with severe mental health problems (Prins, 1999; Waterson, 1999). Safety issues are often linked with case management for work with offenders and older people (Lymbery, 1998). In Britain, Home Office (1998) guidelines for effective practice make this connection between risk and safety:

> Case management is a necessary precondition of effective practice. The lifestyle of the persistent offender is likely to be chaotic, lacking in boundaries and potentially dangerous . . . Consequently it requires a sense of safety and stability. One function of effective case management is to reduce behaviour which threatens safety and stability. . . . (www.homeoffice.gov.uk/hmiprob/)

In *The Practice of Case Management in the Human Services* Moxley (1989) defines case management in purely operational and functional terms. He regards it as a person or team who co-ordinate and sustain a network of formal and informal activities designed to optimise the functioning of service user needs (p. 21). The difference in usage between 'case' and 'care' management is largely a transatlantic one. In Britain what is called care management is referred to as case management in the USA, although sometimes the terms are used interchangeably (Orme and Glastonbury, 1993). However, the Department of Health has been strategic in its preference for the usage of care management, regarding it as more persuasive and conducive to governmental response (Department of Health, 1991a, b; Phillips & Waterson, 2002). Challis draws out the distinction between case and care management as follows:

> I take the definition of case management to be the coordination of care through an identified responsible individual or key worker whose role is to ensure the performance of the core tasks of case management. Care management I take to be 'the management of case management'. It is, therefore, more systematically focused at a higher tier in the organisation than concern with the coordination and organisation of care for individual clients. (1990, p. 10)

By splitting these two functions the managerial lines of responsibility become clear. Phillips and Waterson (2002) beg the important question of whether care management actually constitutes part of the core social work task. They describe the social work role as being reduced to a 'go-between' and as following health-dominated professional agendas. From a sociological perspective Mitchell refers to this current trend in expert intervention as 'case management risk'. The sort of risk rationality at stake is based on qualitative assessment of those targeted individuals and groups who fall within 'at-risk categories' (1999, p. 189). The proliferation of care management techniques is derived from this need to categorise and regulate various individuals and targeted populations. Typical of the care management perspective in social work in the UK is the development of the Care Programme Approach introduced in 1991 as the central platform of the Government's mental health policy. This approach focuses on assessment, care planning and the notion of continuous review for people with serious mental health problems. For those service users considered to be 'high risk', representing significant risk to themselves or others, there is a Supervision Register, which came into force in 1994, which aims to ensure that someone at risk is actively followed up and continuously monitored. In Floersch's (2002) study of the American method of 'strengths case management' which requires a focus on individualised strengths of clients and their desires, he observed that case managers frequently used the categories of 'high functioning' and 'low functioning' to describe clients as part of the mobilisation of situated expertise.

American case management is well developed with the Case

Management Society of America (CMSA), for example, defining the key functions as:

> a collaborative process which assesses, plans, implements, coordinates, monitors and evaluates the options and services required to meet an individual's health needs, using communications and available resources to promote quality, cost-effective outcomes. (www.cmsa.org/)

Here we can see how each major segment of the collaborative process is apportioned within a division of labour and time to achieve some predetermined outcomes. The rational orchestration of procedure is at the centre of this kind of technical-managerial enterprise. In its discussion of effective outcome measures CMSA makes the link between the purpose of case management and calculable performance measures:

> Case managers need to use a consistent set of quantitative indicators of their performance on key outcome dimensions. Good outcome indicators measure the outcome dimensions sensitive to case management practice, have been statistically validated, and are widely used. To build credibility, outcome measures must be scrutinized for their fit with nationally recognized outcome initiatives. A case management 'report card' should specify the outcome measures and their source. (www.cmsa.org/ccma/ccma-main.html)

These kinds of policy statement, which litter the bookshelves of social workers, look very much like programming language in that they see the practitioner qua person as a mere cypher. Such statements amount to a prescribed set of distributed competences within a procedural system. These types of policy statements also amount to what Law & Singleton (2000) call a narrative performance. They are a performance of reality in that they make 'present a *representation* of reality, and at the same time *make* that reality' (p. 1) thereby attempting to persuade readers that it offers reliable and authoritative knowledge.

We can observe that case management typically involves: (1) review and assessment; (2) an individual care plan; (3) discussion of the plan with the service user; (4) monitoring of the service user's progress; (5) review of the individual service user's care plan. Mitchell discusses case management risk more widely, saying that it 'draws upon the techniques of the interview, the exercise of professional judgement, the case note and the file' (1999, p. 189). He describes the way that risk screening and profiling techniques combine with more traditional modes of face-to-face assessment to categorise the needs and levels of risk associated with problems presented by service users. It can be easily discerned in the above definition given by the CMSA how case management is based on the rationalisation of procedure and the separation of means and ends as part of a technological enterprise that combines input–outputs; performance-effectiveness; and quantitative and qualitative modes of assessment. To put it a little differently, case management seeks to build from diverse information an expert structure that may (or such is the aspiration) be devised and controlled from a single place, a case management centre (Law, 1997). This is a process that is goal-oriented and functionalist. Therefore it shouldn't surprise readers to learn that Moxley describes case managers as information specialists and 'processors' (1989, pp. 88–9). This perspective is also reflected in Chapman & Hough's (1999) guidelines on case management for probation officers in *Evidence Based Practice: a Guide to Effective Practice*. The authors argue that case management must be standardised with its effectiveness depending on practitioners who are competent in the skills of: (1) risk assessment and management; (2) supervision, planning and review; (3) co-ordination and sequencing of work through the order; (4) motivating, pro-social modelling and reinforcing progress in learning and change; and (5) using data to assess and adapt practice.

The expectation is that each of the case management components will be 'integrated seamlessly' into an effectively managed plan of work (Vourlekis & Greene, 1992). Front-line workers are expected to produce recorded evidence of the case process that conforms to the plan as it is contracted between the court and the offender. So what is actually happening at the concrete level of front-line practice? Case management is a kind of summing up of all interactions and information through practical devices that are very local to the information at hand. The manner in which materials are ordered is important but it is the practitioner who plays the crucial role in the chains of mediation that take place in arranging and sorting any information or material. Thus the strain is on the social worker in sorting things out, weaving, bending and then patching them together. This means that social workers are constantly engaged in a process of reflexive repair in which they adjust the information and material at hand. The ordering process involved in case management is momentary. This is because the elements that are crafted into a plan or procedure change over time. The plan will thus oscillate, be modified or move into an alternate pattern. At some other moment things will be ordered and sorted out differently (Latour, 1987). Care managers are often caught between functional demands (administrative computer and paperwork) and working relationships with people (Postle, 2002). Moreover they recognise that plans and assessment often don't hold together in a single and coherent way. This is why the emphasis on review and evaluation is so important for these rational planners. But because things are uncertain and change unexpectedly the process of drawing things up and ordering them will be problematic and at best things will not be drawn together very well. This is why Cussins (1998) refers to the process of diagnosis and assessment in healthcare as being more like a dance than a design.

Care management reduces to a form of low-level data input in the regulation of risk. But more importantly it has the net effect of routinising professional work. This type of technologically minded rationality of planning and procedure relieves front-line workers of the burden of having to engage with essentially contestable processes of interpretation that make up the thick stuff of diverse sociocultural practices. Complexity is thus reduced within the low-level data generation process of the administrative social worker. Herewith social meaning is understood only through the functional spectacles of an administrative assessor who is only capable of recognising calculable patterns of information input-and-output that are specific to the individual case. This 'don't think but do' mentality is ultimately deskilling for social workers. Community reintegration of the offender is the overall goal of the case manager in probation, thereby involving her or him in dispatching the individual from the targeted-marginal to the normalised population from which s/he will be required to take responsibility for her or his own actions and choices. It is easy to see how the advancement of case management systems in social work fulfills Castel's characterisation of the social worker as an operative on the ground being a simple auxiliary to the senior case manager. As administrative operatives front-line practitioners will generate and supply data through assessment and review formats with key decisions about risk and need being left to the office of the case manager. There is little evidence to support the effectiveness of case management in improving services, even though it's regarded as the cornerstone of service delivery. Some researchers go so far as to claim that case management has questionable value as a management method and is difficult to justify in resource terms (Marshall et al., 2002).

Risk Assessment and Evaluation

Tanner (1998) claims that the shift towards risk management will increasingly utilise technical managerial skills thus involving a move from 'depth' to 'surface' in social work with a focus on tasks and process at the expense of professional values (Howe, 1996). More specifically, Craddock (2001) traces the emergence of the predominance of risk assessment to particular problems linked with advanced liberalism, 'Namely, the resistance to governing too much balanced against the dangers of intervening too little' (p. 8). The previous chapter drew attention to the manner in which the management and assessment of risk are increasingly based on individualising the calculating rationality of targeted populations. Paul Michael Garrett's (1999a, b) analysis of the Looking After Children system examines how its Action and Assessment Records (AARs) contribute to this normalising strategy of regulation. He argues that AARs are potentially oppressive and contain powerful value-laden categories about 'appropriate' youth lifestyles and the nature of 'work'. Here Garrett is drawing attention to the simultaneity of individualisation and standardisation in the categories that assessment constructs. There is a subtle connection between individualising risk and targeting risk populations in social work. As Craddock points out within the context of child protection work:

> The introduction of the concept of 'at-risk' populations into social work discourse has resulted in a kind of linguistic slippage. Many child welfare programs are targeted towards at-risk populations, but through the looping effect, once a child or family participates in such a program they become the criteria for their entry – often because they have been assessed by way of a gate-keeping checklist. Hence the risks associated with their population are personalized within each particular participant. They cease to be members of an 'at-risk' population and become, instead, 'at-risk' people. (2001, pp. 7–8)

With this perspective risk is essentially characterised by the probability of events or their consequences as well as having powerful labelling effects on certain sections of the population. In the UK the Multi-Agency Protection Arrangements, or MAPA, for reducing the risk to the general public from reoffending by convicted sexual and violent offenders released into the community are symptomatic of these kinds of development. A statutory duty was placed on the police and probation service, under Section 67 of the Criminal Justice & Court Services Act 2000, to 'establish arrangements for

the purpose of assessing and managing the risks posed in that area'
by people previously convicted of sexual and violent offences. Two
standard risk assessment tools are used for offenders in all probation
areas and in all prisons, OASys (Offender Assessment System) and
Risk Matrix 2000. Service users are allocated to one of the four risk
categories of low, medium, high and very high. OASys is regarded
as a central part of evidence-based practice in assisting front-line
practitioners to make what are called 'defensible decisions' about
levels of risk posed by offenders. It assesses an offender's risk of reoffending by systematically examining up to 13 offending-related
factors and underpins 'what works' practice with a pivotal role in
assessment, case management, targeting of intervention treatment
programmes, resource allocation and risk management.

In *Evidence Based Practice: a Guide to Effective Practice* the
authors mirror this increasingly dominant policy perspective:

> Risk assessment is essentially about making calculations about potential harm or
> loss based upon a rational appraisal of what has been learnt from past events. It
> balances the risk of potential harm with the ability to control the risk.
> (www.homeoffice.gov.uk/hmiprob/ebp3.htm#Chapter%203)

The above example neatly expresses the security–regulation pair
in the idea of balancing potential harm alongside the need to control
risk. As Thompson & Dean (1996) suggest, this probabilistic view
(e.g. potential harm) will be most plausible to those managers and
policy makers who work in organisational settings where their job is
to assess probabilities for outcomes that have been judged important
by others. For social workers these judgements are manifest in their
relations with a range of interested parties, including service users,
politicians, journalists, pressure groups and rights campaigners and
their own managers. Therefore it's important to acknowledge that
risk assessment doesn't occupy some value-neutral place in social
work organisations (Smale et al., 1993; Ross, 1997). There may be
some political agenda that determines which risk assessments are
considered more important than others. Objective criteria about
levels of probable risk are unlikely to be the sole criteria on which
priority is given to intervention. Resource rationing and performance targets will determine which risk assessments are given priority. Craddock (2001) suggests that risk calculation in child
protection is appealing to bureaucrats because it allows professional
judgement to be specifically located, tracked and isolated to persons
or teams. The audit process, for example, makes the service user *and*

practitioner undertaking the risk assessment 'visible and account-able' and therefore governable from a distance (p. 14). Thus those risk assessments that feed into the wider parameters (political and bureaucratic) are likely to be preferred over those that disrupt management agendas (Houston & Griffiths, 2000).

Formal approaches to risk assessment have developed fast over the last decade. However, much of what gets called risk assessment is generally 'tick-box' schedules that are practised through the use of standardised guidelines. For the most part these are designed by the local team/department and are pretty crude and blunt instruments (Froggett & Sapey, 1997). Guidelines on risk assessment typically caution social workers to adjust their estimation of probabilities in light of new evidence. As we've seen above, in the messy world of case management they are expected to monitor and review the risk plan and ensure it is recorded. Of course, this perspective on perceived risk assumes that there are such things as 'right' or 'wrong' risk estimates in relation to a particular state of affairs. Yet research shows there is considerable variability between practition-ers using risk assessments. Benbenishty et al. (2002) found consid-erable variability in their study of social workers' decision making when searching for information and using it to reach their risk assessments and their recommendations as to whether to remove children from home. Tuddenham (2000) argues that risk assessment practice in probation and offender work has to all intents and purposes failed. He proposes that probation practice must embrace a more dynamic notion of risk assessment, which has at its centre the concept of 'reflexivity', whereby an expressive, confrontational and dialogic approach is pursued.

Risk assessment is permeated with normative presuppositions. Recognising the normative aspects of risk assessment greatly affects how we use it and what we should expect from it, but, importantly, it also opens up possibilities that might not be foreseen or under-stood if we merely treat it as a probabilistic mechanism. Rarely are such narrow technical and economic frameworks transparent to service users or do they take their views into account (Hardey & Maddox, 2000). Neither do they acknowledge the ethical factors involved in the morally complex situation under consideration (Fritzsche, 1996). Disputes between parents over access to children, for example, are an obvious candidate that involves both ethical considerations and judgements about potential risk. Moreover, it's often been overlooked in the literature that risk assessments can be dangerous and harmful to service users. de Milo Martin (1998) showed, for example, that risk assessment for in vitro fertilisation under-estimated the possibility of jeopardising women's health because it failed to take into consideration the fact that these women were making judgements of their own under conditions of uncertainty that run against objective criteria. Similarly, Houston & Griffiths (2000) argue that in child protection work the emphasis on prediction, control and culpability in risk assessment has failed to provide valid and reliable measures of risk and is a one-sided approach. Social work practitioners often regard the context of cases as crucial in determining risk decision making. It was with this in mind that Shrader-Frechette (1995) was led to conclude that risk assessments should provide 'an independent analysis' of risk and explicitly distinguish conclusions based on facts from judgments based on values. Again Craddock illustrates this tension in child protection with reference to notions of children being exposed to 'too much risk'. He argues: 'the question of what constitutes "too much risk" cannot be divined by means of assessments themselves. Rather, while assessment categories structure and focus child protection inquiries, the question of what constitutes too much risk remains at its root a subjective process of judgment' (2001, p. 14).

Making Risky Decisions

To conclude this part of the chapter I want to reflect on how decisions about risk are really reached in practice. The calculus of risk inevitably reflects the practitioner's confidence that those events are likely to occur. What tends to happen in day-to-day practice with risk assessment is that if several accounts converge and if the informants and information that are mobilised have a high degree of coherence whilst confirming the initial viewpoint, then the social worker will feel more confident in their overall assessment. During the process of feedback on casework with colleagues, supervisors and other professionals story telling is just as important as the factual information obtained during the risk assessment. This is because social workers are away from the setting in which the information was gained and are recalling or often simply remembering how it was when they were in setting *x*. Here then, narrated information – as casenotes, reputation, hunches or gossip – is the bridge, the translator of the risk. Risk claims are not simply propositions but are also moves in a narrative that attempts to develop an argument for or against a particular decision. Throughout this process social workers are responding to a situation, taking up a particular perspective, eliciting value positions and weighing up pros and cons. This important point has been overlooked in much of the literature on risk assessment.

Decisions about risk in social work combine action-at-hand (assessment) with action-at-a-distance (evaluation). As Bruno Latour (1988) says, these kinds of explanations for the way things are perceived can be understood as a 'measure of the distance between contexts'. For Latour this creates the very distinction between practice on the one hand, and knowledge on the other. 'Practice is whatever people do in the setting acted on', in this case, the risk assessment environment; and 'knowledge becomes whatever is mobilised in x to act upon the other setting', in this case, the reporting environment in which evaluative decisions take place. Considerations of risk during the evaluative stage will inevitably involve social workers drawing comparisons between cases and perhaps simultaneously highlighting the distinctiveness of the present case. It is also inevitable that social workers will experience different doubts about risk in identical situations. They know that the past is not necessarily a reliable predictor of the future. It's often underplayed in the literature but hesitancy, procrastination, fuzziness and indecisiveness are the significant elements of such decision making (Lipshitz & Strauss, 1997). Moreover, risk comparisons are likely to be ubiquitous because managers and practitioners have to deal with incessant pressures to focus on some risks and ignore or defer others within a process of rationing limited resources. They focus on the countervailing effects of the same intervention or various risks competing for the same financial and human resources (Finkel, 1996).

From this perspective decision making for risk reduction or aversion is more like a language game than an objective state of affairs in the sense that games have time limits, rules of play, opponents and criteria for winning and losing. Rather than seeing risk assessment as a fact finding exercise, incorporating rational decisions about how to use these facts, we need to acknowledge that fuzzy judgments, bias and even inaccurate data recording permeate each stage of the risk decision making process. A small-scale research study showed that data collection for risk assessment of elder abuse is fraught with error even on the part of the most experienced practitioners (Comijis, 2000). Sometimes relevant data for the risk assessment will not even surface prior to a case review or an important decision making node. Fitzgerald's (1999) study of child protection and computer-networked information revealed some major problems in sharing information for risk assessments. While carrying out some 30 Part 8 inquiries and case reviews, a child protection agency was astonished to find that important information in the records of various agencies had not surfaced while the children were alive and had not been used in the risk assessment. Clearly the way that inter-professional agencies communicate risk is a crucial consideration if effective practice is to be achieved. A Department of Health study (2002) on serious care reviews when a child dies or suffers serious injury also showed that risk assessment techniques are often inadequate in determining levels of risk and that their predictive value is limited (pp. 43–6).

Finally, it's important to recognise the difficulty in finding agreement on how to define risk. In Britain some forward-looking government think-tanks increasingly accept that assessing risks is full of uncertainties; that the science underlying most risk assessment assumptions is inconclusive or untestable; and that probabilistic methods are inadequate. As Vaughan & Seifert note, 'Persistent disagreements about risk appear to have their origin in different belief and value systems' (1992, p. 120), which shape the way people define, weigh, and frame dimensions of risk. A consensus is emerging that risk assessment in its present form can only be used to inform opinion-based decisions and not blindly dictate decision making (Interdepartmental Liaison Group on Risk Assessment, 2000). It's pertinent to remind ourselves of Furedi's (1997) powerful observation that the vicious spiral of blame and preoccupation with security results in a morality of low expectation from others and ourselves. (See Marriott, 2000 for a similar discussion in relation to voluntary work and risk assessment.)

Evidence-based Practice

Evidence-based practice (EBP) has become a major theme within social work (Cournoyer, 2004). This has fuelled a significant debate about its role in reducing risk and its possible impact on definitions of good practice and professional autonomy (Sheldon, 2001; Webb, 2001, 2002). In Britain the upsurge of interest in EBP is reflected in considerable financial investment. In 1996 the Department of Health invested £1.5 million in an initiative designed to help social services departments develop EBP. The Centre for Evidence-Based Social Services at the University of Exeter, led by Brian Sheldon, was established to co-ordinate this initiative with 15 local authority social services departments. In October 1997, the Department of Health also funded research on EBP at the University of Salford as part of the Outcomes of Social Care for Adults initiative. The project identified the links between best practice and effective outcomes for a range of stakeholders using research-minded methods. The project described its aims as 'to strengthen and cultivate evidence-based practice in health care and at the interface of health and social care'. Similar research initiatives have taken place in medicine and health studies. In the late 1990s the Centre for Evidence-Based Pathology was established at the Queen's Medical Centre, University of Nottingham, and the Department of Health Studies at the University of York identifies evidence-based nursing as a key strategic interest. The NHS Research and Development Centre for Evidence-Based Medicine at Oxford has been conducting investigations into the applicability and effectiveness of this approach for several years (see McGuire, 1997 and Geddes, 1998 for a discussion of evidence-based approaches in mental health). Taken together these developments in EBP suggest that the perspective will significantly shape the professional culture of both health and social care. Sheldon pointed out on the web page introduction to the Centre for Evidence-Based Social Services: 'In the US, it has been compulsory for the last few years for all social workers to be trained in the skills necessary to appraise and make use of research evidence' (www.ex.ac.uk/cebss/newsspring98%20.htm). The belief is that the best available evidence is produced from within the experimental paradigm of social science. Inevitably this would result in the contingencies of direct casework being displaced by mechanical expert systems, emphasising an instrumental approach.

In social work there are competing claims about what counts as evidence. A sharp divide has emerged between what Liz Trinder (2000) calls the *experimental* and *pragmatic* approaches to EBP in social work. She points out that:

> Two fairly distinctive approaches are beginning to emerge, one associated with the empirical practice lobby and one associated with a more mainstream pragmatist group of researchers. (p. 145)

The pragmatists claim that EBP involves integrating professional expertise with the best available external evidence from good quality research as well as considering the values and expectations of clients and service users. In some key respects this type of thinking resonates with longstanding calls for social work to become more research-minded in order to enhance its status and identity. Sheldon and Macdonald are leading exponents of the experimental approach in EBP, with both having a longstanding interest in evaluative and empirically based practice. Trinder makes the connection between EBP and the empirical practice movement in social work:

> The empirical practice movement within social work . . . shares many of the aims, methods and models of the evidence based practice movement in health, specifically the emphasis on basing interventions on research evidence derived from randomised controlled trials and meta analysis. (2000, p. 147)

For adherents of experimental EBP randomised controlled trials (RCTs) are the gold standard. The main concern of experimental EBP is that social workers rarely use evidence or models that are falsifiable. That is, that they make little effort to find refutations for their own practice and thus operate according to opinion-based beliefs rather than hypotheses or facts that allow for specific predictions. On the other hand, EBP pragmatists argue that the strict adoption of randomised controlled trials as the gold standard is reductionist and inappropriate for the kinds of social, emotional and value-laden problems faced by social work.

Systematic reviews are considered to be a vital source of information management for EBP – in Britain the Social Care Institute for Excellence (SCIE) commissions such reviews based on a normative and restrictive model. They provide aggregated data from a large volume of targeted/search inquiries which produce relevant information. As Newman (1999) points out, with systematic reviews the criteria for inclusion or exclusion are made explicit in advance; the objectives of the review and methods used are specified; others can replicate the reviews. In medicine the Cochrane Collaboration (National Institute for Clinical Excellence) is a good example of a worldwide network of centres that prepare, maintain and disseminate high quality systematic reviews on the efficacy of health care. These databases allow access to evidence related to clinical practice decisions.

In a statement about 'What is evidence-based social care?' the Centre for Evidence-Based Social Services, in Exeter, suggests: 'the starting point for evidence-based social care is the principle that all decisions in our field should be based on the best available research evidence. Research evidence should inform both our understanding of the origins and developments of social problems and our knowledge of the likely outcomes of different types of service provision' (www.ex.ac.uk/cebbs). Thus EBP is both concerned with the diagnosis of social problems and is a determinant of likely outcomes of intervention. In this sense it moves from the general to the particular.

Social workers are expected to 'know about what works in order to participate effectively in decision making'. The link between evidence as a vehicle for risk, decision making and effective outcomes is transparent in these definitions. It is also offered as an alternative to what is called opinion-based social work practice. In 'Developing empirically based practice in probation' Macdonald (1994) says that alternative approaches are difficult 'to countenance' since they rely 'purely on ideological assumptions and subjective views about the basis of decision-making' (p. 405).

Eileen Gambrill (2003) atttempts to mount a defence of evidence-based social work. She says that 'EBP offers practitioners and administrators a philosophy that is compatible with obligations described in our professional code of ethics and educational accreditation policies and standards . . . as well as an evolving technology for integrating evidentiary, ethical, and practical issues' (p. 1). This is a neat rhetorical move by Gambrill, because it effectively creates a panacea of all admissible parts, thus ruling out the potential for dissension. In constructing the defence of EBP she thinks that most critiques reflect 'narrow views that ignore, misrepresent, or play down the philosophy and related technology of EBP as described in original sources'. My own work is singled out as misrepresenting EBP by aligning it solely with behaviourism, when in fact, I showed that five background sources feed into evidence-based social work: (1) behavioural social work; (2) medical and healthcare research; (3) positivist and empirical science; (4) influence of evaluative research about 'what works'; (5) government and management preoccupation with performance culture. The common thread connecting these five influences is that a formal rationality of practice based on scientific calculation will result in a more effective and economically account-able social work.

Gambrill also misrepresents Taylor & White's (2001) claim that EBP seeks for and assumes the possibility of certainty about know-ledge, by drawing attention to the uncertainty of decision making, arguing that EBP 'highlights the uncertainty involved in making decisions and related potential sources of bias'. So far so good if EBP is about the governance of uncertainty. However, the confusion lies in conflating the epistemology of knowledge claims with the psychology of decision uncertainty, of which Taylor & White were referring to the former. Epistemology and psychology occupy differ-ent logical domains of explanation and reference; for example, one can posit the possibility of knowledge certainty whilst still holding to the view that decisions take place in a field of uncertainty. It was argued that EBP is complementary to 'behavioural decisionist theory' and on this basis attempts are made to predict behaviour 'realistically' on the basis of scientific evidence. This decisionist perspective separates questions of fact from questions of value and assumes that decision making *can* be rational if enforced by evidence and freed from the noise of substantive reasoning. Given this logical separation, and in light of Max Weber's well-known distinction between formal and substantive rationality, it's puzzling to note Gambrill's insistence on integrating evidentiary, ethical, and implementation concerns. The justification for EBP should not rest on selective and partial research. Gambrill (2003) and Sheldon (2001), for example, have thus far ignored research on heuristics as the basis for a critique of EBP.

The scientific evidence against a narrow EBP perspective is over-whelming. Kahneman & Tversky (1973) showed that people failed to be influenced by base-rate evidence in reaching accurate judgments about a given situation. Nisbett & Ross (1980), working on the proposition that 'popular induction depends on the emotional interest of the instances, not upon their number', argue that the effects of consensus evidence are based on subjective opinions rather than the sheer number of instances reported. They demonstrate that 'people are unmoved by the sorts of dry statistical data that are dear to the hearts of scientists and policy planners . . . information that the scientist regards as highly pertinent and logically compelling [is] habitually ignored by people' (1980, pp. 115–16). Research on heuristics undermines the model of social work practice as data-driven information flows, whereby valid and reliable decisions are reached on the basis of empirical research data. *People simply do not act or behave in this way, even when they have evidence at their disposal.* Case conference decision making confirms this, whereby social workers provide reasons, explain decisions or conduct to other professionals or clients. In such situations they are primarily interested in providing a justification, and in putting their acts in a good light. They are also concerned to show that what they did was the right, reasonable, correct and prudent thing to do, and if not, that it was permissible or excusable in some way. McLaughlin (2001) takes this a step further by suggesting that EBP is little more than a rhetorical device used to prop up increasingly fragile professional identities in situations of inter-professional rivalry.

Trinder (2000) asks why EBP has emerged at this juncture. She explains that EBP as a product of its time is complementary to significant changes taking place in risk society. Trinder puts this well in the following:

> The timing of evidence-based practice is not accidental. It has developed within a specific context, particularly the current preoccupations with risk, ambivalence about science and professional expertise, and the concern with effectiveness, proceduralisation and the consumer . . . The response to the critique of science is to place renewed emphasis on science with a constantly revisable and transparent process that excludes uncertainty, and in an age of anxiety, promises security for practitioners, researchers, managers and consumers. Trust is transferred from the fallible individual and placed in a revised system. (2000, pp. 12–13)

We've seen in earlier chapters how risk regulation is joined to expert systems, especially those emphasising the forensic scientist-practitioner. As Jordan (2000) explains, 'the evidence-based approach relies on top-down social engineering, on the power of the expert over the lay person, and on the prestige of official science . . . in order to overcome the resistances of identity, locality, particularism, idiosyncrasy or creativity (p. 76). The paradox entailed here is that more science is required to deal with the internal manufacture of risk by science itself, which is significant in understanding the circular response made by expert systems such as EBP. In true modernist vein it is a technology of care for purportedly making states of affairs more manageable, ordering and predictable. By attempting to create clarity and precision around decision making and the effectiveness of outcomes it narrows down the range of action and marginalises surrounding areas of potentially relevant information. Sanderson (2002) makes the connections between EBP and instrumental rationality explicit when he says that 'there is a danger that the increased emphasis on the role of evidence in policy making is indicative of "technocratic politics" underpinned by instrumental rationality which erodes the normative basis of policy making and undermines the capacity for "appropriate practice"' (p. 1).

Decision Pathway Analysis

This section examines the expanding but controversial area of decision analysis as it relates to social work. Wherever possible the difficult technical language of mathematical and statistical modelling is avoided to make the discussion more accessible to the readership.

Decision analysis is a forensic instrument for decision making processes – either prior to a particular process occurring or as a post-evaluative device – that uses information relevant to justify the decision taken in relation to a particular case (Birch, 1997).

Much of everyday decision making is made on limited evidence. In healthcare literature it is claimed that decision-analytic techniques contribute to problem structuring and the implementation of evidence-based practice. There are numerous sources of unexpectability for social workers. We've seen that many of these lead to the situations involving judgements under conditions of uncertainty. The main problems associated with judgements under such conditions include: (1) risk and uncertainty; (2) intangibles; (3) multiple criteria; (4) long-term implications; (5) inter-professional input and differential vested interests; (6) pooled decision making; (7) value judgments. Decision analysis has developed as a statistical technique to help to overcome such conditions of uncertainty. The taming of chance is a key consideration for this emergent technology. The above discussion on technologically framed risk fits closely with this; as Lindley has argued, 'statistics is *the* study of uncertainty' and 'statistical inference is firmly based on probability alone' (2000, p. 293).

For policy makers decision analysis is intended to supplement EBP in assessing risk. The aim is to provide a scientific method to analyse probabilities associated with decision processes. Some researchers believe decision analysis can provide a framework that is needed to consider the trade-offs and uncertainties of risk. It can be a useful tool for assessing a sequence of decisions made under conditions of uncertainty. And its structuring of a problem requires explicit attention to describing possible uncertain events, estimating the probability of the different outcomes, and valuing each possible outcome. As Rohlin & Mileman (2000) point out, 'the decision analysis approach complements that of evidence-based care by enabling the best empirical evidence to be used in practice. Formal use of decision analysis will promote the rational use of existing knowledge' (p. 453). Some commentators in medicine have suggested that decision analysis is a substitute for the dependency on randomised controlled trials (Sarasin, 1999). Whereas RCTs cannot be applied to individual clients seen in daily practice because they differ in age, presenting problem and background, decision analysis is a technique allowing for multiple outcomes and contributory factors and client preferences.

Decision making in social work would be easy if we could predict reliably what outcome would follow from the selection of which alternative. As previously noted, however, decisions are often uncertain and influenced by attributes of subjective bias (Manning, 2001). Within a decision analysis framework when the outcomes are uncertain, social workers can describe their uncertainty about this state of affairs by using a probability distribution. This is a mathematical form for capturing what we know about the attributes of uncertainties, and how confident we are of what we know. A probability distribution could record, for example, that on the basis of research evidence a social worker estimates that there is a 30 per cent chance of a foster care placement for a five year old child breaking down nine months after the initial placement, whilst there is only a 20 per cent chance of the same outcome occurring with an adoption placement under the same conditions. After assigning probability distributions to each uncertainty, practitioners can examine the uncertainty associated with the outcomes of the decision situation. For example, given probability distributions for age, type of placement, length of time in placement, etc., one can determine a probability distribution for placement outcomes.

Munro (1998) was one of the first to track the relevance of decision analysis for social work. She examines how Bayesian decision analysis is relevant to front-line practice. Using probability inductively and establishing a mathematical basis for probability inference Bayesian models provide a means of calculating, from the number of times an event has not occurred, the probability that it will occur in future. This kind of probability theory provides an optimal approach to such decisions when the uncertainty in the evidence can be quantified in the form of probabilities. Munro uses this model to provide a detailed example of problems associated with conflicting decision indicators at case conferences when information is presented about the risk associated with a child being abused if s/he continues to remain with a family (1998, pp. 147–52). Clearly, the applications of decision analysis are wider than its complementary relation to EBP and can be utilised for case management, risk assessment and process recording.

A service user perspective on decision analysis suggests greater transparency and accountability around decision making. Service users will increasingly be able to monitor the processes involved. Social workers may be required to provide detailed decision pathways for service users showing why discrete decisions were reached at different times in the process. Providing service users with decision maps can be central to ensuring accountability and enable them to discriminate between alternative and conflicting information. On the basis of decision analysis service users may be able to determine the kinds of optimal care package needed or the economic mix of interventions available at different cost prices (see Sheppard & Ryan, 2003, for an embryonic version of this).

To summarise, some researchers believe that decision analysis can rid social work of 'organisational noise', bias and uncertainty in predicting outcomes (Warren & Knox, 2000; McDonald et al., 2001). That is, it can overcome the complexity of decision making by structuring of a problem and provide a formal analysis of the implications of different decision pathways. Decision-analytic techniques will guide the case management process and address wider levels of risk for aggregate groups of clients (Roback & Welch, 2001). It's important to note that decision analysis is not without its critics, the main criticism being that it is derived from rule-driven decision support systems. The critics of rule-driven modelling argue that an unprecedented but distinguishing situation could arise in any application of any rule (Wu, 1999). This leads to the complaint that problems are narrowly defined and artificial in relation to real life situations. Decision analysis is dependent on algebraic techniques that do not address decision making from an information processing perspective; they cannot take account of situational factors (e.g., specific task requirements) and cognitive factors (e.g., memory limitations and specific subject strategies) (Cooper & Fox, 1997). Consequently, decision analysis is restricted in its ability to account for the detailed structure of the decision making process. Although journals such as *Clinical Social Work Journal* and *Journal of Social Service Research* are increasingly publishing research articles on decision and systems analysis, the jury is still out on these methodologies and their relevance to social work.

Networked Information Technologies

This final section focuses on the way that new information and communication technologies (ICTs) increasingly structure social work practice in attempts to reduce or manage risk. It shows how new information technologies may form the basis for networked convergence of actuarialism, decision pathways and evidence-based practice in social work. This link between technologies and networks is important in order to understand future directions that may occur in social work. According to Castells (2000) networks are the fundamental stuff of which new organisations will be designed.

The imperative, however, is a networked system designed to reduce uncertainty rather than encourage adaptability or greater worker and stakeholder democracy.

As new technologies of care converge the causal power of networked information becomes more important than the specific interests it represents, the flows of power. It becomes vital to be present in a network and not to be excluded from it. Castells reckons that this leads to a new mode of development called informationalism or what he refers to as 'networked society'. This is 'the attribute of a specific form of social organization in which information generation, processing and transmission become the fundamental resources of productivity and power' (2000, p. 211). Network analysis has emerged to measure the occurrence or frequency of relationships between the members of a network (Knoke et al., 1996).

The network is a portable concept that can be applied to any public arena. The notion of networks – organisational and knowledge-based – is becoming very fashionable in health and social care. Primary care trusts, as providing the basis for integrating health and social services, are required to develop networked systems of collaborative working (Hampton, 2001). Although not a solution in itself, it's assumed that new information technology will facilitate the flow of case and performance data along various care networks so that information sharing between inter-professional agencies is managed more efficiently. Unfortunately, the information architectures and classification tools that underlie many of the new technologies impacting on front-line practice are designed by a small elite, with decisions on what is represented and what is not being made behind closed doors. This is a top-down approach to modelling practice that excludes social workers.

Computers have a mixed reputation in social work. Information technology is often poorly understood by large numbers of care workers. Therefore the implementation of ICTs for the provision of social services requires trust, and has implications for the way trust is understood and managed. Practitioners need to be involved in decisions about design and implementation. Burkert has remarked: '[u]sing computers and communicating electronically are dependent on trust: trust in people, in organizations, in technology (1994, p. 239).

In the future successful social care organisations will be predicated on being able to generate knowledge and process information efficiently through networked technologies. It is believed that public sector investment in this sort of hi-tech networked organisation will automate inefficient ways of doing things and make them more flexible. Gould

(2003) comments that the Department of Health (2000) in *Information for Social Care* anticipated that British social work would be overwhelmed by the new information technology agenda that is making radical demands for change on service provision and delivery. Gould notes the 'swamped' feeling comes from several sources:

> From the centre, or 'top down' there is: an e-government expectation that all transactions should be capable of being carried out electronically by 2005; all records should be held electronically; there must be interoperability (compatibility) of systems, and the service user should experience the delivery of services as seamless; initiatives such as Quality Protects and Best Value support performance assessment and monitoring regimes which have an information component; the emerging health modernization agenda implies the development of information strategies to support national service frameworks; and a range of cross-departmental policy themes such as social exclusion, economic competitiveness and democratic renewal all have implications for the social care information agenda. (2003, p. 45)

These policy initiatives are dependent on new technologies: telecommunication networks; powerful laptop and desktop computers; adaptive, self-evolving software; new, mobile communication networks for on-line links; digitised automation and recording equipment; and virtual presence environments. In their article 'Living in cyberspace' Gonchar & Roper Adams (2000) argue for a framework for social work assessment 'that demonstrates the utility of considering client Internet use as part of an assessment of client functioning' (p. 86). No less ambitiously, the Department of Health offered a virtual pen-picture of what front-line practice might look like in 2005. In 'Forward look to 2005' it posited that:

> There is an electronic in-tray, which contains not only their own email, but also a diary and a reminder of jobs due over the next few weeks. This can be accessed from the palm top computer or mobile phone as well as the PC on the desk. The reviews to be arranged and the childcare visits to be made are listed, awaiting scheduling in to the diary. They know the team manager will get a report of any visits or reviews that go overdue, and this will be raised at the next supervision session. (www.doh.gov.uk/scg/infsoc/2005/index.htm)

The manner in which the material in this example is ordered is important. It constructs a representation of the relation between worker and machines as the embodiment of new technology itself. The image of the job as 'expert' is nicely conveyed. It makes a series of inter-connected processes (from palmtop computer to PC on the desk) that are safely punctualised through their simplicity. The pen-picture gives the impression that new technologies are systemic procedures or means of achieving specific goals. As such they are projected as basic facts of working life. Hard copy is replaced by electronic dataflows that have the effect of grafting the undoubted logic of technological practice onto daily tasks. Throughout the rationality of ordering is mediated by information technology. The rhetoric of time is important – planning, making lists, scheduling and reporting, all figure significantly. Working life becomes a networked enterprise. Performance is dependent on its connectedness and communication on its consistency. Any lacuna is filled by a power of accountability or what might be called the governance of visibility through the lens of technology. Any lapses of efficiency are monitored in advance and the prospect of the team manager discovering these prior to supervision looms large.

As part of its drive to implement its Information for Social Care initiative, the Department of Health commissioned a number of demonstrator projects from various local authority social services departments. A process model was developed aimed at both non-technical managers and IT specialists. This sets out core processes as they relate to data management and information technology for delivering adult and children's services. A brief glance at some of the demonstrator projects is enough to underscore the point made by Gould about the rapid transformations taking place. In Bristol, for example, integrated electronic recording of data and text information by practitioners in children's services; in West London, a secure Extranet that transfers the service delivery information of a client who moves from one local authority to another; Dorset proposed an electronic collection of visit data in respect of domiciliary care services provided to all service users; Hounslow was developing Multi-Media Profiling for people with learning disabilities; Newcastle-upon-Tyne will develop a care plan using Oracle forms that produce a structured Care Plan document translated into a user-chosen language; and Camden is giving service users, concerned parties and partner organisations electronic access to care planning process (specifically RAP) (Department of Health, 2002a). Each of these initiatives confirms what Sanderson (2002) calls the 'techno politics' occurring in new directions in social care provision. It is relevant to note that two important international research policy groups have also contributed to this rapid development of new information technologies in social work. HUSITA (Human Services Information Technology Applications) and ENITH (European Network for Information Technology in the Human Services) have produced a number of influential publications and guidelines on implementing new information technologies. However, in spite of all these initiatives, as Gould (2003) goes on to explain, thus far there is no unified or coherent perspective about how the deployment of new information technologies is occurring.

We've seen how front-line practice, particularly, in local authority social services departments, is being transformed into an objective component of administrative, technical and financial systems organised in networks (Sapey, 1997). This is tantamount to what many refer to as the 'tick-box culture' wherein only assessment and evaluation figure in low-level data generation. New ICTs become a crucial part of the machinery for achieving these ends. As Suzanne Iacono (1996) poignantly notes:

> From information acquisition and anxiety to information warfare and weapons, there are few areas of social life that are left untouched by the mechanistic and instrumental rhetoric of computational information processing and the associated ways we humans traffic and trade in it. (p. 449)

Gould confirms that at the level of front-line practice 'social work is an inherently complex and fuzzy activity' and that 'the process of social work cannot be modelled algorithmically. Despite the claims of evidence-based practice, the core business of social care cannot be characterised in terms of technical rationality' (2003, p. 46).

New information technologies are themselves phenomena entailing vast uncertainties. Very little is understood about the long-term effects of changes in organisational structure and practices in technology-driven social care. The hypermediacy of ICTs is attractive because it promises, unlike the immediacy of face-to-face work, a built-in reflexivity that purports to give us control over the interface and, by extension, over networked information itself. The suggestion is that controlling the interface gives control over the information it mediates. Again we can observe how these tools of control can be used to rationalise and simplify social work activities, to make them more readable for decision makers, and to direct them toward achieving a narrow set of predetermined goals.

Conclusion

This chapter has highlighted a number of important developments in social work that are indicative of the hardening of technical planning and of the rational orchestration of procedural rules for practice governance. It's been suggested that these changes may offset the longstanding tradition of social casework and emphasis on core social work values. In its preoccupation with rationalising risk social work is increasingly constructed and rendered into a technical calculable form. By increasingly decontextualising expressive and proximal social relations, this kind of instrumentally oriented rationality in social work may inhibit collaboration, trust and mutual recognition, especially when the interaction is not evaluated in a wider socioecological context.

The technologies of care discussed rely on an instrumental rationality that is supposed to be reliably grounded in empirical support and which at a wider level attempts to manage and regulate public and individual activities. These are comprised of networks of practice methods which objectively reframe clients' experiences through the accomplishment of dynamic operating systems that are supposed to produce more effective interventions (Robards & Gillespie, 2000). Ulrich Beck refers to these kinds of developments as 'scientific authoritarianism' with welfare as the control centre (1992, p. 230). Policy makers regard the deployment of these technologies as increasing public trust in social work and removing professional uncertainty in decision making. Whilst technologies of care aim to produce a more systematic way of mapping risk within social work they need to be understood within the political parameters of neoliberal rule. Most notably we've seen they form part of the governance of uncertainty based on the control of risk and targeted populations. Technologies of care effect the reflexive ordering of social work by attempting to regulate and manage risk populations. They may result in administrative executants who are trained in some narrow specialisation rather than in a broadly cultured and interpretive framework for professional practice. Thus the open spaces for professional judgement and autonomy become fewer and reduce the prospects of seeing beyond the enclosing technical framework itself.

6

Management and Organisation of Social Work

Introduction

Talk about risk is widespread in public sector management parlance. 'Risk regulation', 'risk transfer', 'risk accountability', 'risk culture', 'risk management', 'risk tolerance', 'risk governance' and 'risk aversion' are all common. In Britain the Association of Local Authority Risk Managers (ALARM) was formed in 1989 to ensure that a risk management culture was embedded throughout the public sector, and to avoid liabilities and increase trust and reputation. The British government published *Risk: Improving Government's Capability to Handle Risk and Uncertainty* (Cabinet Office Strategy Unit, 2002) to help improve risk management in the public sector and to encourage managerial responsibility and choice in effective risk decision making. Lupton (1993) argues that risk assessment and risk communication have become growth industries in the management of public sector organisations. The argument developed in this chapter is that the management and organisation of social work is best understood as a risk regulation regime within neo-liberal welfare (Hood, 2001).

In situating the organisation and management of social work within risk regulation regimes the chapter explores how risk is mapped, structured and processed so that we can begin to understand decisions and management strategies at different levels. Few studies, for instance, have focused on how risk differentially affects senior and middle managers in social work. This is surprising given that public sector managers work in an unforgiving environment in which to take risks. In social work, risk is distributed across and through the organisational nets that carry out public policy as well as through individuals and groups. Responses to risk are rationed within an inter-organisational network as public attention, risk regulators and political priorities shift from one type of risk to another. Whatever level of safety – the inverse of risk – social work agencies are able to achieve is accomplished in the everyday work routines of organisations. The norms and rules governing safety within an organisation, whether explicit or tacit, are at the heart of a deepening risk-averse culture in social work (Pidgeon, 1991; Cooper et al., 2003).

The chapter also outlines some key British government policy directives in social work showing how risk regulation and neo-liberal market economics are inter-dependent elements in shaping management practice. This is because neo-liberal political programmes convey late modern conditions as unambiguous with a blind faith in technical rationality, planning and calculation. Policy directives implicitly assume that risk can be anticipated, controlled and governed. It will be shown how because of certain intractable problems this leads to a fundamental contradiction in the management of social work. This in turn leads me to conclude towards the end of the chapter that risk cannot be controlled or apprehended by public sector management strategies or government policy, but is subject to what are called 'wicked problems' or silo effects in the transfer of risk. Thus managed care entails an ideological partisanship that is driven by a false trust in technical rationality, planning and ordering.

The neo-liberal programme of managed care is described as a combination of economic reasoning with decisionist behaviourism. That is, in order to secure its ends neo-liberalism needs to regulate professional power and autonomy in the public sector by breaking it down into measurable performance-based components that can be regulated via efficiency and accountability criteria. The solution is not to govern bureaucracy better but rather, as Rose (1999) explains, 'to transform its ethos from one of bureaucracy to one of business, from one of planning to one of competition, from one dictated by the logics of the system to one dictated by the logics of the market and the demands of customers' (p. 142). With the advent of new public sector management a main focus is on capturing and controlling knowledge to avert risky situations and allow for greater organisational efficiency. This is done through various techniques of risk regulation, accountability, explicit standards and measures of performance, desegregation of functions into cost units operating with their own budgets, contracts and competition. The basis of the neo-liberal economy is 'knowledge work', and the workhorse of this economy is the knowledge worker. Knowledge is regarded as the key asset of the knowledge organisation. Organisational memory extends and amplifies this asset by capturing, organising, disseminating and reusing the knowledge created by its employees (see Conkin, 1996). We shall see that the production, categorisation and management of knowledge become crucial in countering risk and attempting to improve performance within the neo-liberal framework: crudely put, new public sector managers are the knowledge engineers, care managers are knowledge technicians and front-line practitioners are knowledge workers in the social handling of risk. Information gathering and handling becomes the central feature of planning various care pathways for front-line practitioners from the point of referral to identifying need and making recommendations about resource provision.

New Public Sector Management

Changes in the management of local authority social services have been occurring over a number of years in the UK, and in many other countries. These changes have been driven largely by economic and political factors. Some writers treat New Labour's modernising agenda for the public sector as an endorsement of 'populism' and 'pragmatism' (Department of Health, 1999b). It simultaneously tries to woo, rather than direct, front-line practitioners, service users and managers through a populist strategy. At the same time it adopts a pragmatic 'what works' approach to joined-up partnerships between health, education and social care (Powell, 2000). This is regarded as an ambivalent attempt to press ahead with Thatcherite Conservative social policy, on the one hand, whilst furthering some semblance of redistributive justice and democracy, on the other. Many writers feel it does nothing to directly tackle structural inequalities and poverty or allow for the redistribution of wealth (Lister, 2001).

During the 1980s there was an acute loss of confidence in the capacity of government to deliver public services and priority was given to cutting public spending. This led to an increased role for private and non-profit organisation and encouraged competitive markets based on corporate models. Based on the success of

American neo-liberal policy, stakeholder power and competition were seen as the key to successful services, with budgetary limits providing sharper incentives for public sector organisations. Independent regulators were introduced to regulate risk and sharpen performance and accountability (Alaszewski, 2000).

The management style associated with organisational change in social work is described by Hood (1991, 1995) and other writers as 'new public management'. According to Hood (1995) the central features of the new management style are based on principles of risk regulation, in which 'lessening or removing differences between the public and the private sector and shifting the emphasis from process accountability towards a greater element of accountability in terms of results' (p. 94). The move towards new public sector management in the 1980s required a shift in ethic from public service to one of private management. No longer was the public sector able to legitimate itself through ethical claims, such as the helping or caring ethic, but was judged according to its capacity to produce results and meet customer demand. Public sector organisations like those of social work were required to make themselves transparent and accountable to both service users and quasi-governmental regulatory bodies. Described as a regulatory logic, this is regarded by Rose as the development of a 'new grid of visibility' which means that decisions about costs and performance:

> [a]re no longer unique: they have been made inscribable and comparable; aggregated, related, plotted over time, presented in league tables, judged against national averages, and utilized for future decisions about the allocation of contracts and budgets. Arbitrary powers seem to have been tamed and liberalized through the neutrality and objectivity of accounting. But if experts have, in the process, been rendered governable, this has changed expertise itself, financial vocabularies, grammars and judgements have infiltrated the very terms in which experts calculate and enact their expertise. (1999, p. 153)

By adapting the risk analysis framework of Mary Douglas, Dunleavy and Hood (1994) analyse the shift towards new public sector management as moving 'down group' (de-differentiating between the private and public sector) and moving 'down grid' (from process to outcome requirements and performance accountability). Hood (1995) summarises the 'down grid' concerns as entailing several key characteristics which include: more emphasis on visible hands-on top management; explicit formal measurable standards and measures of performance and success; and greater emphasis on output controls. The process of incorporating ever tighter risk regulation regimes in public sector management was required because 'it reflected high trust in the market and private business methods . . . and low trust in public servants and professionals . . . whose activities therefore need to be more closely costed and evaluated by regulatory techniques' (Hood, 1995, p. 94). The programming of professional action, to which risk regulation techniques are inextricably linked, is at the heart of the 'down grid' movement in social work management reforms.

This explanation of organisational restructuring in the public sector fits closely with Michael Power's (1997) analysis of what he calls the shift towards an 'audit society'. The development of audit society is seen by Power as a technical response to risk and regulatory failure and he warns against the obsession with audit becoming nothing more than 'shallow rituals of verification' (1997, p. 123). The development of audit society needs to be understood in relation to the breakdown of trust, as Parton notes: 'audit responds to failure and insecurity by the managerialization of risk' (1998, p. 20). Audit society seeks to mimic via administrative means certain paradigm conceptions of appropriate market-based relations, the routinisation of work and enterprising selves. The effect in public sector organisations is to make 'a greater investment in formal generalizable systems of control rather than by developing non-standard capabilities for acting on informal sources of intelligence' (Power, 1997, p. 141). Systems audit, compliance audit, performance audit, user satisfaction audit, value-added audit and strategic HRM audit are now intrinsic to the operations of public sector organisations. The measurement of outcomes, performance and target setting are central to reorganisation in audit society.

There is little proof that people work better when their performance is measured at intervals against a regulatory standard. As we'll see below, in British social services these regulatory shifts were set in motion by a whole raft of policy guidelines and legislation, such as New Labour's modernisation agenda (Jessop, 1999; Powell, 1999; Perri 6 & Peck, 2004). In her discussion of the *NHS Plan* (Department of Health, 2000c), Kerri Hampton of the Office for Public Management confidently reported that as part of strengthening relations between health and social work 'Every part of the service is required to conduct a full performance and modernisation audit with key targets which health and social services are expected to meet' (Hampton, 2001). It is argued here that such 'modernised' public sector systems increasingly employ robust technical methods that undermine professional discretion and autonomy. In this neo-liberal shift towards quasi-markets, formal systems of regulation and mixed economies of care, little attention is given over to the limitations of this dominant perspective. There has been little consideration of the limits to which the balance of social care can be pushed in the direction of enterprise or any single vision of organisational ordering. We know that in practice things are more complex, messier than can be grasped by this single vision of neo-liberal economic ordering. We also know that public sector employees are leaving their professions in droves. In 2002, the NHS, for example, had 20,000 vacancies for nurses and was resorting to employing nurses from Thailand, the Philippines and Spain to fill to gap (BBC 2 Television documentary, *Costa Nurses*, Tuesday 9 April 2002).

Organisational Change in Social Work

The post-1990 reforms in the organisation and management of social work resulted in quasi-markets, centralised funding and an acceptance of top-down managerialism. This process was started by the British Conservative government's (1979–97) attempts to undermine bureaucratic administrations, through the economic levers of contracting and the market. These changes were complemented by the slogan 'let the managers manage', resulting in discretion for public sector managers and executives and not too much daily interference from the political leaders (Kettl, 1997). This is sometimes referred to as 'managing by objectives' whereby the cascade effect of organisational objectives (or mission statements) is devolved functionally to regions or specific areas of responsibility, then ultimately to smaller teams. Richard Sennett (1998c), a sceptic about team working in the context of both corporate and public sector organisations, refers to this as 'the work ethic of a flexible political economy'. According to Sennett, team work rests on 'the fiction of harmony,' stressing mutual responsiveness at the expense of creative thinking. Unity requires the team to confine its members to specific tasks and superficial processes, without much reference to either the experience or perspective of individuals. Sennett argues that 'in the team context, you no longer have a boss – you have a "leader"'. This obscures ordinary power relationships and leads to a condition which he calls 'power without authority' (2000, pp. 41–2).

In Britain devolution of responsibility and discretionary control of a social work agency by managers who are free to manage formed part of the post-1990 reforms. However, as Christensen and Lægreid (2001) point out, the cost of managerial devolution has been a more formal and rigid hierarchic control system by extensive use of contracts in the public sector. Through contracts political leaders specify targets and objectives more clearly, and performance is controlled by use of quantitative indicators for monitoring results and for measuring efficiency. Historically, the template for these policy shifts was initially outlined in the White Paper *Caring for People*, published by the Department of Health in 1989. The government replaced the rigidity of red tape with another administrative edifice of financial transactions, contracts, performance management and regulations within social work. This led to the development of quasi-markets and mixed economies of care, which in turn fed directly into the shaping of a new public sector management culture. Siddall (2000) summarises important aspects of this neo-liberal shift as including 'change: from assessment of need to consumer demand; from state provision to increasing provision by voluntary and private sectors; from acceptance of existing services to the need to promote quality; and from state direction of welfare to partnerships' (p. 26).

These shifts in the organisation of welfare provision aimed to create simulated market environments using actuarial techniques based on contracts, competence-based management, end user empowerment and quasi-markets. It should be stressed that these changes have affected the voluntary as much as the statutory sector. As Stephen Osborne (1996) points out, strategic management, business planning and market pricing are now central in the management of charitable and voluntary sector organisations. In 2001 the Cabinet Office's Performance and Innovation Unit (PIU) in Britain began a review of voluntary sector regulation. The aim of the review was to consider how the regulatory and legal framework can help meet performance measures for new types of organisation (www.cabinet-office.gov.uk/innovation). Discussions about 'venture philanthropy' in the UK underline the increasing influence of corporate culture on the voluntary sector. This new-fangled approach, advocated as early as 1995 by Christine Letts, recognises that too many voluntary and charity organisations are dependent on grant-assisted funding. Venture philanthropy aims to attract entrepreneurs to invest in the non-profit sector of social care – sometimes demanding a return on their investment – and use best business practices to achieve outcome-led performance. The venture philanthropist assumes the risk of voluntary sector costs for an agreed time period with a specified set of returns. This means taking managed risks, developing tools to track effectiveness, and generating measurable returns. In a BBC radio discussion the National Council for Voluntary Organisations applauded this market-oriented venture philanthropy (BBC Radio 4, 8 April 2002).

In Britain organisational changes to social work were influenced by the Griffiths Report recommendations and the onset of what Rose (1999) calls the purchaser–provider split which had a dramatic effect on the mix of social care provision (pp. 146–7). Concepts of the market are bound up with complex projects concerned with how to know, regulate, manage and govern social work (Wistow et al., 1994; Osborne, 1997). Increasingly, the market comes onto the social work agenda as much through the everyday practical concepts of an advertising agent – 'what is our market?' – as through a health service bureaucrat applying the rhetoric of marketisation to the relation between hospital departments or through the formal algorithms of risk and decision making models (Slater & Tonkiss, 2000). As Bamford (2001) explains, however, a strict purchaser–provider split in social services didn't produce any visible improvements and has decreased in popularity. This resulted in the purchasing function being accommodated by a broader commissioning role. As will presently be discussed the Best Value policy of New Labour has softened the compulsory competitive tendering of the Tories with its four C's – challenge, compare, consult and compete – policy for the modernisation agenda. Local councils are no longer forced to put their services out to tender, but are required to obtain best value through commissioning, internal audits and external regulation. Bamford says commissioning 'involves decisions about the mix and pattern of services to achieve the policy objective; it involves decisions . . . about the use of a mixed economy of welfare provision to achieve the objectives; it involves securing quality standards in provision and monitoring performance . . .' (2001, p. 21). He goes on to claim that the social work role is much more about commissioning than direct service provision. In local authority social services there has been a mixed and varied response to commissioning: some authorities have embraced it wholeheartedly, others have shunned it and simply made the right kinds of noises. Tom White (1992) offered a word of caution about contract commissioning from the point of view of voluntary agencies:

Such contracts, with their detailed specification, may be appropriate for road construction, where materials and design can be scientifically determined, or for street cleaning, where standards can be set and monitored, but not, in my judgement, for the kind of human services that we are engaged in. (p. 28)

As we'll see below, these moves are aimed increasingly at developing joint commissioning between health and social care as part of the drive to integrate adult services provision under Care Trusts (Joyce, 2001).

Modernisation and Best Value Policy

In 1999 the Labour government developed the Best Value policy as a significant part of its modernisation agenda to improve and regulate standards in the public sector (see Section 7 of the Local Government Act 1999). This was formalised under the Local Government Act in 2000. Pressures were on New Labour to get rid of compulsory competitive tendering so they came up with something called 'best value'. Under Best Value, local authorities are required to assess their own performance and put in place measures to ensure continual improvements in their services. Year-on-year improvements are required which are audited according to tightly regulated performance plans (see Department of Health, 2000b). Best Value emphasises New Labour's conditional or contractarian welfare approach to managed care (Powell, 2002).

With Best Value the managerialist imagination feeds on the idea of continuous improvement delivered through quality assurance measures. Five performance areas of Best Value are used as an organising framework for all assessment data and information. The Audit Commission's Directorate of Inspection incorporates the Best Value Inspection Service to enforce this policy (Jones, 2001). Evaluations can follow with in-depth Social Service Inspectorate inspections and Audit Commission Joint Reviews covering the full breadth of social services in evaluating the performance of a regional or unitary council. The Best Value paradigm is not only potentially very divisive, but also unintelligible since local authorities don't actually know what a 'best value authority' looks like, particularly in relation to quality and cost (Langan, 2000). They also find it difficult to pin down the indicators of best value. The Best Value policy has, however, significantly hardened the public sector management paradigm. Bamford summarises the modernisation agenda as follows:

The modernization agenda in social services aims to achieve higher standards and greater consistency across the country . . . Best Value will provide a tool with which to secure improvement in poorly performing authorities. As Best Value will itself be subject to external inspection, the room for independent action on the part of local authorities is becoming more circumscribed. Social services departments are increasingly seen by government as delivering a national service which is locally administered. (2001, p. 9)

Delivery of this standardised national service means that statutory and voluntary sector agencies have to aggressively engage in corporate business practices, such as continuous quality improvement (Curry & Herbert, 1998). During the 1980s marketing was also advocated as a necessary business strategy for social work. There was also a clash of marketing orientation with public sector cultures, which was largely based on notions of trust. As Bovaird & Rubienska (1996) argued, public sector organisations emphasised 'paternalism and the importance of trust and dignity which seemed to deny any attempt at marketing. In addition, marketing was seen as superficial in attempting to deny the increasing losses of citizens' rights' (1996, p. 51). However, the resistance to marketing in social work has largely ebbed away, and it is now widely advocated as essential to improving performance as markets became more important in the destiny of public sector organisations. The management of market research to help supply the growing need for customer-oriented social work is now undertaken as a matter of routine in statutory and voluntary sector organisations (Luck et al., 2000).

Nowhere is the eclipse of the British social services role as direct service provider more evident than with the advent of contracting and tendering. Bamford's (2001) helpful little book has a chapter devoted to contracting which spells out the difference between block contracts, spot contracts, call-off contracts and cost-and-volume contracts. As Bamford points out, by glancing through any issue of *Community Care* many advertisements for tendering from local authorities can be found. For instance, Suffolk County Council Procurement and Commissioning department has developed E.L.T.O.N. (Electronic Tendering On-Line), allowing them to issue tenders electronically, and companies to submit bids and proposals via e-mail. Their web page has customer and supplier areas, the latter having details of tenders for the supply of a whole range of services including: supplying occupational health services; maintenance of hospital beds; sanitary disposal units and even funeral undertaking (www.suffolkcc.gov.uk/procurement/suppliers.html).

New Labour's Best Value policy has had a mixed reception in social work. Some believe that effective performance indicators are valuable as sources of motivation for staff, and of planning and control for managers within social work. Many people in public sector services, however, remain unconvinced of the need for such rigorous inspection, seeing it as a further example of central government's lack of trust in those working in health and social care (Martin, 1999). Best Value doesn't really provide a machinery for dealing with resource shortages or resource allocation, crucial issues when money is scarce in social services. Buchanan (2000) argues that the user voice has been diminished by New Labour's increased reliance on regulation and inspection in Best Value.

Performance Management and Audit Culture

Social work is now saturated with market-driven performance measurement evaluations. The quasi-market process of performance is not regulated directly by government but by quango institutions, such as the National Care Standards Commission and the Audit Commission, which focus on results. These agencies are part of the widespread development of a performance culture aimed at regulating and auditing social care. The regulatory function they perform, as Rose says, involves 'setting targets, promulgating standards, monitoring outputs and undertaking audits' (1999, p. 146) which conform to what are described below as risk regulation regimes.

Performance management is a regulatory tool for controlling and managing resources and requires definitions of 'outcomes' for social work policies and programmes using quantitative indicators to monitor the effectiveness and efficiency of services (Tilbury, 2004, p. 228). It's easy to get a flavour of this performance culture at work in social care. Notably, the Personal Social Services Research Unit (PSSRU) at University of Kent and the Business School at Aston University have a flourishing industry of research papers on performance indicators, evaluations of social care plans, quality-of-life measurements and the economic costs of various 'anti-social' behaviours (Kendall & Knapp, 2000). This work has been extremely influential on the Department of Health and has shaped policy guidelines, notably in areas of care management, unit costing and performance management. Netten and Curtis (2000) compiled unit costs of health and social care, claiming that the quantification of care economies is part of 'the drive towards using performance measurement as a means of raising standards and increasing efficiency' (www.ukc.ac.uk/PSSRU). In the discussion paper 'On the targeting of care management' Bleddyn Davies, another member of PSSRU, tells us they already have good local targeting policies based on quantified knowledge, but all that is needed now is a consortium of agencies to 'establish *the laboratories* in which we could develop, analyze and use the *minimum data set for care-managed* community care' (www.ukc.ac.uk/PSSRU; my emphasis). A plethora of evidence-based findings based on PSSRU's 'production of welfare' approach gives details of care-managed performance and the study of cost performance units and costs of a 'typical episode of care, comprising several hours of a professional's time'. This is absorbing stuff and PSSRU reports even provide glossaries, defining such key terms as: agency overheads; annuitising capital investment; capital overheads; care package costs; cost function analysis; discounting; marginal costs; oncosts; and opportunity costs. The emphasis on stakeholders means it's likely that new customer satisfaction indexes and focus group feedback will also be used as measures of particular units of social services performance (Cabinet Office, 2000).

In local authority social services the Performance Assessment Framework (PAF) was initially introduced by the Department of Health as part of the government's *Modernising Social Services* White Paper (Department of Health, 1999b). As Jordan (2000) cynically notes, the modernisation policy is primarily 'concerned with regulating local authority departments, through a series of new supervisory and monitoring bodies: with setting new standards and targets against which to measure performance; and agencies to enforce these' (2000, p. 8). The PAF allows for comparison of all authorities across the country on a range of standardised measures on an annual basis. Local authorities are then judged according to their performance within their socioeconomic target group (e.g. regional or unitary) and league tables are produced. Good Management Information Officers are crucial in producing this very detailed performance information, which is often decontextualised. Scores are given, for example, for placement stability of children with three or more moves within a year; children leaving care with one GCSE with Grade A to G; and units of residential care for children. Quantitative targets are to be achieved based on the notion of continuous improvement: 'the percentage of looked after children who obtain GCSEs and GNVQs should be high and rising: the rate of admissions of elderly people to residential homes should not be rising; the proportion of disabled people living independently should be steadily increasing' (Humphrey, 2003, pp. 12–13).

There are significant methodological problems regarding the collection of performance data and serious concerns about the validity of individual indicators and their relevance to service delivery for clients. The data are descriptive and tell the readers very little about the quality of the service. Statistical anomalies easily occur because of the scale, ratio and numbers involved in the database. In a small unitary local authority, for instance, five individuals being removed from a hundred on the child protection register can produce a statistically significant percentage shift. These problems are compounded because local authorities collect their statistics in different ways and the Department of Health pays little attention to this and its potential distortions. Hood (2001) has noted that cheating and interest-based strategic action are common with performance measures and they can only be sustained in a narrow range of social conditions. As a further layer of performance management Position Statements run in parallel with and are intended to complement the PAF measures. The methodology for these self-monitoring health checks contrasts with the raw data approach of PAF by having a more descriptive, mission-type and qualitative feel to them. Position Statements are submitted to the regional Social Services Inspectorate (SSI) twice, at the beginning and end of each year. (The Commission for Social Care Inspection replaced the SSI in April 2004 in monitoring services.) They tell the SSI where the local authority considers it is performing well and where it is performing poorly, and are cross-referenced with PAF returns.

Performance culture has hardened in social services over the past ten years. In childcare, for instance, PAF was proceeded by the Department of Health's 'Quality Protects' Management Action Plans, which set benchmarks for funding based on the necessity to meet specific targets such as educational standards of children in care, placement stability, placement choice. A further stream of performance reviews preceding PAF and still ongoing are the annual statistical returns for the Department of Health on Looked After Children and Child Protection (colloquially referred to as '903' and 'CPR3' returns). In fact, this was the original framework for annual performance reporting in children and family services. It included, for instance, the number of child protection investigations carried out by a local authority, number of children on the child protection register; number of children added or removed during that year; types of category of registration, ethnicity, age, duration on the child protection register, assessments completed within set time-scales. A national profile is produced by the Department of Health from these figures.

For Joan Orme (2001) the resultant effects of this combination of performance culture with public sector managerialism are deeply worrying. She considers that it will increase competition and deepen the regulatory culture of social work:

> The use of reviews, performance plans and user satisfaction surveys involves the collection of data, mechanisms to record delivery of services and development plans to improve them. This generates an industry of constant monitoring and information collection . . . Best Value league tables and 'beacon council' awards not only precipitate fragmentation through competition rather than collaboration, they also represent a form of surveillance of social care workers. (2001, p. 619)

The establishment of the Cabinet Office's Performance & Innovation Unit (PIU), which reports directly to the Prime Minister, has added another policy layer to the performance culture in social care. The PIU is particularly concerned with performance and resource productivity in the public sector. It is currently undertaking a review of factors contributing to better performance management and leadership in the public sector. Most significantly, perhaps, this review focuses on encouraging greater entrepreneurship and risk within the public sector. As will be seen presently, the balance between risk aversion and risk taking in public sector management is beginning to shift in favour of the latter as managers are increasingly expected to demonstrate entrepreneurial talent especially at executive officer level (www.cabinet-office.gov.uk/innovation/leadershipreport).

A variety of fragmented performance evaluations are apparent throughout the social care sector. Performance targets are set for the time required to undertake assessments and new call centres and help desks are introduced to improve performance. Disabled facilities grants provided by housing authorities have to be approved within a time-limited six months. Gloucester Social Services were delighted, for instance, that 38 service users used direct payments in 2000, and by the end of March 2001, this figure had increased to 52 service users (Gloucester Social Services 'Better care, higher standards' leaflet, 2001). Adding 14 more enterprising service users to the tally in a year was seen as an improvement in the quality of service provision. All local authority social services departments are required to produce management action plans which include performance indicator tables with headings like 'helping people to live at home'; 'targeting needs and arranging services'; and 'reductions in the number of looked-after children'. Computerised information systems are introduced to plan decisions and underpin these quality assurance systems. Performance targets are also set for front-line social workers in terms of the number of cases they are carrying. In adult services, particularly in work with older people, this has created a 'case closing culture' in which social workers are pressurised to prematurely close cases in order to demonstrate high volume turnover. This has undoubtedly increased tension between front-line workers and their supervisors who are caught up in the chain of command for delivering these volume capacity targets. Performance pressures for quick high volume turnover are compounded by the introduction of new methods for detailed measures of work-place activity. The Children in Need Census is a good example of this at work. It aims to develop the use of activity and cost information in the management and planning of children's social care. Here each local authority is required to pick a specific week and monitor its entire activities within the time-frame. Every worker in the authority completes time management records. When the raw data have been collated, compiled and categorised, annual reports are routinely submitted to the Department of Health.

In performance culture task definition increasingly becomes standardised, measured and outcome-oriented. Within this context social work is largely conceived in terms of low-level assessment and planning functions. This has the effect of reducing professional discretion and autonomy, particularly in adult services. The latter, especially in work with older people, is essentially focused on transaction time and cost units, the key questions being: are enough assessments being done and are enough services being provided at value for money? Maddock (1998) summarises the effects of contracting in mixed economy care as follows:

> The impact of contracting generally has been to create a smaller core of better paid managers who have a strategic role in commissioning and purchasing; service practitioners are undermined by intrusive measurement and increased workloads; support staff have, in general, lost security and are now often on short-term contracts. The flexibility required by new developing agencies has been introduced at the expense of staff security and morale. (p. 16)

Performance audit in social work is a process that is based on complex and sometimes tense relations between people. In other words, it's a reflexive process of monitoring, not simply a matter of collecting and punching in relevant data. Inside social work organisations the buzz words for care managers are targets, performance, efficiency, responsibility and resources. There is, however, a strain towards surveillance and authoritarian regulation. John Law (1994) captures the reflexive aspects of relations between power and risk entailed in performance audits:

> How do you get the best out of your people? The enterprise strategy is to give them resources and require that they perform. And then it is to monitor performance. It is to monitor performance for two reasons: to see how well they are performing; and second, to foresee, so far as possible, if anything is going to go wrong. The strain in other words, is towards a self-reflexive space, a place of discretion. And it's towards the disciplinary surveillance of subordinate performance. (pp. 176–7)

Increasingly, the concentration on audit and performance shapes the types of relationship that develop between care managers, frontline workers and service users (see Salauroo and Burnes, 1998). As Power says, 'the assumption of distrust of the person being audited, which is built into external audit, can seriously damage the relationship between practitioners and those they serve' (1997, p. 143). The performance culture encourages competitive forms of behaviour that tend towards prioritising immediate results and a quick turn-around of service rather than emphasising qualitative processes or holistic organisational learning. Aggressive competition between teams and units of service delivery is likely to occur as the emphasis on 'provider agencies' adopting an 'entrepreneurial' approach to service users and contractors hardens. Work-place bullying, intimidation and harassment are common in such highly competitive environments. Adult services in social care are particularly prone to the development of this type of entrepreneurial culture.

The deepening of performance culture in social work has meant that the role of managers, senior practitioners and front-line workers has significantly changed. Care managers, for example, as commissioners, act as knowledge brokers, providing technical information for profit or not-for-profit organisations tendering to deliver home care for the elderly or respite care for the disabled. According to Rose (1999) the reconceptualised role for social care is derived from knowledge management and networked information paradigms:

Experts, as knowledge workers, no longer merely manage disciplinary individualization or act as functionaries of the social state. They provide information –
for example, risk assessment – that enables quasi-autonomous agencies to steer
themselves. They tutor in the techniques of self-government . . . They provide
information that will allow regulatory agencies to assess the performance of
these quasi-autonomous agencies. (p. 147)

The knowledge worker, unlike the blue-collar and traditional
white-collar worker, is an actuarial expert, because to be effectively
applied, knowledge must be specialised. As a consequence, knowledge workers must routinely come together to solve complex problems in a functional and technical manner. The information provided
by social knowledge workers is reduced to a series of tasks that are
decontextualised rather than ecologically grounded. We've seen how
performance management becomes a key indicator of 'value for
money' for these front-line knowledge experts. Knowledge workers
are changed by the information in their environment, and they in
turn seek to change others through information (see Performance &
Innovation Unit, 2001). From the above we can see how performance is a sub-set of complex relations between determinate and inde-
terminate outcomes.

Let's try to anticipate some future directions in the organisation
of social work. Presently we are witnessing a convergence of adult
services in health and social work that was set in motion under the
guise of Care Trusts. Some suspect this inevitably means the end
of local authority social services departments. Government policy
is also increasingly focused on 'joined-up working', recognising
that many of the services people rely on the public sector to
provide are the responsibility of more than one agency or department (National Audit Office, 2001; and Richards, 2001). It's
argued that joint working will lower costs, speed up the process of
intervention and increase the transparency and reliability of the
system. What is becoming clear it that the dominant healthcare
partner will increasingly come to shape adult care as the pace
towards full integration increases. The kind of neo-liberal governance envisaged is based on what Halachmi and Bovaird describe
as 'business process re-engineering'. Here attempts are made to
put 'rationality and systematic thought back into management
transformation efforts, rather than relying on vaguer notions of
inspirational leadership and culture change' (1997, p. 227; also see
Di Maggio & Powell, 1991).

Risk Management Policy Making

The New Labour government placed a great deal of faith in ever expanding risk regulatory regimes in attempting to make social work accountable (Humphrey, 2003). In July 2001, the Prime Minister, Tony Blair, instructed the Performance & Innovation Unit to examine how the government's management of risk could be improved. Announcing the review in response to a Parliamentary Question, the Prime Minister said:

> Effective management of a wide range of risks is essential both for the delivery of improved public services and for the achievement of the Government's wider goals. Government is concerned with managing risks to the public (including public health, social, environmental and safety risks) and also risks to the delivery of specific objectives and programmes (including financial, operational and technological risks).

The PIU project identified best practice in decision making on risks and the best methods for promoting this within public sector organisations, such as health and social care. Government policy think tanks such as the PIU aim to make recommendations to improve the management of risks to the public and to the delivery of specific objectives and programmes. In a similar vein the National Audit Office, which is responsible for scrutinising public spending on behalf of government, reported that risk management can promote innovation and lead to improved value for money for tax payers. Public sector organisations are advised to devise and implement effective risk management strategies (www.nao.gov.uk/publications/nao_reports/9900864es.pdf). Social care organisations use a range of methods to manage risk including: action plans for implementing decisions about identified risks; evaluations of controls to prevent or minimise the likelihood of risks materialising; and assessing the costs and benefits of addressing risks. Policy guidelines recommend that it's increasingly important for care agencies to include risk reports as an integral part of their departments' organisational planning and management processes.

Risk issues in social work are unarguably contentious. Managers and executives will evaluate risks in incompatible ways and put forward conflicting proposals for mitigating or litigating risk issues. The sources of contention between, say, senior managers, middle managers and front-line workers are multi-layered. Sometimes professionals differ in their judgement about risk because they have different information; sometimes they differ because they have incompatible interests and values; sometimes individuals will differ because they have competing agendas. The contentious nature of risk become even more problematic when we realise that there are multiple conceptions of risk and little agreement about how to define it within the organisational context. Broadly speaking risk is almost always defined within management parlance in terms of loss and uncertainty. Whichever way we turn in trying to stipulate definitions of risk or provide a general conception of risk, its clear that policy makers and public sector managers regard risk management as bound up with notions of better performance and better service delivery. The PIU project on risk and uncertainty states:

> Effective management of the risk to government business can help departments improve their performance. It can lead to better service delivery, more efficient use of resources, better project management, help minimise waste, fraud and poor value for money.
> (www.cabinet-office.gov.uk/innovation/2001/risk/scope.shtml)

Not surprisingly, the policy discourse of the PIU risk project adopts a positivist account of risk. It takes a purely scientific conception of risk which admits of complete characterisation and analysis through data collection and quantitative methods. This positivist position of public policy makers interprets risk as referring objectively to circumstances in the physical world of the organisation. Their definition of risk is consistent with the classical positivist model of the probability and utility of events based on 'significant *harms* to or *costs* falling upon individuals or organisations, or *obstacles* to the achievement of the goals of the programmes of government' and 'where there is reason to believe that the *severity* of those harms, the scale of those costs or obstacles is great enough to cause wide public concern' (PIU, op. cit., emphasis in original). This is referred to in the literature as a 'decision-theoretic' treatment of risk, which holds that the utility or value of a choice to a decision maker is a function of the relative value of potential outcomes (Starr & Whipple, 1980). Douglas & Wildavsky (1982), strong critics of this approach, argue that a rational-objective approach to risk is pointless because risk is always contextualised within a specific time-space configuration and its associated political culture. They argue that the specific content of beliefs about purity, danger and risk are arbitrary but that probability theory acts as a general framework for structuring our reasoning about risks and the management of risk. Similarly

Adrian Smith argues, 'Any approach to scientific inference which seeks to legitimize an answer in response to complex uncertainty is . . . a totalitarian parody of a would-be rational human learning process' (1990, p. 141). We've seen in an earlier chapter how social reasoning is in fact based on forms of bounded rationality and what were referred to as heuristic devices. From the PIU's decision-probability perspective risk management is construed as a structured process that seeks to arrive at predictively informative evaluations about possible events and probabilities which, should they transpire, could pose a potential threat to the health and safety of service users, workers or the organisation itself.

The PIU project identifies two types of risk management relevant to public sector organisations: (i) *anticipation*: identifying risks in advance and putting in place measures to prevent those risks, or at least reduce their probability or severity; and (ii) *resilience*: creating generic organisational capability for flexible response, when harms, costs or obstacles do fall. The implications of the government strategy on risk for social work is that risk management should be integrated into planning, feedback and decision processes. However, as Hood & Rothstein (2000) argue, in their report commissioned by the National Audit Office, risk management should avoid the 'tick-box' culture that dominates social work assessment. This low-level functionalist culture gets in the way of sound judgement and interpretive skills in social work. The Department of Health (2002) study of serious case reviews of child deaths and serious injury or neglect highlighted the drawbacks of this administrative mentality from the point of view of one respondent:

> There's a tendency to translate a rather big issue into something that can be measured and ticked because of all the frenzy about outcomes at the moment. (2002, p. 43)

Hood & Rothstein insist that risk evaluation requires fostering intelligent and analytical deliberation that is markedly different from the sterile, unreflective routinised tick-box style. This means 'designing deliberative procedures that require careful attention to be paid to likely second-order effects as well as first-order effects of risk management, and to reflective practitioner processes' (2000, p. 29). By second-order risk effects they mean, for example, that if all paedophiles on release from prison are electronically tagged and their movements around child-sensitive locations excluded against, the possible emergence of an alternative route, such as the use of

internet technology, can spring up in response to measures to control
the risks of established social movement (Relph & Webb, 2003).
Hood & Rothstein claim that successful business managers often
stress that risk management is an art or craft and that if risk management procedures are overly rationalised they can unintendedly exacerbate blame-avoidance tendencies in public bureaucracies. Hood &
Rothstein point to a reflexive stance that conjoins knowledge and
experience in an active immersion confined only to the risk material
offered and not some distant notion of planned outcome. The
process of understanding the risk material is based on a progressive
self-correcting that emphasises the imaginative capacity for discovery by reconfiguring the risk material at hand. This suggests a
balance is needed between proceduralised or legalistic approaches
and more informally structured risk management discussions.

We've seen throughout this discussion that the 'decentralised
approach' associated with risk regulation regimes in social work has
spawned a proliferation of audit and inspection activities which have
over-burdened the care system, and which are likely to reduce rather
than enhance the public interest. Moreover, the saturation of social
care agencies with risk regulation regimes leads to conservativism
and risk aversion by public sector management and front-line practitioners alike. This kind of management conservatism involves a preference for erring on the side of over-stating as opposed to
under-stating risk under conditions of uncertainty (Perhac, 1996).
This discussion shows there are clear limits to the extent to which
caring agencies can be pushed in the direction of enterprise and
market criteria of performance – or indeed towards any single vision
of organisational ordering. Both front-line practice and management
in social care are larger, more complex, and messier than can be
grasped within any particular logic of regulation. In summary, this
form of risk governance in social work takes the form of the
'machine' of continual contractualisation – with institutions, stakeholders and front-line practitioners – that creates a continuous call for
authority through regulation, performance and audit (Hutton, 1998).

Wicked Problems, Silo Effects in Social Work

This section will show that the organisational response to certain
types of social risk cannot be easily planned, predicted or accounted
for. The predominance of the kind of organisational thinking based on

a traditional linear approach to problem solving – in which we gather data, analyse them, formulate a solution, and implement that solution – is rooted in a flawed linear and mechanistic view of the social world. With the linear model planning methods are expected to allow a smooth, straight ride from well-understood problem to final solution. Here progress is quantitative, marking distance from the organisational objectives. Public sector management is rooted in this rational organisational model, as is evidenced in its risk regulation regimes, performance reviews and audits of accountability. A different organisational paradigm is required which takes into account non-rational intractable problems. Rittel and Webber (1973) characterised some salient aspects of expert knowledge or knowledge work that are highly pertinent to some of the organisational issues in social care. They identified a class of problem that they termed 'wicked', in contrast to 'tame' problems. Wicked problems are often derived from issues of organisational complexity and competing value positions within organisations. Rittel and Webber argued that:

> Diverse values are held by different groups of individuals – that what satisfies one may be abhorrent to another, that what comprises a problem-solution for one is a problem-generation for another. Under such circumstances, and in the absence of overriding social theory or overriding social ethic, there is no determining which group is right and which should have its ends served. (1973, p. 158)

It's noteworthy to observe how wicked problems are necessarily coupled to the twin processes of uncertainty and complexity as features of changing organisational environments (Clarke & Stewart, 1997). There are parallels between wicked problems and what cognitive psychologists refer to as 'irreducible uncertainty', defined by Hammond (1996) as referring to 'uncertainty that cannot be reduced by *any* activity at the moment action is required' (p. 13). Uncertainty in the formation of social policy and organisational planning makes error inevitable. Tame problems are not necessarily trivial problems, but by virtue of the maturity of certain fields of intervention, can be tackled with more confidence in a greater level of predictability by experts. Traditional planning and problem solving methods are adequate for any of the tame problems encountered in organisational life. Unless, however, we can distinguish between tame and wicked problems we are likely to be using tame problem solving methods on all our organisation and policy problems in social care. Without an understanding of the weakness associated with tame problem solving methods for the purpose of policy planning there is a danger, easily observable in the history of child abuse scandals, of blaming persons for not accomplishing what their tools will not allow them to accomplish. Wicked problems display a number of distinctive properties that violate the assumptions made in using tame problem solving methods. It can be difficult to recognise a wicked problem. Many problems that appear tame, are not (see King, 1993). Confusion and disagreement among the stakeholders are signs that the problem on which you are working is, in fact, wicked. Also, the number of instances of public sector organisations determining the definition of the problem, rather than the reverse, gives rises to wicked problems.

This basic distinction between wicked and tame problems has been highly influential in recent public policy research on governance and used to good effect to explain policy failure and success. According to Rittel & Webber (1973), wicked problems display a number of distinctive properties that violate the assumptions made using 'tame rational planning' and problem solving methods. They defined their key characteristics as follows – to which I've added examples from social work:

● *cannot be easily defined so that all stakeholders agree on the problem to solve*; there are many stakeholders – people who care about or have competing interests at stake in how the problem is resolved (child protection case conferences; school truancy and refusal; persistent youth offending; paedophiles' right to privacy, Area Child Protection Committee meetings)
● *require complex judgements about the level of abstraction at which to define the problem* (work with refugees and immigrants, ethnoculturally differentiated child rearing and parenting practices, inner-city race riots)
● *have no clear stopping rules* (domestic violence; drug misuse, panic attacks)
● *have better or worse solutions, not right and wrong ones*; the constraints on the solution, such as limited resources and political ramifications, change over time ('good enough' parenting, unemployment among the socially disadvantaged, inner-city areas; poor housing, social isolation and rough sleeping)
● *have no objective measure of success* (home visits for elderly service users; emotional support for distressed clients; playgroups and drop-in centres)

- *require iteration – every trial counts* (using respite care to prevent family disruption and breakdown; parental contact following divorce)
- *have no given alternative solutions – these must be discovered*; here you don't understand the problem until you have developed a solution (preventing street crime; lack of domestic hygiene; disruptive behaviour)
- *often have strong moral, political or professional dimensions, particularly for failure* (child sex abuse; violent service users with mental health problems)

The connection between wicked problems and social work intervention is readily apparent. Such problems are those typically faced on a daily basis by managers and front-line workers in social work. Wicked problems and their related 'silo effects', described below, are endemic features of the care system, rather than a merely superficial phenomenon. We've seen that wicked problems are inter-related components of organised complexity and cannot be solved in isolation from one another. They also hinge on differing sociopolitical values that clash in the political arena of organisational life. The wicked problems are multiple and inter-locking deep-seated social problems relating to drug misuse, abusive relationships, low skills, poor housing, street crime, poor health and unemployment. Given the range and depth of wicked problems associated with the social work task it's inevitable that errors of judgment will be made, some of which will turn out to have very serious consequences. Front-line workers and managers frequently find themselves caught up in the dilemma of making decisions in these highly contestable areas of social policy and with much public and political scrutiny at stake.

The difficulties associated with wicked problems are compounded by the organisational structures designed to deal with them. The dominant organisational model in social work has been to design structures and provision around specialised areas of knowledge and professional skill – functional specialisation – classically illustrated in the separation of adult and children and family services, or in the distinction between community psychiatric nursing and mental heath social work (a distinction incidentally that is becoming increasingly blurred). As we'll see this model of service delivery is particularly prone to fatigue, breakdown or collapse when it comes to dealing with wicked problems. The longstanding features of this dominant model of organising social services are beneficial if the problem to be dealt with lies within one area of professional knowledge, but it creates a major set of obstacles in handing service provision issues with cross-professional or specialist domains. At a systems level the problems identified with these organisational limitations have been described as 'silo effects'. Richards (2001) argues that wicked problems are an effect of the silo structures within an organisational network. According to Richards, public sector organisations are preoccupied with performance and measurement outcomes and thereby transfer the risks associated with wicked problems from one organisation to another in order to meet targets and outcomes:

> The term 'wicked problems' was identified as a product of the silo structures, occurring because rational efficient behaviour – narrowly defined – had consequences for other policy or service areas, creating irrationality and inefficiency at an overall systems level. The classic example is the difficult pupil, excluded from school by the head teacher who needs to improve his or her school's performance measurement and thus position on league tables of measured outputs. The young person then frequently becomes a charge on the criminal justice budget in the first instance, and then later on the social security budget as they face adult life ill-equipped for modern employment conditions. (2001, p. 63)

A good example of this is where the probation service is shifting the focus of its activity, from reducing involvement with people who commit minor offences to increasing activities with people at risk of going into custody, to improve its performance outcomes (Nash & Savage, 1995). Richards defines silo effects as a process whereby risk is transferred around from one public sector organisation to others, or within an intra-organisational setting from one department to another. She says they are 'obviously the product of the perverse incentives created by narrowly defined, output driven performance management systems, and the term wicked problems has been used to refer to this' (2001, p. 63). The Sure Start programme, for example, designed to deliver integrated services to young children and their families in areas of disadvantage is specifically outcome-focused and performance-related. With silo effects service users typically fall into a limbo between the performance regimes of different social work agencies. Examples include: young people leaving care; disabled and mentally ill people trying to lead a normal life; young people alienated from a service which they would otherwise benefit from in making their way into adult life. Similarly, as we've seen, the service inspectorates (such as the Social Services Inspectorate) which have become central mechanisms for performance management exert their pressure for improvement primarily in a 'professional silo' position, and thus from the point of view of wicked problems are part of the problems rather than part of the solution. There are thus two distinctive ways of understanding how wicked problems impact decisively on the organisation of social work: the first refers to the types of intervention social work is typically involved with, that is, a set of intractable social and economic problems which no one knows how to solve; the second refers to problems that persist because the organisational design and priorities of the public policy system hinder their solution (Jervis & Richards, 1997). Let's look in detail at examples of these kinds of silo effects as reported by the Department of Environment, Transport & the Regions (DETR) report (2000) on 'cross-cutting issues'.

Community safety involves wicked problems derived from the silo effect of organisational design. The DETR report (2000) notes that it is also linked to a criminal justice system that fails to operate as a 'system'. The various criminal justice agencies – police, prosecution service, courts, prisons and probation services – pull apart as much as pulling together, and serve their own professional values and orientation. The silo effects are most obvious in relation to issues around domestic violence, where different departments have responsibility for different aspects of the issues: multi-agency partnerships are dealt with by the DETR, perpetrators are the responsibility of the Home Office (Probation), service needs of women as victims are the responsibility of the Department of Health (which is co-ordinating a government strategy on violence against women) as well as voluntary agencies such as Women's Aid; and issues concerning the well-being of children are dealt with via personal social services staff in the Department of Health. Value conflicts are often in evidence in domestic violence work. The three main professional groups in this area are social workers, probation services and the police. The first two are like-minded and tend to approach the issue of gender and power in the same way. The police have a different kind of professional orientation, although those involved in domestic violence work over a period of time tend to become 'incorporated' into the social model and develop a similar 'world-view' about male violence. A key problem is that budgets are divided into separate silos for social work, probation services and the police and whilst the vertical links between the agencies might be strong, the horizontal links are either weak or non-existent.

The DETR report suggests that public sector agencies need to develop a more strategic approach to these silo effects and that the case of disaffected young people illustrates the problems of developing 'ownership' across inter-professional agencies and of matching existing organisational priorities and budgets to meet the targeted needs of this group of people. Unfortunately, service provision for young people is functional and based on highly specialised divisions of expert labour within a fragmented set of policies and political interests. In other words there is too much vertical integration and too little horizontal integration of care governance provision for young people.

What possible solutions are there to these complex wicked problems? How do we organise social work to deal with diverse values and expectations about the purpose, resources and provision of care? Yankelovich (1991) asserted that the answer lies in the notion of informed governance. That is, forums are required where front-line practitioners and managers can learn, question, debate, and come to an informed judgment as to what choices are best. In *Coming to Public Judgment*, Yankelovich also determined that the most critical barrier to making effective and informed choices in a complex world is the lack of public forums in which the process of 'working through' value differences and preferences can occur. Rittel & Webber (1973) also concluded that wicked problems could only be tackled through what they termed an *argumentative* method.

Understanding how to frame wicked problems is the key to finding solutions to them: what are the key questions, values and priorities? Wicked problems are necessarily an inter-professional issue and therefore require a creative and critical dialogue between professionals that will inevitably lead to conflict, negotiation, debate and compromise.

The government policy efforts to remedy silo effects and wicked problems in social work are based on developing the strategy of 'joined-up' governance within a variety of inter-professional or multi-disciplinary contexts. Here the short-term emphasis is on structuring care provision around solving problems rather than integrated services and functions. By this I mean that policy targets a specific problem, say street crime in ten inner-city black spots, sets targets and time limits, and then throws all its resources at it. Does this sound familiar? It should do: it's exactly in line with New Labour's zero tolerance street crime reduction policy. For social work the prescription is for it to engage in joined-up practice across boundaries in partnerships or public–private contracts to deal with specific problems. There are, however, no easy structural solutions for cross-cutting issues, a matter often overlooked in the rhetoric of inter-professional practice. Restructuring around client group, for instance, such as adult or children services, simply redraws the boundaries of the silos. Integrated management, change leadership and joined-up practice are thought to be the key to solving intractable and structural organisational problems in social work.

Earlier discussion of contracting and tendering showed that public sector managers are already buying in key components in the supply chain for care services from other sources. Structural boundaries have already become more permeable, and will become increasingly so. As the DETR report (2000) argued, the key principles of organisational structuring need to be process-related, fluid and flexible in connecting across boundaries, with care services being delivered through vertical and horizontal supply chains. There is, however, one significant problem with joined-up social work governance, in that the risk regulatory regimes discussed above can have the effect of undermining increased horizontal integration in organisational processes (Cope & Goodship, 1999).

Conclusion

This chapter has explored the relationship between risk and the management and organisation of social work. It has shown how the managerialist imagination in recent neo-liberal ideology and policy feeds on the idea of continuous improvement through quality assurance measures, audit and performance indicators. Some key British policy directives in care management and social work organisation have been outlined to elucidate how risk regulation and neo-liberal market economics are inter-dependent elements in shaping management culture. A double alliance was identified in social work between a re-fashioned technical rationality, emphasising science and technical know-how, and a market rationality focusing on economic performance and flexibility. As Bourdieu (1998a) notes, 'the absolute reign of flexibility is established' with employees being hired on fixed-term contracts or a temporary basis, repeated organisational restructuring, and within the organisation itself, competition between autonomous divisions as well as teams to perform multiple funtions. Bourdieu argues that neo-liberal management extends to individuals themselves, 'through the individualization of the wage relationship, individual performance evaluations, permanent evaluation, individual salary increases or granting of bonuses as a function of competence or merit, strategies of delegating responsibility and individualized career paths' (1998, p. 15).

Neo-liberal managed care in social work increasingly resembles the consequences set out by Bourdieu. Its self-legitimation rests on the fantasy of hyper-rationality, progressive improvement and efficiency. We've seen how it assumes a rational paradigm of organisational life which relies upon, and is the application of, rational techniques such as the gathering of empirical data in performance reviews, the systematic specification of aims and objects in business planning, cost-benefit analysis in the resourcing of service provision, and economic modelling. Such a perspective is highly problematic in social work in confusing the ideal case (or the programme) with the actual processes, and assumes that policy makers and managers have learnt from past experience. This perspective is also steeped in a positivitist epistemology, that acts on the premise that there are readily identifiable problems that can be addressed through planning and structuring. Recent initiatives which herald the so-called learning organisation and knowledge management for social work are shown to fit with this neo-liberal managed care. The central features of this are based on risk regulation, in which differences between the public and the private sector are gradually erased by shifting the emphasis from process accountability towards a greater element of accountability in terms of results. The crucial link between the effective management of risk and the preoccupation with regulation, performance, audit and accountability has been addressed in relation to the important role of New Labour's Performance & Innovation Unit. Performance management uses indicators to gather data and information that are assigned meaning, and is therefore a social construction, rather than an objective measure (Tilbury, 2004). We've seen how it forms part of an audit culture which is based on regulation and management accountability rather than social work. For front-line practitioners and case managers there is little hope of escaping the performance management treadmill which relentlessly pushes on in its absurd quest for 'continuous improvement'. Typically, social workers tend to adopt a coping strategy based on 'sitting out' a government programme they mistrust, reflecting demotivation, low morale and a strategy of avoidance.

The final section discussed the inevitability of wicked problems and silo effects in social work. These phenomena occur because so-called 'rational efficient behaviour' has consequences for other policy or service areas, creating irrationality and inefficiency at an overall systems level. In other words risk, as a cross-cutting issue, is transferred around from one unit of an organisation to another, or to another partnership agency. Clearly, power is an important factor in our understanding of attempts to regulate systems and provide inter-professional 'joined-up' practice. The arena of health and social care is one of constestation and agencies inevitably pull apart as much as pulling together. It's been argued here that the organisational handling and management of risk are key factors driving changes in social work, as well as driving practitioners apart. It's important to recognise, following Kemshall (2000), that there is considerable dissonance between stated policy, inter-professional and manage-ment objectives and practitioner views on risk, 'with managers and policy-makers valuing actuarially based knowledge for its consist-ency and accountability, and practitioners valuing professional, indi-vidualised judgement for its flexibility and responsiveness to individual factors' (p. 52).

7

The Practice of Value

Introduction

In a society in which the narrow pursuit of material self-interest is the norm, adherence to an ethical stance is more radical than many people realise. This for me is one of the defining strengths of social work and something that makes it most distinctive. It holds on to values of compassion, justice and caring in the face of a culture of self-interest. Most significantly it retains a commitment to an ethical core. So far this book has concentrated on social-theoretical issues at the expense of moral and ontological issues, but the latter are very important for a project that aspires to recast social work along ethical lines. It is this ethical dimension to which I now turn.

Social work is not ethically indifferent even though the tide of mass culture and self-interest becomes ever more pervasive. It refuses to drop the notion that society can be a vehicle for the translation of private troubles into public concerns and the democratically generated search for community, solidarity and the good life. As standardly conceived, the pursuit of self-interest, implicit in neoliberal ideology, is a life without any meaning beyond our own pleasure, choice or individual satisfaction. One can only hazard a guess about the likely long-term effects this egocentric world view will have on child rearing practices, care for the elderly, teenager lifestyles, vulnerability to mental illness and so forth. There is little room for co-operation and felt solidarity in what Bourdieu (1998) calls a neo-liberal 'programme of the methodical destruction of collectives' (p. 12). Such a life increasingly erodes our capacity to think in terms of co-operative and common interests. It is against this drift of hardening neo-liberal political rule that I wish to situate the significance of social work in terms of the practice of value. My starting point for this derives from the writings of the Canadian philosopher and sociologist Charles Taylor, and especially his idea that human beings lead their lives and assess themselves in light of broadly ethical standards. As we shall see it is striking that in the face of neo-liberalism social work remains morally committed and in fact has the potential to deepen its ethical impulse via the practice of value. Here I emphasise the importance of social work ethics in terms of care, recognition and virtue and in generating social capital.

Putting Values First

The chapter aims to provide a validation of social work in terms of an ideal-typical ethical practice. It argued that we must not lose sight of the importance of ethics in social work and as a profession should be more musical in matters of moral discourse. Here I concur with Bisman (2004) about the primacy of values and her contention that it's time for social work to embrace a core ethical framework. It's my view that to pose questions of ethical practice for social work is the first step towards reawakening these values. This can contribute to the enrichment of ethical practice in social work by activating moral sources – drawing on sociological and philosophical perspectives – underneath the rampant economic individualism of neo-liberalism. Developing such a perspective is also important because of the increasing tide of neo-conservative critiques of social work that castigate the profession precisely for adhering to core values. (See Payne, 1998, for an example of this kind of neo-conservative perspective on social work.) My starting point is to concentrate on what social workers do or can do and in particular what sort of ethical engagement is carried forth in professional practice, rather than concentrating on preconceptions about what social workers ought to do (see Jordan, 2004). In this section I want to introduce two caveats before proceeding to define the ethical good of social work.

Firstly, I want to suggest that ethical commitment emerges in sustained and proximal social relations. Societal changes such as the impact of globalisation, risk technologies and the growth of corporate capitalism produce conditions of profound uncertainty which impacts on ethics and politics. Social ties are increasingly loosened between people. Bauman holds that the terrain of late modernity 'is a territory subjected to rival and contradictory meaning-bestowing claims and hence perpetually ambivalent' (1992, p. 193). In emphasising ambivalence Bauman (1998) locates ethics at the centre of social relations, but an organic and practical ethics based on facing ambiguity and making hard moral choices, rather than one based on an external moral law. In this way, Bauman wants to replace the notion of society with an affirmative form of sociality. By using the term 'sociality' he wishes to emphasise an ethics based on durable and proximal relations. Bauman, as a defender of social work, is concerned not just with the social glue that holds society together but with the ethical commitment that emerges in sustained and proximal social interaction. Sociality is about having a concern for people in their fullness and is contrasted with short-termism in social relations that reduces encounters between people to instrumental self-interest, requiring them to constantly make everything anew through fragmented, partial and intermittent membership of groups and social networks. It is a minimal condition for producing trust and solidarity, allowing us to perceive the social world as more stable and create coherence out of contingency (Misztal, 1996). We've seen that proximal and sustained interaction sits at the centre of traditional social work interventions and mirrors Bauman's plea for sociality. To believe in the inherent sociability of individuals implies that one redefines the ends of society, and the institutions, like social work, that are used to meet those ends.

In the second place, I want to claim that ethical practice should not be rule-bound or based on codes of conduct. Ethical prescriptions for social work often start from rule-bound or duty-based moral prescriptions that are set up to be validated in practice. For example, the former Central Council for Education and Training in Social Work (CCETSW) said that 'a value determines what a person thinks he *ought* to do' (1976, p. 14). A key problem here is, who tells you that there are moral laws to which our conduct ought to be liable? And as with many child abuse scandals, who tells you that what never happened ought to have happened? Moreover, the social worker who does the task because he or she is obliged – is duty-bound – to do it, lacks commitment as a self-responsible being pursuing the good life. Foucault, too, recognises that codified ethics is in decline:

> The idea of a morality as obedience to a code of rules is now disappearing, has already disappeared. And to this absence of morality corresponds, must correspond, the search for an aesthetics of existence. (1990, p. 49)

Supplication to duty leaves the social worker without moral identity because he or she is acting for the sake of others, that is the social work agency or client. If a social worker doesn't recognise his or her moral identity and calling, then one may wonder whether such a person ought to do social work at all. It is easy for professional associations and bodies to preach morality but difficult to establish any basis for it. As we'll see the starting point for the practice of value is based on what is given, and thus on what actually happens or can happen in order to arrive at an ethical standpoint. It is better to start from the professional context in which practitioners find themselves to see if they encounter any experiences which can be significantly labelled 'moral' in a sense that they and their clients understand.

The Self and the Good

Let's begin rather boldly. The social worker has an ethical disposition to do the best for clients and insofar as they have the resources to do so, they try to use these to maximise ethical ends. This is not about adherence to duty-bound rules or a set of prescribed codes of conduct. That is conformity. Practising values and believing in them are acts of an ethical disposition or will. Commitment to an ethical practice is a virtue because it indicates the seriousness, necessity and deliberative nature of some direction of action.

Why are social workers committed to an ethical life? The short answer to this is that they are what Charles Taylor calls 'strong evaluators'. This concept needs some careful explanation if we are to properly understand the relation between social work and the ethical good. These ideas haven't been explored before in the social work literature, so let's look closely at the way Taylor vividly brings theory and practice together in accounting for an ethical life and how it can provide the basis for reframing of social work values. He is not just interested in what it is right to do, but what it is good to be. The starting point for Taylor's account is derived from existential phenomenology, which holds to the view that human beings are essentially embodied agents. This means that human experience is not merely a representation of objects or a disinterested contemplation of things, but entails an *encounter with things that concern us* (Smith, 2002, p. 87).

Taylor is concerned about the malaise of late modernity and wants to sort out the good from the harmful in the cultivation of the self. His starting point is to insist that the human condition is distinctive in that we lead our lives and evaluate ourselves in light of broad ethical standards. He thinks that the rich moral background can be retrieved without giving in to the undesirable consequences of technical, disengaged and political rationality. For Taylor the character of the self is constituted by ethical concerns, that is, the self is constituted in and through the taking of moral stances (see *Sources of the Self,* 1989, p. 41). His concern is *how* we orient ourselves in relation to the good, and the way in which we negotiate and move in the ethical space we inevitably find ourselves in as human agents. Taylor begins to articulate this position by distinguishing between what he calls 'weak evaluation' and 'strong evaluation'. The former is about the manner in which we weigh up the way we want to satisfy our desires and decide which desires we want to satisfy best. This might involve thinking about whether you want to buy a new car or instead take a holiday. As Smith points out, 'The decisive issue in my evaluation is just what I happen to feel like' (2002, p. 89). Taylor refers to this as 'weak evaluation'. In weak evaluation the statement that that 'A is better than B' remains inarticulable, because there is nothing more to articulate. I just like A better, it just feels that way, it is just a matter of de facto desires or preferences.

Taylor recognises, however, that another kind of evaluation is at play in the way we think about ourselves. Sometimes we find ourselves evaluating desires in terms of what they are worth. He calls this 'strong evaluation'. Using the previous example, if one starts to give reasons for one's preference in terms of the good-making properties of A and B, one is actually engaged in strong evaluation. As Smith goes on to explain, 'What counts now is the way I locate or interpret the feelings, that is, how I characterize them as something base and petty, or as something higher and more admirable' (2002, p. 89). Roughly speaking to characterise this type of evaluation refers to the times we beat ourselves up over things we do to ourselves or others. It involves a standard or judgement of worth or what some call conscience. Taylor says that when we strongly evaluate our action or motive we 'classify it in such categories as higher and lower, virtuous and vicious, more and less fulfilling, more and less refined, profound and superficial, noble and base' (1985, p. 16). He wants to show the importance of this distinction for our understanding of the ethical self in the modern world. Smith gives some examples of the difference between strong and weak evaluators in terms of practical reflection:

The strong evaluator has a depth and articulacy lacking in the weak evaluator. This is obviously true for the quality of their practical reflection. Faced with a choice, the weak evaluator has a sense of which outcome he [sic] would prefer – a sense that he would rather have one of his desires satisfied than another – and he can reflect on the likelihood of satisfying his desires through the course of action he adopts. But he only has an inarticulate sense of what it is that makes one desire superior, or more worth going after than another. All he can say is that there is a certain 'feel' to it which appeals to him. The strong evaluator, on the other hand, can articulate his sense that one desire is more worth satisfying than another by locating the desires in a qualitative contrast – such as the contrast between a mean or generous spirit – that enables him to have a more nuanced and refined understanding of the options available to him. (2002, p. 90)

This has a very familiar ring to it in our late modern lives, and arguably, as part of the neo-liberal scheme of things, we are increasingly faced with a culture of weak evaluators. How often do we hear of people saying 'don't argue with me, it's my right' and 'it just feels right to me – so don't you dare challenge or insist on me accounting for myself'? Or the even shallower 'don't be bullying me by asking me to justify why I want to do – it's my choice!' Wilful and selfish might properly define these kinds of asymmetrical weak evaluative statements.

Taylor is not only claiming that strong evaluators are more considered and careful about their options, or that they are capable of having a deeper kind of self-reflection; more than this, he is saying that their reflection upon value engages with the heartland of desires and purposes themselves. Strong evaluators exercise an ethical sensibility and judgement that's based on their ability to contrast the value or worth of things. This provides them with standards and characteristics by which they judge the quality of human life. Taylor's argument runs such that certain social actors owe their identity to the role played by strong values in their life. It seems to me that this perspective, by offering an ethical dimension to practical reflection, goes significantly beyond the reflective practice model offered by Schon and others, which has been so uncritically taken up by social work in recent times. Schon and adherents of reflective practice have very little to say about ethics in the context of social work. My argument is that reflection, or better still reflexivity, is necessarily an ethical evaluation whereby the practitioner 'confronts herself' as part of a process.

For Taylor, then, value is inescapable in that the process of judging, ascribing, affirming or even denying value, in short, the process of evaluation, can never be avoided. What is at stake is the kind of evaluation that takes place. Seen in this way, the practice of value is intimately bound up with motivation and purpose of every kind. From this perspective we can map acts of ethical practice as involving first of all judgements of an agent, whether oneself or another, in terms of whether a motive or an action is proper to the given situation of that agent; if it is, we evaluate that the motive or action has merit, otherwise demerit. We do this irrespective of whether the situation is past, present or future (see Connor, 1993).

Taylor distinguishes three dimensions that count as strong valuations or ethical concerns. These broadly correlate with the three elements of care, virtue and recognition discussed below, and fit neatly with the framework developed for ethical practice in social work. First, in every sociocultural formation we find practices that express some aspect of concern, love or respect for other people. This group of ethical goods includes duties, obligations, and responsibilities towards others as caring concern. As Smith explains, 'People fall short of the standard set up by this class of life goods when they are cruel to others, betray them, humiliate them, wrong them and so forth' (2002, p. 91). The second category or class includes the aspiration to human flourishing, living a meaningful and fulfilled life that is acknowledged as having virtue, as opposed to a shallow, empty or purposeless life. As something emanating in the relation between self and Other it involves those special moments of tenderness, compassion and concern for others. The final dimension Taylor distinguishes refers to human dignity and recognition. Again Smith elucidates this as 'dignity elicits the respect of others, a respect born not so much from the duty of care or responsibility for the other as from the recognition of something like nobility' (p. 92). This is not a form of personal understanding of self-fulfillment but an individual dignity or form of life that is acknowledged as something we look up to, aspire to and recognise as having value.

At the risk of being labelled as naively idealistic, another distinctive move needs to be made in order to validate the ethical dimension of social work. Firstly, I want to position social workers, in general, as strong evaluators. Secondly, and this is the added dimension, I wish to locate the identity of social work as a profession as one that has the potential to be a reflexive moral source for the articulation of strong evaluative goods. This of course begs questions about the ethical relation between social work and the social worker.

Here again, I draw from Taylor who identifies the moral sources that are the constitutive ground of things we strongly value. In the broadest sense we can argue that social work is a *constitutive socioethical good* that has generative power for the social worker, in that it permits an ethical life to be articulated and channelled towards that which has intrinsic worth. Taylor recognises how problematic and difficult it is for us to articulate constitutive goods, but doesn't think this is a sufficiently good reason for eschewing the task. For Taylor the constitutive good is an articulation of the Idea of the Good itself, or that which is immanent in it. The constitutive good of social work provides for social workers the constituting ground of their worth or goodness. In other words, social work as a narrative moral source has the capacity to empower and energise social workers to do good. As Taylor explains, the articulation of 'modern understandings of the good has to be a historical enterprise' but notwithstanding this 'high standards need strong sources' (1985, p. 516). Therefore, there is an important ethical correspondence between the strong evaluations of social workers and the traditional source of core values in social work itself that is embedded and realised in its narrative history.

Positioning social workers as strong evaluators may mean that they are different from, say, politicians, shop keepers, bankers, business people, lawyers and the police. I accept that this kind of claim requires some empirical justification but it wouldn't be too difficult to devise questionnaires that test the differences between strong and weak evaluators. Similarly, we are aware that there are strong and weak evaluators within social work. The weak evaluating practitioner is a simple weigher of alternatives, an opportunist making discrete judgement-by-judgement decisions, who takes no stand at all concerning the qualitative worth of different options. They are unconcerned with the evaluative aspects of the objects of evaluation. We've seen that strong evaluators can articulate the reasons for their preferences on the basis of qualitative distinctions of worth. For social work this means that judgements concerning the worth of options are not merely of theoretical interest, but are practically relevant in determining the worker's commitment, compassion and authenticity. To move back to the personal level, strong evaluation makes a difference to one's motivation. The difference to one's motivation is not simply on a judgement-by-judgement basis, but rather, one has strong attachments to certain strongly valued ends. Taylor suggests that it is because I see certain of my other properties as admitting of only one kind of strong evaluation by myself, because these properties so centrally touch what I am as an agent, that is, as a strong evaluator, that I cannot really repudiate them in the full sense. For I would be thereby repudiating myself, inwardly riven and hence incapable of fully authentic evaluation. (1985, p. 34)

One can misread this passage as Taylor advocating the following kind of reasoning: 'because I am filthy rich, I would be repudiating myself if I were an egalitarian, so the value of equality cannot be applied to me.' Or, 'I am not a nice guy, so demands of considerateness do not apply to me.' Clearly, when identified with one's factual characteristics these can play a central role in justifying one's evaluative judgements. The point here is that one's dignity or personal worth is in internal connection to one's motivations.

Social work is the commitment to certain 'higher' or more basic constitutive goods and thereby provides social workers with the capacity to locate themselves, to establish an identity, determine the qualitative significance of various relationships, events and things in terms of values and most importantly to articulate ethical ideals. It entails depth in its seriousness, emotional involvement and capacity to respond in the right way to complex situations involving strong values. By acting within an ethical framework social workers have a 'sense' of qualitative distinctions in which some basic evaluative commitments orient them in positive terms and give horizons to the constitutive ground of their professional identity. In other words, such a sense permits an enactment of the special relationship between self and Other along ethical lines. Taylor explains:

We sense in the very experience of being moved by some higher good that we are moved by what is good in it rather than that it is valuable because of our reaction. We are moved by seeing its points as something infinitely valuable. We experience our love for it as a well-formed love. Nothing that couldn't move me in *this* way would count as a hyper-good. (1989, p. 74)

According to Taylor we cannot live without either valuing a way of life or feeling guilty about living at odds with such values. It strikes me that social work does value such a way of life and thinks deeply and seriously about it, such that it believes it to have a higher standing or constitutive ground than other ways of life.

Notice that in the above discussion I've mostly used the term 'ethical' instead of 'moral'. There is good reason for this. Following the work of feminist writer Drucilla Cornell, I want to establish a hierarchical relationship between ethics and morality. Morality, which is subordinated to ethics, is regarded as a set of behavioural norms and generator of system-bound rules and duties. 'Don't think for yourself, just follow the rules' is the message implied in moral codes. The ethical relation, on the other hand, is rooted in a deeper value framework that includes care, virtue and recognition. Cornell remarks:

> . . . 'morality' designates any attempt to spell out how one *determines* a 'right way to behave', a behavioural norm which, once determined, can be translated into a system of rules. The ethical relation, a term which I contrast with morality, focuses instead on the kind of person one must become in order to develop a nonviolative relationship to the Other. The concern of the ethical relation, in other words, is a way of being in the world that spans diverse value systems and allows us to criticize the repressive aspects of competing moral systems. (1993, p. 13)

This idea of the kind of person one might become in terms of ethical character is picked up in the discussion below on virtue ethics. For now we should acknowledge that the 'ethics of care' is not used in the narrow proceduralist sense of universal rules of conduct but in the broader and more basic sense of appropriate concern for others. It will be shown below that care as ethical practice, which is inducible by intentional actions, is commonly recognised as promoting the interests of a recipient by the recipient and the provider – mutual recognition. Here we acknowledge how social work contributes to a practical, compassionate and reflective ethics that is grounded in care, virtue and recognition (McBeath & Webb, 1997).

The ethical justifications raised above are crucial if we are to convincingly argue for a sustained social work role in neo-liberal risk society. In the discussion that follows social work is defended on *practico-ethical* grounds with five distinctive elements identified:

- ethics of the care
- socially affirming ethics of recognition
- virtue ethics as the basis for professional ethics
- generating social capital as a networked human resource
- life planning for risk, uncertainty and insecurity

These linked core elements will be elucidated from a practical standpoint, that is, what social workers actually do, or can do, in proximal, direct, inter-subjective relations. For each aspect I develop key sociological connections to buttress the social work agenda. Taken together these components enlarge upon and fit with Taylor's

concept of the ethical self. They also form part of a social work tradition of core values that can combat the drift of neo-liberalism at one
level and the instrumental rationality that is taking hold within the
profession at another level. The underlying connection here is a
communitarian humanistic tradition, in which Taylor broadly situ-
ates his work, which was constituted in the same spirit as the project
of ethical democracy. We can conceive of the practice of value in
social work as forming part of this project. I'll return to this concept
of neo-humanism towards the end of the chapter, but for now it's
worth noting that it rests on the German word *Bildung* which is
roughly translated as the formation of human character, that involves
an evaluative dialogue or a discourse between self and Other, aimed
at cultivating self-knowledge through an understanding of the lived-
world of other people. *Bildung* or the cultivation of the self is a
holistic concept in which individuals must perceive themselves in
their totality, develop practical judgement and integrate their selves
with the external world of other people, society and nature.

Neo-humanist projects rest on the elevation of a particular type of
ethical self other than my own as the ultimate ethical goal and the
preference for acts freely chosen over ones performed under
constraint (Simpson, 2001). Thus it becomes incumbent upon social
work to resist political ideologies or rationalities that attempt to
undermine this humanist ethical practice. This may seem a rather
grand ambition to some readers, but it may be just a matter of focus.
Resistance is intrinsic to all types of professional practice. It seems to
me that social workers spend as much time twisting, evading, bending and reinterpreting rules as they do being guided by or conform-
ing to them. However, if social work is to be a vehicle of resistance
against dominant neo-liberal agendas a hard dose of realism is
required. We mustn't get too carried away about the potential emancipation from neo-liberal rule, since public sector institutions like
social work are inevitably no match for the deep penetration of global
capitalism and its pervasive political ideology. Nevertheless, it will
be shown that we can begin to develop valuable ways of thinking and
acting that militate decisively against the neo-liberal hegemony.

The Ethics of Care

The value of the caring relationship lies in its potential for compassionate ethical reciprocity. It generates an understanding of the value

of 'the Other', and ultimately, a *structure of concern and understanding between recipient and carer*. This kind of relationship occupies the central ground in social work ethics and is a primary commitment. The primary sense of care is found in the phrase 'taking care'. Care should not be equated with protection, as negative freedom, nor should care and protection be coupled together – for example, as in 'need of care and protection' – in a regulatory framework. Rather, the activity of caring as concern and taking care occupies a definite ethical space between self and Other. As Sevenhuijsen (2000) points out, 'care is a social activity in itself and . . . caring activities and caring moral orientations are crucial for the provision of basic needs' (2000, p. 14).

In Britain one of the most prominent and persistent research findings across the last four decades is that clients really value the caring relationship of social work. Practitioners frequently comment on how clients often need a few gentle words of encouragement, reassurance and someone to share their problems with. Personal qualities of warmth, trust and support are crucial in this respect. Bleach and Ryan (1995) point out that it is the human interpersonal qualities, rather than technical skills and competence that influence the degree of trust and satisfaction between clients and social workers. Similarly, Maluccio (1981a), from an American perspective, concluded that clients' definitions of good social work always involve inter-personal dispositions of warmth, acceptance, honesty and trust. Caring and trusting relations are core values highly regarded by clients, with personal qualities identified as paramount in service user satisfaction surveys. In part, it is precisely because inter-personal relations are among the concerns of social workers that they adopt high ethical standards. Smith (2001) recognises the important link between ethics of care, inter-personal relations and trust. She says that in social work 'material services will be accompanied by the need for interpersonal help in the form of emotional support, reassurance, understanding, comfort and guidance. These situations call for people to give something of themselves, to increase their vulnerability and to risk a dismissive, insensitive, and judgemental or . . . uncaring response. In other words, these situations create the conditions for trust' (2001, p. 300). Giving something of oneself is valued because it amounts to a form of mutual disclosure which is the basis of trusting relations in modern relationships. Care as expressed through actions is a very important element of trust and reciprocity. The willingness to trust and the ability to restrain self-interest in meeting the needs of other people flow, in some sense, from the attachments of people to each other. This stands in clear contrast to the material self-interestedness of neo-liberal consumerism.

Social workers frame relationships of trust by mutual proximity and listening; finding answers and solutions to troublesome situations, encouraging participation and responding to grievances through supportive advocacy. This amounts to what Giddens calls a situation of 'active trust'. That is, trust that has to be energetically developed, handled and sustained. In the context of the caring relationship active trust is geared towards evaluating the integrity of the social worker. Integrity cannot be taken as given, it has to be worked at; this is perhaps why clients value stability and reliability in their relations with social workers. The importance of trust in marking out reciprocity is indicative of why people wish to be involved in decision making. For Giddens, this kind of trust helps initiate new forms of voluntary solidarity in risk society (1994, p. 186). Recurring face-to-face interaction that rests on trust is the basis for the voluntary, supporting insight into the human likeness of the Other. It has also been suggested that effective responses to fateful moments are deeply embedded in an inter-personal face-to-face context. To develop a caring relationship is to achieve a reciprocal understanding and thus validation of the care that is taken. It is this recognition or understanding that consolidates sympathy between carer and client and thereby moves beyond the rule-based prescriptions of impersonal regulation, duties and obligations. Caring is valued as an important ethical practice in it own right (Harris, 2002). It is also an essential component of social work skills that are increasingly devalued and submerged by the demands of low-level data generation, administration, budgeting and the management of the delivery of services.

It is inevitable that some relationships between client and social worker rest on what Richard Sennett (1980) calls 'false love'. That is, an authority of paternalism which operates a parade of benevolence existing only insofar as it's in the interest of selfish motivations and dominant vested interests, requiring passive acquiescence on the part of clients as the price of being cared for. Such a tendency, however, is not representative of the major part of front-line practice. The value of the caring relationship lies in the contribution it makes to a kind of inter-personal democracy that is critical for human flourishing. Better still, perhaps, we might say that the caring relationship fulfils important aspects of concern and recognition through an 'ethics of care'. Feminist writers such as Carol Gilligan, Nell Noddings and Seyla Benhabib have positively discussed the ethics of care. Such an ethics is not impartial or objective, but is concerned with the subjective evaluation of persons, motives and character. Gilligan (1982) identifies two frames, 'the ethic of justice' and 'the ethic of care', that result in the division of the moral field into the masculine and the feminine. Her observation reads the masculine ethic according to a deep 'justice' orientation, and the feminine ethic according to a deep 'care' orientation. Gilligan's ethics of care emphasises notions of attachment over equality, relatedness over individuality, and commitment over autonomy, thus representing an important shift in the language of morality, while remaining concerned with the kinds of reciprocal relations featured significantly in social work. Orme (2002) argues that these related concepts of gender, social justice and care have been woefully neglected in the social work literature on professional values and ethics.

An ethics of care contradicts the Kantian rule and duty-bound ethics of the British Association of Social Workers (BASW) and the General Social Care Council (GSCC) Code of Conduct (Webb & McBeath, 1989). 'You can do your duty, because you must do it' is how Kant formulated the categorical imperative. The usual negative corollary of this formula found in codified social work morality is 'You cannot, because you should not.' An ethics of care is quite different. As Marilyn Friedman (1991) argues this involves a fundamental commitment to persons individually, often at the expense of strict obedience to moral rules

> ... the so-called 'ethic of care' stresses an ongoing responsiveness. The ethic of care *is* about the nature of relationships to particular persons grasped as such. The key issue is the sensitivity and responsiveness to another person's emotional states, individuating differences, specific uniqueness, and whole particularity. The 'care' orientation focuses on whole persons and de-emphasizes adherence to moral rules. (p. 106)

Practice in child protection, young offender and mental health work is caught within this legally ascribed mandate of moral obligation and duty. We've seen how these form part of regulatory regimes that normalise and exclude marginal populations. Few would be naïve enough to deny that social work is inevitably caught up in networks and relations of power in such circumstances. Social workers are given the capacity to act, as well as actually acting as social workers, due to several legitimating powers. They are also involved in influencing, persuading and cajoling their clients and colleagues as to the validity of their judgement or opinion. Thus, it's important to recognise the centrality of power relations in social work. However, we must stay clear of the Nietzschean post-modernist position in social work, which reduces identity/difference to mere constructions of power and discourse. The point is that an ethics of care works against the grain of those modernist preoccupations of legitimising unequal power relations and normative moral rules. Moreover, as will be considered below, the caring relationship, in terms of its ethical substance, can give a vital purchase on the phenomenon of community and social support.

The ethical identity of social work is dispositional rather than functional. Fiona Williams (2000) juxtaposes an ethics of care against those sorts of legalistic ethics based on duty and obligation. She argues there is something distinctive and qualitatively different in modern caring relationships from more traditional social arrangements. Seyla Benhabib has contributed a powerful conceptual revision of Gilligan's ethics of care along the lines of dialogical ethics. Benhabib's (1992) reformulation of Habermas's discourse ethics envisions moral relationships in terms of an ongoing conversation that is less concerned with rational agreement or consensus than with 'sustaining those normative practices and moral relationships within which reasoned agreement as a way of life can flourish and continue' (p. 38). She criticises Habermas for his over-emphasis on principles of justice which might exclude ethical dialogue about what communities and individuals conceive as a good life (White, 1990). Community development work falls within this framework. Benhabib argues for a softening of distinctions between judgements of justice and those of the good life. In this way an ethics of care becomes a democratic procedure for sustaining ordinary moral conversations where the participants have some insight into 'what it means to be an "I" and a "me", to know that I am an "other" to you and that likewise, you are an "I" to yourself but an "other" to me' (1992, p. 52). Thus the dialogic encounter between social worker and client is a reciprocal encounter. Ongoing and sustained face-to-face relations of this kind invariably lead to mutual respect (Sennett, 2003).

For Williams the source of an ethics of care rests on this meaningful and valued reciprocity. She points out that 'the care relationship is often but not always an intimate one; the intimate relationship is usually, but not always, a relationship of care.' She goes on to say that the intimate sphere covers relationships based upon family ties, friendship, sexual relationships, as well as paid care relationships. A number of significant changes occur in the context of caring relationships in late modernity. To paraphrase Williams, they are less about duty and more about mutually agreed commitment; they are less about achieving status and more about negotiating an identity; less about authority and more about consent; less about tradition and more about trust; they are less about honour and more about respect. In short they point to a kind of what Giddens (1994b) calls an 'emotional democracy', constructed around significant moral qualities and character.

Certain types of social work, such as group work, family therapy and counselling, are democratising as dialogic modes of social co-operation and solidarity. Giddens is terribly optimistic about the prospects of deepening and extending democratic forms of life in late modernity. Potentially though, this kind of optimism opens an ethical space for social work by showing how caring relations of concern can contribute to 'emotional democracy'. As Giddens (1994) explains, democracy, as David Held has shown, is linked to a principle of autonomy. Here autonomy is promoted by the capability to represent one's interests and by the possibility of resolving clashes of interest through dialogue. Thus the emphasis is on promoting autonomy and not empowerment or self-reliance. Giddens goes on to say:

> . . . we see the potential emergence of 'emotional democracy' in the domains of sexual relations, parent–child relations and friendship. To the degree to which the pure relationship becomes dominant in these spheres, a relation of equals, organized through emotional communication coupled to self-understanding, becomes possible. Emotional democracy as it does progress, promises a great deal for the reconstruction of civic ethics as a whole. (1994b, p. 193)

This idea of emotional democracy rests on the assumption that the self (client) and other (social worker) are ethically inter-dependent, thus running contrary to the neo-liberal idiom of individualism. It also rests on the view that repeated proximal interactions among clients and social workers are a way of establishing mutual reciprocity and respect. Interactions between practitioners and clients, as they develop from initial expectations about their counterparts, are crucial in accommodating reciprocity and the durability of the caring relationship.

It is through the constitution of *caring relations* and not *caring actions* that ethical commitment becomes significant in front-line practice. The former is synonymous with reciprocity by entailing inter-subjective concern. Care implicitly arises out of the same logic as a concern for things and for other human beings. In caring relations people reveal themselves dialogically in their unfolding and their becoming with others (see Parton, 2003). But caring is not merely a matter of being around things or people. The opposite is suggested by the notion of being 'untogether' or lacking the sureness of ontological security (Cooper, 1989). From this perspective caring is not only a matter of well-being or satisfying needs but of becoming through interactions with others. It is not a fixed state, but one that privileges mobility and the unfolding of caring concern. It's stating the obvious to say that direct work fits this caring relationship, whilst low-level data generation and assessment fall within caring action. Sevenhuijsen (2000) contends that care should be conceived as an inclusive democratic practice that should be more centrally discussed in Third Way politics (pp. 27–8). She concludes that 'when caring is acknowledged as a valuable social activity in its own right, we can further our sensitivity towards everyday forms of mutual responsibility and their failures and successes' (p. 30). This begs the question, what is the relation of ethics to experience in social work? Could the latter, in some way, produce the former? The next section addresses these matters in relation to social work and the concept of an ethics of recognition.

Ethics of Recognition – Having a Sense of Ourselves

There is another important ethical contribution given in social work that stands in sharp contrast to the economic and instrumental rationality of neo-liberal calculating practice. This different view starts from a *relational ontology* that is structured through time and circumstance. It is referred to in the literature as an ethics of recognition (Fraser & Honneth, 2001). It will be shown that caring relations are structured around the Hegelian notion of 'reciprocal recognition' as a manifestation of ethical identity. Social work thereby plays a role ethically affirming of clients' phenomenological presencing in the social world and their relations with others.

An ethics of recognition is concerned with affirmative forms of social relationships. These relations contribute towards the mediation of an ethical identity. According to Hegel, freedom requires recognition of the other for its realisation: thus the threshold of the ethical is attained when the other (persons) are not regarded as mere 'things' but come to count as self-determining ends in themselves. Therefore the nexus of freedom and recognition is important for the realisation of human rights (Williams, 1997). From this standpoint it's argued that inter-subjective relations as mutual recognition constitute the general structure of ethical life. This is to be distinguished from the neo-liberal preoccupation with personal autonomy and categories of self-interest. It's my contention that this general structure is privileged and accentuated in some forms of social work practice. In *The Struggle for Recognition* (1995) Axel Honneth claimed that human beings have two types of needs in relation to their inter-subjective relations: we need both respect and recognition. In social work, the former is well catered for in various liberal Kantian tracts such as BASW's and the former CCETSW's code of ethics. Respect for persons, as a moral duty, is one of the defining concepts of social work ethics (Webb & McBeath, 1989). Recognition, on the other hand, has not acquired a clear determination in the social work literature, even though it's implicit in much of the practice of value.

In terms of recognition, individuals or communities wish to be understood in their singularity. Honneth contrasts the ethics of recognition with the dignity needs of respect for persons. He claims that recognition is based in 'affective needs and the reciprocation of social esteem from concrete others' (1995, p. 15). This is how the French philosopher Emmanuel Levinas describes an informed ethical practice. He recognises that we are never wholly alone in the world, nor are we part of a totality to which all others belong. For Levinas our temporal encounter with others and the realisation that we must negotiate sharing the world with them is the moment ethical life begins. Recognition is a feature of several levels and dimensions: the unity of the family is a communal unit of recognition; property is the legal relation of recognition between individuals and institutions; love is a primary relation of intimate recognition. In this respect we can understand the distress caused by misrecognition; as for example, when single women are accused of being bad mothers, older people are told that they are incapable of looking after themselves, or ethnic minority communities are stereotyped as disengaged. Social work, to its credit, does much to counter this sort of misrecognition. Implicit in much front-line practice is the perspective that physical and affective needs are validated through the proximity of direct work possessing affirmative acceptance, support and encouragement. Social work fosters a positive attitude to clients out of which increased self-esteem and trust in oneself emerge. We saw in Chapter 3 how the home visit provides a bridgehead for confidence building and trust as well as a mode of emotional presence between client and practitioner. This process cements co-operation and the felt solidarity through social proximity. As the structure of intimate and caring relations changes in risk society, social work is strategically placed to mobilise an ethics of recognition in respect of changing lifestyles.

Clients consistently report, as Howe (1993) confirms, the need for acceptance and positive regard, and the search for understanding. It enables them to acquire a measure of self-esteem that is found in solidaristic acceptance and ethical concern (Honneth, 2001). Recognition denied or refused, on the other hand, has been a powerful catalyst for criticising some aspects of social work, especially in children's services. Alternatively, anti-social behaviour achieves its purpose through the social misrecognition it claims. Taken together, these spheres of recognition form a network of normative presuppositions that change over time and place. Honneth claims that modern societies need a principle of voluntary solidarity based in recognition as much as on redistribution (e.g. respect, equality, dignity) (Lash & Featherstone, 2001). Cynically, perhaps, it's easy to see how the social need for recognition fuels the rhetoric of New Labour's stakeholder society (Hutton, 1998).

It is this encounter with otherness in the democratisation of modern culture, family, community and personal life that provides a progressive ethics for social work. It runs against the grain of modernist attempts to legislate for morality. An ethics of recognition is not a singular ideology or for that matter a form of mediation but a moral perspective that holds the potential for new forms of social connectivity in late modernity. It acts as a holding check on the dominant material self-interestedness of consumer culture and the rationalisation of the life-world as technical performance. The relevance to social work should be fairly clear, since such an ethics gives moral meaning to modes of practice in everyday life whether in personal or professional settings. The practice of recognition developed through experience, reflection and circumspection is the very stuff of good social work. These situated factors provide criteria for a profoundly human ethical theory which is not perfectionist in its ambition, but rather is defensible in terms of the 'good enough'. This is precisely because the structures of human encounter, of setting, and of policy horizons are variable and dynamic. Only in a static world is perfection possible, and of all worlds the social work world is no utopia. Thus an ethics of recognition fits well within the contingencies and uncertainties of risk society.

Virtue Ethics and Good Judgement

It was noted above that the practice of value is socially dependent and cannot be impartial or objective, but is concerned with the evaluation of persons, judgements and character. This leads to my contention that social work ethics needs to recast the moral identity of the social worker in terms of virtue ethics (McBeath & Webb, 2002; Houston, 2003). The basic question asked is not just what is good social work, but rather, what is a good social worker? We noted earlier the importance of Taylor's concept of strong evaluation and it's easy to establish the relationship between this and virtue ethics. Virtue ethics emphasises the priority of the moral agent who has acquired virtues commensurate with the pursuit of a revisable conception of the good life – the *well-fare* of all in a defined community. The virtues are the acquired inner qualities of humans – character – the possession of which, if applied in due measure, will typically contribute to the realisation of the good life or *eudaimonia*. Virtue ethics is especially distinct from its rivals by pointing the ethical way back to the need for the cultivation of character, and thus to the precedence of the quality of the actor over that of the action.

We've seen that doing the right thing in social work is not a matter of applying a moral rule, it is not the work-as-activity that is morally right, but rather the worker-as-agent expressed in the range, and subtlety of use of the virtues. In this sense the virtues are not specific moral concepts, but generalisable capacities of self, the application of which is acquired via training and experience. The morality of the agent emanates from evaluative dispositions to do the best s/he can in the circumstances conjoined to good judgement and perception. Good judgement in social work entails a process of reflective equilibrium, of striking a balance between concept-driven and practice-driven patterns of thinking and moral intuitions primed by factual and counter-factual framing of the situation. We mustn't forget that judgement itself has a moral character in that it requires mental effort, commitment to thinking, and consideration of the state of affairs obtaining. Morality under virtue ethics has an intellectual and motivational content that culminates in practical value.

So, if we want to find ethical constants in a risk society we have to look to the reflected-upon character of the ethical agent in terms of her/his dispositions, and not the actions s/he actually does or that s/he will always do in similar cases (under her/his terms of recognition of what is similar). The individual's character and judgement are the stable reference point, not the actions. In the case of the actions s/he actually does, these could be spontaneous and only coincidentally fit the circumstances – i.e. they would be pure luck and thus have no ethical value whatsoever and further, contain little possibility of being repeated in some way. When we try to abide by the virtues, we try to act as best as we can in a manner and to a degree appropriate to the situation. We judge the situation and what is needed and this takes the successful action beyond mere serendipity. In social work one tries to work with the grain of the social and cultural situations of individuals and families, and not impose an abstract moral solution. In a virtue ethics for social work the role of perception, judgement, and flexibility is emphasised. Implicit in this is that social workers should be striving to reach goals which are set for their own sake, that is due to conscious commitment and not only because someone said so. Further, the task is done well because it will be best fitted to doing good social work for the client. Such dispositions of virtues carry the agent of social work forth to realise best practice. Thus we can conceive of a social work ethics having a far more inclusive notion of what it is to be human than either legal, psychological or strict moral conceptions which have at various times prevailed in social work. The morality of the social worker comes from qualitative dispositions to do the best they can in the circumstances, conjoined to good judgement and concern. Morality under virtue ethics has an intellectual and motivational content that culminates in practical ethics. The conjunction of a conception of the good life with one's virtues and resulting actions establishes the morality of things.

The idea of virtue works within an ecological picture of society as a complex of interacting parts in which social workers strive to promote ethical practice and do the best for their clients without violating any virtues. The integrity of the social worker is not found in consistent action across cases, nor in carrying out agency policy or the law accurately, rather it is found in the consistency of a fundamental orientation of good-will towards those whom one works for and works with, and towards the activities in which one engages. The worker self-understandingly comports herself towards her own field of possibilities, striving to realise the best outcome where such striving has becomes a virtuous property of character.

Virtue ethics, then, is not some doctrine of utilitarian relativism where each situation has a rationally calculable maximising solution pursued by the social worker. Virtue ethics draws upon capacities of self, of perception, judgement and measure, and not just upon an automated response. The possibility of the virtuous self is primordially a question of what it is to be human, and not a function of moments in our lives determined by pure self-interest. To be virtuous is prior to any particular configuration of life. The development of the virtues is rather like the development of our use of the senses. We have an inborn capacity to use our senses, but we can still be trained to use them effectively. We can be given guidance as to how to see things better if we stand here rather than there and so on. We can be shown how to judge and we come to realise that this basic virtue can be used in any number of cases. This is a dialogical concern with peers and supervisors alike, not to find out how this case could have been handled better, but to explore how one might go about thinking, judging, reflecting, and imagining the aspects of social work. That is, to get a sense of what is possible as a social worker qua human actor in various situations and settings.

A virtue ethics relies on a call to conscience in the social worker, and is a function of reflection, deliberation and self-understanding. Resistance to the idea of virtue signals a bad conscience. Virtue calls upon the inner sense of the essential rightness of one's stance commensurate with the situation and the determination of a moral dialogue with the rest of society.

Ties that Bind – Generating Social Capital

There is a burgeoning literature on social capital, even though it's relatively new, with the major literature beginning in the early 1990s and developed from the writings of the French sociologist Pierre Bourdieu (Bourdieu, 1999; Anheier et al., 1995). It is inter-disciplinary, joining theoretical and empirical concerns of economists, political scientists, sociologists, social anthropologists and social psychologists.

Social capital consists of 'informal social networks and formal organizations used by individuals and households to produce goods and services for their own consumption, exchange or sale' (Putnam, 1993). For Putnam social capital refers to connections among individuals' social networks and the norms of reciprocity and trustworthiness that arise from them. Thus, social capital is not merely the sum of network processes which underpin relationships; more importantly, it is the glue that creates cohesion. Small shops, pubs, leisure centres or youth clubs where local people hang out are examples of focal points that fertilise this social glue. Crucially, social capital depends on bonds of trust, reciprocity and obligation that hold communities, friendships and individuals together (Banks, 1997). We've seen in the discussion above that reciprocity is to a large extent dependent upon trust and respect from others. In this way social capital is an emergent property that can transform self-interested and conflictual situations into ones that are based on co-operation and stability, thus encouraging voluntary collective behaviour (Newton, 1997). Social capital also helps ameliorate the effects of the privatisation of risk and the morality of low expectation. It's my contention that social work can play a significant role in this kind of social support networking.

Social proximity and inter-personal contact facilitate the generation of social networks. In their study of mobilising American ethnic minority urban groups to develop social capital, Portney and Berry (1997) showed these processes to be heavily dependent on long-term face-to-face work. Social capital is built through repeated inter-subjective exchange, a process that social work embodies in direct work with clients. According to Putnam:

> The central premise of social capital is that social networks have value. Social capital refers to the collective value of all 'social networks' and the inclinations that arise from these networks to do things for each other. The idea is that a wide variety of quite specific benefits flow from the trust, reciprocity, information, and cooperation associated with social networks. Social capital creates value for the people who are connected and – at least sometimes – for bystanders as well. (1993, p. 15)

Politically, it's worth noting that the left version of the social capital paradigm runs counter to the privatisation of risk and material self-interestedness of neo-liberalism. For Putnam, social capital emphasises not just the kinds of caring relationships and social recognition discussed above, but above all the importance of supportive social networks. This has close parallels to the influential work of Mark Granovetter who argues that most behaviours are closely embedded in networks of inter-personal relations. For Granovetter networks of social relations, rather than institutional arrangements or generalised morality are mainly responsible for the production and maintenance of trust and order in social life (Granovetter, 1985).

Social capital draws attention to a wide variety of quite specific benefits that flow from the trust, reciprocity, information, and co-operation associated with the networks that people forge and maintain. It also underlines the importance of resources that people develop, build upon and then use later. In this sense social capital can be understood as a resource stored in relationships that can be drawn upon to achieve some ends. It's important to recognise that the types of action involved in mobilising social capital are continually evolving an ever widening pool of 'ways that work'. These are passed on and consensually validated by the action of other individuals and communities. Bullen and Onyx (1999) offer a different definition emphasising social capital as a bottom-up process involving civic engagement:

> Social capital is the raw material of civil society. It is created from the myriad of everyday interactions between people. It is not located within the individual person or within the social structure, but in the space between people. It is not the property of the organisation, the market or the state, though all can engage in its production. Social capital is a 'bottom-up' phenomenon. It originates with people forming social connections and networks based on principles of trust, mutual reciprocity and norms of action.

The social goods produced by capital are largely an effect of unintended consequences, such as cohesion, proximity and trust. Bullen and Onyx suggest that community-based social work should develop a framework to determine whether its projects, in addition to accomplishing material or personal life planning, can contribute to changes in practice that transcend crisis-based work or regulatory protection. The aim should be to improve the potential for generating social capital via the ecology of the communities in which social work operates. This sounds very much like community patchwork, but is referred to in this literature as 'bridging social capital', which enables clients to connect to mainstream resources and services. Social workers can act as brokers between structural holes across groups. Given greater homogeneity within than between groups, people whose networks bridge the structural holes between groups have earlier access to a broader diversity of information and have experience in translating information across groups (Burt, 2004). The concept of social workers as knowledge brokers might have greater utility in the sense that the broker position links two or more otherwise unconnected individuals in a network. The network influence of a social capital pool often depends on social workers' welfare knowledge. As Healy and Hampshire (2002) note, social workers, as brokers, are thus able to route and direct capital between a distributed network of events. Conceived in this way, firstly, a broker often has better access to a broad scope of relevant and resource-intensive knowledge than other people and secondly, a broker is quicker to be informed about new initiatives. In addition, social workers, through assessment skills, can also assist in strategically identifying where and what type of social capital is missing in local communities and families.

Social capital is likely to be especially important with working-class families and communities on the fringes of the money economy. We've observed how the impact of risk society bears heavily on those least able to negotiate its uncertainties and insecurities. For poor people or impoverished communities social capital is no real substitute for human or financial capital. However, it can be viewed as part of a family's stock of resources, e.g. friends who may be able to loan money as and when a loan is needed; or extended kin and neighbours who baby-sit, caring for children while people work. An important study of African American ghetto communities showed that they adapted to their poverty conditions by forming large, resilient, life-long support networks based on friendship and family that were very powerful, highly structured and surprisingly complex (Stack, 1974). Through the use of social network analysis this study debunked the misconception that poor families were unstable and disorganised. Similarly, social support networks are important in the role they play for women in achieving effective care during pregnancy and child-birth; for older people returning to the community after hospital; overcoming social isolation by meeting new friends; and for abused women seeking support following domestic violence (Mandel, 1983). Social capital can deepen trust and reciprocity for people. It can also improve various levels of attainment. Research has shown, for example, that a father's social activities in the community can have positive effects on children's educational attainment and that if parents invest less direct social capital with their children, the child's educational performance suffers (Buchel & Duncan, 1998).

Social capital is not possessed in the way that knowledge or money is. It gains its cohesion in sets of flows and patterns among networked people. These relationships are productive to the extent that they are based on a common set of expectations, norms of reciprocity, and a sense of trust among people. Norms of reciprocity (mutual aid and self-help groups) are dependent on social networks. Putnam refers to these as facilitating bonding or bridging networks that connect people. Simply put, social capital creates value for the people who are connected. Some might regard this a fashionable re-working of the community development and generic social work paradigms of the mid 1960s, but lacking the midwifery of Keynesian universal welfarism to underscore it. In other words, it by-passes by default the severity of economic disadvantage, social division and 'underclass' poverty through planned welfare programmes.

A sceptic may also contend that social networks are not comprised of egalitarian or innocent parties all working co-opera-tively together to achieve mutually desired ends. Such a perspective, it can be argued, is apolitical and doesn't take account of wider structures and relations of power. Neighbourhood Watch schemes are good examples of networks involving bias and self-interest. Such networks involve self-segregation that is inclusive. Typically, people push the network in particular ways to reveal elite patterns of social capital based on the influence of group leaders or key players pursu-ing their own interests. It might be argued, for instance, that freema-sonry or the Mafia are optimal networks for generating social capital. Clearly, we need to be aware of this kind of criticism and the role that entrepreneurial divisions play in the formation and devel-opment of social capital networks. Networks of social capital may be good for those inside the network, but the external effects of social capital will by no means always be positive (Putnam, 2000, pp. 350–3).

The argument pursued here is that people are linked in social groups, geography and positions within networks, with caring professionals helping to generate social capital through participation in these links. These are sometimes referred to as 'capacity building strategies', which Adkins et al. (2003) show at work with homeless women, or the 'strengths perspective', which is an approach to working with clients that rejects problem-based assessment and concentrates on developing the ecological resources individuals and communities possess (see Kisthardt & Rapp, 1992; Saleebey, 1992; Rudolph & Epstein, 2000; McMahon, 2002). Adkins et al. identify capacity building as including 'clients' lack of confidence in approaching government departments over issues such as bond loan debts and priority housing, access to information about various housing tenures and options, financial skills and budgeting and tenancy database listings' (2003, p. 11). Social work has a long and respected history of generating social capital through community work and development, as well as through neighbourhood patch teams and informal groups (Hadley & McGrath, 1980; Meyer, 1985). It has long recognised that relationships with kin, neighbours and friends are an important safety net, and are crucial to survival when formal safety nets are absent or inadequate. Family, community and day centres, social support and self-help groups, respite and domiciliary care, befriending and community development schemes all contribute to these informal social networks that generate social capital.

Social work often works in partnership to help people and their local communities build or maintain their social capital. Family centre staff and volunteers, for example, bring high levels of connection with their neighbourhood and communities and high levels of the social capital building blocks. They facilitate co-operation through face-to-face informal networks and proactive projects that spill over into the formation of community associations and crime reduction schemes (Fukuyama, 1995). It's been advanced that frontline practitioners can act as knowledge brokers and bridging facilitators in the advice and guidance they give clients, ranging over a whole set of matters such as entitlements to welfare benefits, the availability of local nursery places, how to secure an application for meal-on-wheels or identify the contact person for the local neighbourhood watch scheme. Again we can see how this deepens and expands the social capital of people whilst creating a supportive environment.

There are obvious links between the social capital, strengths-based and ecological approaches to social work, most notably advanced in the work of Garbarino, Jack and Saleebey (Garbarino & Sherman, 1980; Saleebey, 1992; Garbarino & Kostelny, 1993; Jack, 1997; Jack & Jordan, 1999; Jack, 2000). Jack developed an ecological framework to examine the mutual influence of various systems that impact on family life and childhood. The identification and development of sources of informal social support available to families living in impoverished circumstances are seen as key tasks for social workers and other welfare professionals. He identifies features of networked resiliency found amongst children and families in coping successfully in high-risk environments and uncertainty. Whilst concurring with the above, Jack goes further to suggest that 'there is sufficient evidence available to demonstrate the potential for community social work strategies, which enhance the social support networks to significantly reduce the incidence of child abuse' (1997, p. 109).

Drawing on the work of Garbarino, Jack discusses the links between social ecology and personal well-being in high-risk environments. This permits him to draw up a geography of vulnerability linked to place, resources and the specificities of local lifestyle. He sees social ecology as a root metaphor for community life. It is a webbing of inter-dependencies embedded in expectations, obligations, actions and interactions. Jack draws on a considerable body of research to show that child development is powerfully shaped by social capital. As Putnam claims, 'research dating back at least fifty years has demonstrated that trust, networks, norms of reciprocity within a child's family, school, peer group and larger community have wide-ranging effects on the child's opportunities and choices and, hence, on his behaviour and development' (2000, p. 296). We also know that high levels of social capital create safer and more organised communities, creating a sense of continuity and responsibility for local residents (Jacobs, 1961). Much of the research has focused on the negative effects on children and families where there is a deficit of social capital. The guiding principle for social work is that it can provide ecological frameworks from which to support and facilitate the generation of social capital. The suggestion is that people whose lives are rich in social capital cope better with old age, disability, poverty, trauma and illness. Social work does a great deal to widen awareness of how fateful moments are linked and can be supported. It also goes some way towards helping people develop active and trusting relations with others as well as encouraging strategies to resolve inter-personal problems. Jack contends that the ecological approach to social work cannot be simply added to the practice 'toolkit' to be used selectively as and when required. Instead he says it should be considered holistically as the toolkit itself (Jack, 2000, p. 715). Jack also argues that the key role for social work with an ecologically minded perspective is to strengthen community, family and kin networks, not supplant them or create new systems.

Life as a Planned Project

There are plenty of good practical reasons for advancing the case of
social work in neo-liberal risk society. We've seen how it can act as
a safety net, buffering people from the uncertainties and insecurities
of life. This penultimate section returns to the discussion about life
planning and the provision of safety nets and security as a key function of social work. Some caution, however, is required in this
respect. Firstly, because as discussed in previous chapters, a narrow
hyper-rationalist and individualisitic version is unacceptable, and
secondly, because as conceived in terms of Giddens's life politics
project, I concur with Garrett that it 'fails to recognize social work's
regulatory and authoritarian role' (2004, p. 578). Similarly, we must
acknowledge the effects of 'conveyor-belt social work' in which
provision is rationed, taking place within resource-constrained
organisations that are shaped by economic and political interests
(Garrett, 2004, pp. 584–5). Differential social care structures
circumscribe the agency of front-line practitioners. Squeezing strategies delay, deny and speed up care. In social work rationing formu-
lates a particular linkage between allocative decisions and resources
which can work to support certain interests (e.g. those of children
over the elderly) against others.

We've seen in the above discussion on social capital how social
work is best understood in social and ecological and not psycho-
individual terms (Wittel, 2001). Front-line practitioners assess and
evaluate social situations; support people during difficult times;
convey information about rights, benefits and resources; make
services available; communicate the needs of people to service
providers; encourage action by people and help ameliorate risk and
uncertainty. They help vulnerable people cope with difficult and
risky circumstances. Within the constraints outlined above, the role
of the social worker can be understood in terms of life planning
during fateful moments. We must adopt a critical perspective on the
emergent trend towards having all kinds of planners, coaches, advisors, visiting officers, counsellors and mentors in risk society. In
Britain the *Sunday Times* ran advertisements for how to become a
life coach, described as 'a synthesis of a mentor to believe in you
and help you set bigger goals for yourself . . . A manager to break
down the goals into "do-able bits" . . . A personal trainer that will
keep you moving along your path' (www.resultslifecoaching.
com.au/what/coach.html; *Sunday Times*, 6 October 2002). Such

planning rests on assumptions that in the presence of complete information about the initial situation, a plan is simply a sequence of
actions that takes the individual from the initial situation to the state
which satisfies a given goal. Claiming that life is tenuous, life
coaches and advisors are paid to show consumers how realistic planning is one of the keys to solving problems, achieving goals and
defining their purpose in a life of burgeoning risk. Effective holistic
planning is thought to make the difference between a life of security
and one filled with the anxiety of uncertainty and chaos (Hansen,
1996).

We've seen that life is precarious and disorientating in late
modern times. There has always been uncertainty, but now it is
deliberately woven into the everyday practices of triumphant neo-
liberalism. In *The Corrosion of Character* Richard Sennett (1998)
discusses the effects of modern society on the long-term organisation of daily lives and personal narrative, finding in both cases a lack
of mastery over one's life. Focusing on the relation between work-
place and personal experience Sennett describes how people feel
pressured to change jobs frequently. They take risks; they gamble
without knowing what the odds are. Predictable work is essential to
plan our lives, make commitments and provide a social anchor. But,
according to Sennett, it is becoming increasingly unpredictable for
many who feel their lives are determined by market or employer
whims. The frequent shuffling of the work-force breaks up bonds
between worker communities. Thus social solidarity is undermined,
with unstable work-place experiences making for unstable homes
and societies. In our grabbing society a trend is evident whereby the
ideals associated with long-term relations are increasingly stagnat-
ing. Without a sense of shared fate, Sennett suggests, society is
weaker because we are not required to be reliable and accountable to
others. Short-termism in markets reduces all social relations to those
of instrumental self-interest, devaluing other relations of mutual
dependency and care. Short-termism, instrumentalism and weak
evaluators combine to reproduce an impoverished organisational
culture in social work. Not believing in the prospects of a return of
traditional community, Sennett argues that individuals are increasingly forced to find temporary refuge in privatised encounters of
friendship, intimacy and love. For some an existential identity of
angst, loneliness and banality looms large in this advanced liberal
spectacle (Baudrillard, 2001). There are links between Sennett's
characterisation of modern life as fragmented and decentred and

Ferguson's plea for a repositioning of social work within a life-politics of self-actualisation in the face of existential uncertainty:

Such interventions provide a 'methodology of life planning' which enables people to make crucial decisions about who they are and how they want to live in a context of a new kind of life politics involving increased lifestyle choices. (2003, p. 17)

Marthinsen (2002) similarly takes up the notion of life politics and detects a key role for social work, seeing 'the social worker entering the field – as a negotiator of sustainable identities in a context of competing life politics' (p. 2). He claims that social work can make a positive contribution in the construction of life politics and in doing so promote certain ways of living as better than or preferable to others. Clearly the way that such normative judgements are reached would be a matter for negotiation between client and social worker.

In social work life planning may provide a sense of security and safety for clients. We've seen, however, that the redistributive role of social work has changed from a focus on need and poverty in the 1960s, to one based on risk reduction and protection. This changing risk-dominated role tends toward a justification of Rose's defamatory and one-sided description of social workers as 'petty engineers of human conduct' (1999, p. 92). In an earlier chapter it was discussed how the term 'safety nets' encompasses various social work programmes designed to play both a redistributive and a risk reduction role with vulnerable individuals, families and communities. The redistributive role is intended to reduce the impact of insecurity and vulnerability and the risk reduction role is in protecting people against threats, anxieties and fatal moments. The purpose of a safety net is to protect people from ultimate harm. But it also equips clients with certain reflexive techniques for acting upon themselves in order to adjust or reform themselves

A social safety net comprises a set of programmes, benefits, and support networks designed to ensure that people can cope with fateful moments and the uncertainties of late modern life. Ulrich Beck (1997) argues for something similar in his thinking about ways to re-invent radical politics in late modernity. Beck calls for the revival of a public or social work that requires 'active compassion', 'practical critique' and 'active democracy'. There is much scope for social work in engaging with and developing Beck's manifesto. Culpitt (1998) describes these three components as radical features of a 'new welfare reflexivism' which he defines as: (1) active compassion, meaning some form of public work, a blend of politics, care for others, mutual recognition and everyday co-operation; (2) practical critique, referring to deliberative decisions by professionals such as social workers to use their planning skills in some socially useful way and to be rewarded by some form of public recognition; and (3) active democracy, meaning practices of social self-help, supported by social workers, that involve grassroots political organisation and solidarity (1998, p. 110). As we'll see in the final section the axis for this is a renewed public sector/social state alliance in promoting alternative forms of ethical life.

The life planning model of social work is endorsed by leading British leftist think tank the Institute for Public Policy Research (IPPR) in their *New Visions for Social Care* manifesto, suggesting that:

> One way of assessing how demand for social care will change is to take a 'life-course' approach. This involves identifying different stages or points of an individual's or family's lifecycle when a social care intervention might be required. These life stages may be very different from in the past.

The important links between self-identity and life planning are to the fore here. Social work can play an important role in helping people work through important life-course changes. In an earlier chapter life planning was discussed in relation to care pathways, planning and management. As a method it was criticised for being overly rational and procedural in its approach to the fateful moments experienced by clients. Such attempts to regulate the lives of other people, particularly when high-consequence risk is at stake, remain a necessary and feasible project, but we must recognise that such projects will be prone to many displacements and flows of disruption, whether for good or ill (Van der Veen, 2000). We've also seen that social work intervention can act as a safety net of security for vulnerable people and those in need of social protection from risk or harm. This is the direction that social work should strike out in and continues to lay claim to. A concern for the well-being of the client, the establishment of trusting relations and a sense of belonging through feeling secure sit at the heart of much of front-line practice. We've seen, however, that this kind of life planning should be based on intensive and sometimes long-term work. As Richard Sennett (1998) observes, the 'no long term' which is all-pervasive in modern life is a principle that corrodes trust, mutual recognition and solidarity. He says that the short-term frame of experts and modern institutions

limits the ripening of informal trust and the possibility of co-operation. Strong ties, alternatively, rely on long associations and depend
on a voluntary willingness to make commitments to people. Short-
term care or actuarial crisis work, as framed by neo-liberalism,
threaten to corrode the possibility of constructing meaningful ethical
relationships with clients. These kinds of relationship bind human
beings together and furnish people with a sustainable self in the face
of neo-liberal risk society.

What Is to Be Done?

In his penetrating but disturbing essay 'The essence of neo-liberalism' the French sociologist Pierre Bourdieu (1998) outlines the
logic, consequences and rationality of this dominant political
ideology for modern societies. He is hard-pressed to identify any
serious counter-vailing trends or a sociopolitical movement that is
capable of stopping what he calls this 'infernal machine'. For
Bourdieu the transition to neo-liberalism 'takes place in an imper-
ceptible manner, like continental drift, thus hiding its own effects
from view. Its most terrible consequences are those of the long term'
(1998). Nevertheless he identifies what he calls an 'old order' that
paradoxically helps both to conceal the effects of neo-liberalism and
offers a potential space for resistance. The old order Bourdieu is
referring to is the social state and its public sector institutions like
social work and education that are currently being dismantled by
neo-liberalism. To quote at length, Bourdieu tells us that

> We are faced with an extraordinary paradox. The obstacles encountered on the
> way to realising the new order of the lone, but free individual are held today to
> be imputable to rigidities and vestiges. All direct and conscious intervention of
> whatever kind, at least when it comes from the state, is discredited in advance
> and thus condemned to efface itself for the benefit of a pure and anonymous
> mechanism, the market . . . But in reality what keeps the social order from
> dissolving into chaos, despite the growing volume of the endangered population,
> is the continuity or survival of those very institutions and representatives of the
> old order that is in the process of being dismantled, and all the work of the cate-
> gories of social workers, as well as the forms of social solidarity, familial or
> otherwise. (1998)

Thus for Bourdieu, social work assists in maintaining the social
order and holding it together, even though a rampant and destructive
neo-liberal politics calls into question any social solidarities and

collective goods that serve as obstacles to the logic of the pure market. Interestingly, he is suggesting that a field of moral-political conflicts lies hidden and festering beneath the veneer of neo-liberal capitalist integration. And yet, Bourdieu concedes that these 'same forces of conservation . . . are also from another point of view, forces of *resistance* to the establishment of the new order and can *become subversive forces*' (1998, emphasis in original). In echoing my earlier comments identifying social work not merely as an affirmative social entity and evaluative constitutive good, but as 'unruly practices' that can actively sabotage, resist and challenge neo-liberalism, Bourdieu wants to appeal to public sector institutions like social work to take a deliberate stance against the dominant forms of political rule in advanced capitalist societies. We need to take steps to reawaken core ethical practices and activate the moral sources of social work, thereby harnessing the logic of resistance to neo-liberal rule both within and outwith the profession. Using a British example, a very obvious instance of this might be for educators and practitioners to lobby the General Social Care Council and National Occupational Standards bodies insisting on the reinstatement of social work ethics, as central rather than marginal to the prescribed curriculum of the new social work degree.

In this final chapter I've maintained that the practice of value as part of an ethical matrix of strong evaluation in social work is crucial in respect of Bourdieu's political critique. He offers a glimmer of optimism when says that 'If there is still cause for some hope, it is that forces still exist, both in state institutions and in the orientations of social actors (notably individuals and groups most attached to these institutions, those with a tradition of civil and public service) that . . . will be able to invent a new social order. One that will not have as its only law the pursuit of egoistic interests and the individual passion for profit and that will make room for collective oriented ends' (1998). Thus we must think of social work as occupying a specifiable ethical location in social space that belongs to a traditional order underpinned by strong evaluators and social solidarity. It is at the same time expansive in having acquired ethical identities and political skills to counter the hegemony of neo-liberalism. If you want to stick a label on this project call it 'neo-humanism', in acknowledgement of the longstanding European tradition of humanism with its various considerations of shared moral understanding, the cultivation of self, mutual reciprocity, social virtues and the common good. This tradition adhered to the belief that shared understanding of the good is possible within society and that human beings can be cultivated to recognise and make sacrifices for that good. By emphasising the significance of care, recognition and virtue I've located the ethics of commitment as strong evaluation in social work and as a significant feature of its historical legacy.

Bibliography

Abbott, A. (1988) *The System of Professions: an Essay on the Division of Expert Labor*, University of Chicago Press, Chicago.

Abbott, A. (1995) 'Boundaries of social work or social work of boundaries?' in *Social Service Review*, Vol. 69, pp. 545–62.

Adkins, B., Barnett, K., Greenlagh, E. & Heffernan, M. (2003) 'Women and homelessness: innovative practice and exit pathways', paper presented to National Homelessness Conference 'Beyond the Divide', Australian Federation of Homelessness Organisations, Brisbane, April.

Adorno, T. & Horkheimer, M. (1979) *Dialectic of Enlightenment*, Verso, London.

Ainley, P., Barnes, T., & Momen, A. (2002) 'Making connexions: a case study in contemporary social policy' in *Critical Social Policy*, Vol. 22, No. 2, pp. 376–84.

Ainsworth, F. & Maluccio, A. N. (1998) 'Kinship care: false dawn or new hope?' in *Australian Social Work*, Vol. 51, No. 4, pp. 3–8.

Ainsworth, P. (2001) *Offender Profiling and Crime Analysis*, Willan, London.

Alaszewski, A. (2000) 'Restructuring community care: risk, decision-making and control' in *Managing Community Care*, Vol. 8, No. 1, February, pp. 22–6.

Alaszewski, A., Harrison, L. & Manthrope, J. (1998) *Risk, Health and Welfare*, Open University Press, Buckingham.

Allen, I (ed.) (1992) *Purchasing and Providing Social Services in the 1990s*, Policy Studies Institute, London.

Allen, I. (ed.) (1997) *Best Value: Regulation and Risk*, Policy Studies Institute, London.

Anderson, E. (1990) 'The ethical limitations of the market' in *Economics and Philosophy*, Vol. 6, No. 2, pp. 179–205.

Anheier, H. K., Gerhards, J. & Romo, F. P. (1995) 'Forms of capital and social structure in cultural fields: examining Bourdieu's social topography' in *American Journal of Sociology*, Vol. 100, No. 4, pp. 859–903.

Anheier, H. K. & Kendall, J. (2000) 'Trust and voluntary organizations: three theoretical approaches' in *Civil Society Working Paper 5*, London School of Economics, London.

Aronowitz, S. & DiFazio, W. (1994) *The Jobless Future: Sci-tech and the Dogma of Work*, University of Minnesota Press, Minneapolis.

Association of Psychiatric Social Workers (1956) *The Boundaries of Casework*, APSW, London.

Association of Psychiatric Social Workers (1956) *The Essentials of Social Casework*, APSW, London.

Aust, A. (1996) 'Applying risk in practice: case studies and training materials' in *Good Practice in Risk Assessment and Risk Management*, Kemshall, H. & Pritchard, J. (eds), Jessica Kingsley, London.

Ayers, J. & Braithwaite, J. (1992) *Responsive Regulation: Transcending the Deregulation Debate*, Oxford University Press, Oxford.

Bamford, T. (2001) *Commissioning and Purchasing*, Routledge, London.

Banks, E. (1997) 'The social capital of self-help mutual aid groups' in *Social Policy*, Vol. 28, No. 1, pp. 30–9.

Barry, J. & Jones, C. (eds) (1994) *Medicine and Charity before the Welfare State*, Routledge, London.

Baudrillard, J. (2001) 'Dust breeding' in *CTheory*, www.ctheory.net/ text_file.asp?pick=293

Bauman, Z. (1989) *Modernity and the Holocaust*, Blackwell, Oxford.

Bauman, Z. (1991) *Modernity and Ambivalence*, Polity Press, Cambridge.

Bauman, Z. (1992) *Intimations of Postmodernity*, Routledge, London.

Bauman, Z. (1998) 'What prospects of morality in times of uncertainty?' in *Theory, Culture and Society* Vol. 15, No. 1, pp. 11–22.

Bauman, Z. (2000) 'Am I my brother's keeper?' in *European Journal of Social Work*, Vol. 3, No. 1, pp. 5–11.

Bauman, Z. (2001) *Community: Seeking Safety in an Insecure World*. Polity Press, Cambridge.

Beck, U. (1992) *Risk Society: Towards a New Modernity*, Sage, London.

Beck, U. (1997) 'Capitalism without work' in *Dissent*, Vol. 44, No. 1, pp. 51–6.

Beck, U. (1999) *World Risk Society*, Polity Press, Cambridge.

Benbenishty, R., Segey, D., Surkis, T. & Elias, T. (2002) 'Information-search and decision-making by professionals and nonprofessionals in cases of alleged child-abuse and maltreatment' in *Journal of Social Service Research*, Vol. 28, No,3, pp. 11–16.

Bendle, M. (2002) 'The crisis of identity in high modernity' in *British Journal of Sociology*, Vol. 53, No. 1, pp. 1–18.

Benhabib, S. (1992) *Situating the Self: Gender, Community and Postmodernism in Contemporary Ethics*, Routledge, New York.

Bensmaia, R. (1986) 'Foreword: the Kafka Effect', trans. Terry Cochran, in G. Deleuze & F. Guattari, *Kafka: Toward a Minor Literature*, trans. Dana Polan, University of Minnesota Press, Minneapolis.

Benso, S. (2000) *The Face of Things: A Different Side of Ethics*, State University of New York Press, Albany.

Berman, M. (1983) *All That is Solid Melts in Air: the Experience of Modernity*, Verso, London.

Bernstein, P. (1998) *Against the Gods: the Remarkable Story of Risk*, John Wiley, New York.

Beveridge Report (1942) *Social and Allied Services,* Presented to Parliament by William Beveridge, November, CMND 6404, HMSO, London.

Bhaskar, R. (1986) *Scientific Realism and Human Emancipation,* Verso, London.

Biestek, F. P. (1961) *The Casework Relationship,* Allen & Unwin, London.

Biggs, S. (1987) 'Quality of care and the growth of private welfare for old people' in *Critical Social Policy,* Issue 20, Autumn, pp. 28–39.

Birch, S. (1997) 'As a matter of fact: evidence-based decision making unplugged' in *Health Economics,* Vol. 6, No. 6, pp. 547–59.

Bisman, C. (2004) 'Social work values: the moral core of the profession' in *British Journal of Social Work,* Vol. 34, pp. 109–23.

Black, J. (1983) *Social Work in Context,* Tavistock, London.

Blaug, R. (1995) 'Distortion of the face to face: communicative reason and social work practice' in *British Journal of Social Work,* Vol. 25, No. 2, pp. 423–39.

Bleach, A. & Ryan, P. (1995) *Community Support for Mental Health,* Pavilion, Brighton.

Bloom, A. (1987) *The Closing of the American Mind,* Penguin, Harmondsworth.

Bourdieu, P. (1998) 'The essence of neo-liberalism' in *Le Monde Diplomatique,* December, www.monde-diplomatique.fr/1998/03/BOURDIEU/10167.html

Bourdieu, P. (1999) *Acts of Resistance: Against the New Myths of Our Time,* Polity Press, Cambridge.

Bourdieu, P. & Wacquant, L. (1992) *An Invitation to Reflexive Sociology,* University of Chicago Press, Chicago.

Bovaird, T. & Rubienska, A. (1997) 'The clashing cultures of marketing and organizational learning: some emerging contradictions in the public sector' in *Annals of Public and Cooperative Economics,* Vol. 67, No. 1, pp. 51–83.

Bowlby, J. (1951) *Maternal Care and Mental Health,* World Health Organization, Geneva.

Braithwaite, J. (2000) 'The new regulatory state and the transformation of criminology' in *British Journal of Criminology,* Vol. 40, pp. 222–38.

Braye, S. & Preston-Shoot, M. (1995) *Empowering Practice in Social Care,* Open University Press, Buckingham.

Brearley, C. (1982) *Risk and Ageing,* Routledge & Kegan Paul, London.

Brewer, C. & Lait, J. (1980) *Can Social Work Survive?* Maurice Temple Smith, London.

Briggs, A. (1976) 'Social welfare, past and present' in *Traditions of Social Policy,* Halsey, A. H. (ed.), Basil Blackwell, Oxford.

Broadie, A. (1978) 'Authority and social casework' in *Philosophy in Social Work*, Timms, N. & Watson, D. (eds), Routledge & Kegan Paul, London.

Browne, K. & Saqi, S. (1988) 'Approaches to screening for child abuse and neglect' in *Early Prediction and Prevention of Child Abuse*, Browne, K. et al. (eds), Wiley, Chichester.

Buchanan, I. (2000) 'User participation now: evidence-based practice in best value' in *Managing Community Care*, Vol. 8, No. 4, August, pp. 11–15.

Buchel, F. & Duncan, G. J. (1998) 'Do parents' social activities promote children's school attainments? Evidence from the German Socioeconomic Panel' in *Journal of Marriage and the Family*, Vol. 60, February, pp. 95–108.

Bullen, P. & Onyx, J. (1999) *Social Capital: Family Support Services and Neighbourhood and Community Centres in NSW*, Concord West, New South Wales, www.mapl.com.au/A12.htm

Bullock, R. (1990) 'The problems of managing the family contacts of children in residential care' in *British Journal of Social Work*, Vol. 20, No. 6, pp. 591–610.

Bulmer, M. (1987) *The Social Basis of Community Care*, Unwin Hyman, London.

Burkert, H. (1994) '"Electronic trust" and the role of law: a European perspective' in *Applications and Impacts – Information Processing 1994*, Brunnstein, K. & Raubold, E. (eds) (Proceedings of the IFIP 13th World Computer Congress, Hamburg, Volume II), Elsevier, Amsterdam.

Burkitt, I. (1992) 'Beyond the "iron cage": Anthony Giddens on modernity and the self' in *History of the Human Sciences*, Vol. 5, No. 3, pp. 71–9.

Burt, R. S. (2004) 'Structural holes and good ideas' in *American Journal of Sociology*, Vol. 110, No. 2, pp. 349–99.

Buzan, B. (1991) *People, States and Fear*, Harvester Wheatsheaf, Hemel Hempstead.

Byrne, D. (1995) 'De-industrialisation and dispossession: an examination of social division in the industrial city' in *Sociology*, Vol. 29, No. 1, pp. 95–115.

Cabinet Office (2000) *Consumer Focus for Public Services: People's Panel Wave 5. Research Study Conducted for the Modernising Public Services Group*, March–April, London.

Cabinet Office Strategy Unit (2002) *Risk: Improving Government's Capability to Handle Risk and Uncertainty*, London.

Carew, R. (1979) 'The place of knowledge in social work activity' in *British Journal of Social Work*, Vol. 9, No. 3, pp. 349–64.

Castel, R. (1991) 'From dangerousness to risk' in *The Foucault Effect: Studies in Governmentality*, Burchell, G., Gordon, C. & Miller, P. (eds), Harvester Wheatsheaf, London.

Castel, R. (1994) '"Problematization" as a mode of reading history' in *Foucault and the Writing of History*, Goldstein, J. (ed.), Basil Blackwell, Oxford.

Castells, M. (2000) *The Information Age: Economy, Society and Culture. Volume I. The Rise of the Network Society*, Second edition, Blackwell, Oxford.

Cawson, P. & Martell, M. (1979) *Children Referred to Closed Units*, Research Report No. 5, Department of Health and Social Security, HMSO, London.

CCETSW (1973) *Training for Residential Care*, discussion document, Central Council for Education and Training in Social Work, London.

Challis, D. (1990) 'Care management: problems and possibilities' in *Care Managers and Care Management*, Allen, I. (ed.), Policy Studies Institute, London.

Challis, D. (ed.) (1999) *Organizing Public Social Services*, Ashgate, Aldershot.

Chambon, A., Irving, A. & Epstein, L. (eds) (1999) *Reading Foucault for Social Work*, Columbia University Press, New York.

Chapman, T. & Hough, M. (1999) *Evidence Based Practice: a Guide to Effective Practice*, Home Office, London.

Christensen, T. & Lægreid, P. (2001) 'New public management: the effects of contractualism and devolution on political control' in *Public Management Review*, Vol. 3, No. 1, pp. 73–94.

Christie, A. & Mittler, H. (1999) 'Partnership and core groups in risk society' in *Children and Family Social Work*, Vol. 4, pp. 231–40.

Clarke, M. G. & Stewart, J. D. (1997) 'Handling the wicked issues: a challenge for government' *INLOGOV Working Paper*, University of Birmingham, Birmingham.

Clarke, P. (1978) *Liberals and Social Democrats*, Cambridge University Press, Cambridge.

Clough, R. (ed.) (1994) *Insights into Inspection: the Regulation of Social Care*, Whiting & Birch, London.

Colley, H. & Hodkinson, P. (2001) 'Problems with *Bridging the Gap*: the reversal of structure and agency in addressing social exclusion' in *Critical Social Policy*, Vol. 21, No. 3, pp. 335–60.

Colton, M., Vanstone, M., & Walby, C. (2002) 'Victimization, care and justice: reflections on the experiences of victims/survivors involved in large-scale historical investigations of child sexual abuse in residential institutions' in *British Journal of Social Work*, Vol. 32, pp. 541–51.

Comijis, H. (2000) 'The quality of data collection by an interview on the prevalence of elder mistreatment' in *Journal of Elder Abuse and Neglect*, Vol. 12, No. 1, pp. 57–72.

Conkin, J. (1996) 'Designing organizational memory: preserving intellectual assets in a knowledge economy' in *Group Decision Support Systems*, www.gdss.com/DOM.htm

Connor, S. (1993) 'The necessity of value' in *Principled Positions: Postmodernism and the Rediscovery of Value*, Squires, J. (ed.), Lawrence & Wishart, London.

Cooper, A., Hetherington, R. & Katz, I. (2003) *The Risk Factor: Making the Child Protection System Work for Children*, Demos, London.

Cooper, J. (1989) 'From casework to community care' in *British Journal of Social Work*, Vol. 19, No. 3, pp. 177–88.

Cooper, R. (1989) *Thresholds Between Philosophy and Psychoanalysis*, Free Association Books, London.

Cooper, R. & Fox, J. (1997) 'Learning to make decisions under uncertainty: the contribution of qualitative reasoning' in *Proceedings of 19th Annual Conference of the Cognitive Science Society*, Shafto, M. G. & Langley, P. (eds), Palo Alto, pp. 125–130.

Cope, S. & Goodship, J. (1999) 'Comparing regulatory regimes in new governance', paper presented at the Annual Conference of the Political Studies Association, University of Nottingham, March.

Corby, B. (1996) 'Risk assessment in child protection work' in *Good Practice in Risk Assessment and Risk Management*, Kemshall, H. & Pritchard, J. (eds), Jessica Kingsley, London.

Cornell, D. (1993) *The Philosophy of Limit*, Routledge, New York.

Corrigan, P. & Leonard, P. (1978) *Social Work under Capitalism*, Macmillan (now Palgrave Macmillan), London.

Coulshed, V. (1988) *Social Work Practice: an Introduction*, Macmillan (now Palgrave Macmillan), London.

Cournoyer, B. (2004) *Evidence-Based Practice: Skills Book*, Allyn & Bacon, New York.

Craddock, G. (2001) 'Risk, morality, and child protection: technologizing social work' in *Technologies of Uncertainty Workshop*, Cornell University, Ithaca.

Craddock, G. web page, www.iisgp.ubc.ca/community/gerald.htm

Cruikshank, B. (1995) 'Revolutions within: self-government and self-esteem' in *Economy and Society*, Vol. 22, No. 3, pp. 227–44.

Culpitt, I. (1998) *Social Policy and Risk*, Sage, London.

Curry, A. and Herbert, D. (1998) 'Continuous improvement in public services – a way forward' in *Managing Service Quality Review*, Vol. 8, No. 5, pp. 339–49.

Cussins, C. (1998) 'Ontological choreography: agency for women patients in an infertility clinic' in *Differences in Medicine: Unraveling Practices, Techniques and Bodies*, Mol, A. & Berg, M. (eds), Duke University Press, Durham, NC.

Dale, P. & Morrison, T. (1986) *Dangerous Families: Assessment and Treatment of Child Abuse*, NSPCC/Tavistock, London.

Davies, M. (1994) *The Essential Social Worker*, Third edition, Arena, Aldershot.

Davis, A. (1996) 'Risk work and mental health' in *Good Practice in Risk Assessment and Risk Management*, Kemshall, H. & Pritchard, J. (eds), Jessica Kingsley, London.

Dean, M. (1999) *Governmentality*, Sage, London.

Delanty, G. (1999) *Social Theory in a Changing World: Conceptions of Modernity*, Polity Press, Cambridge.

Deleuze, G. & Guattari, F. (1987) *A Thousand Plateaus: Capitalism and Schizophrenia*, trans. B. Massumi, University of Minnesota, Minneapolis.

de Milo-Martin, I. (1998) 'Ethics and uncertainty: *in vitro* fertilization and risks to women's health' in *Risk: Health, Safety and Environment*, Vol. 9, Summer, pp. 134–41.

Denzin, N. K. (2002) 'Social work in the seventh moment' in *Qualitative Social Work*, Vol. 1, No. 1, pp. 25–38.

Department of Education and Science (1974) *Child Guidance*, Circular, 3/74, DES, London.

Department of Environment, Transport and the Regions (2000) *Cross Cutting Issues in Public Policy and Public Service,* February, DETR, London.

Department of Health (1988) *Protecting Children: a Guide for Social Workers Undertaking a Comprehensive Assessment*, HMSO, London.

Department of Health (1989) *Caring for People: Community Care in the Next Decade and Beyond*, Department of Health, London.

Department of Health (1991a) *Care Management and Assessment: Managers' Guide*, HMSO, London.

Department of Health (1991b) *Care Management and Assessment: Practitioners' Guide*, HMSO, London.

Department of Health (1991c) *Working Together Under the Children Act 1989*, HMSO, London.

Department of Health (1994a) *Developing Managers for Community Care: Interagency Management Development Techniques*, HMSO, London.

Department of Health (1994b) *Guidance on Discharge of Mentally Disordered People and their Continuing Care in the Community*, HMSO, London.

Department of Health (1995) *An Introduction to Joint Commissioning*, HMSO, London.

Department of Health (1999a) *Framework for the Assessment of Children in Need and their Families*, Consultation document, September, HMSO, London.

Department of Health (1999b) *Modernising Social Services: Promoting Independence, Improving Protection, Raising Standards*, Department of Health, London.

Department of Health (2000a) *A Quality Strategy for Social Care*, HMSO, London.

Department of Health (2000b) *Information For Social Care: a Framework for Improving Quality in Social Care through Better Use of Information and Information Technology*, HMSO, London.

Department of Health (2000c) *The NHS Plan: A Plan for Investment, A Plan for Reform*, HMSO, London.

Department of Health (2002a) *Demonstrator Projects 2002–03: Proposals for Information for Social Care*, HMSO, London.

Department of Health (2002b) *Learning from Past Experience: a Review Of Serious Case Reviews*, HMSO, London.

Department of Social Welfare (1998) *Towards a Code of Social and Family Responsibility*, Wellington, New Zealand.

DeSwann, A. (1990*) The Management of Normality*, Routledge, London.

Di Maggio, P. & Powell, W. (eds) (1991) *The New Institutionalism in Organizational Analysis*, University of Chicago Press, Chicago.

Dingwall, R. (1997) 'Conclusion: the moral discourse of interactionism' in *Context and Method in Qualitative Research*, Miller, G. & Dingwall, R. (eds), Sage, London.

Dingwall, R. & Eekelaar, J. (1982) *Care Proceedings: a Practical Guide for Social Workers, Health Visitors and Others*, Basil Blackwell, Oxford.

Dingwall, R. & King, M. (1995) 'Herbert Spencer and the professions: occupational ecology reconsidered' in *Sociological Theory*, Vol. 13, No. 1, pp. 14–24.

Dixon, J. & Hoatson, L. (1999) 'Retreat from within: social work education's faltering commitment to community work' in *Australian Social Work*, Vol. 52, No. 2, pp. 3–9.

Donzelot, J. (1991) 'The mobilization of society' in *The Foucault Effect: Studies in Governmentality*, Burchell, G., Gordon, C. & Miller, P. (eds), Harvester Wheatsheaf, Hemel Hempstead.

Douglas, M. (1986) *How Institutions Think*, Syracuse University, Syracuse.

Douglas, M. (1990) 'Risk as a forensic resource' in *Daedalus*, Vol. 119, No. 4, pp. 1–16.

Douglas, M. & Wildavsky, A. (1982) *Risk and Culture*, University of California Press, London.

Downing, J. D., Wells, S. J. & Fluke, J. (1990) 'Gatekeeping in child protective services: a survey of screening policies' in *Child Welfare*, Vol. 69, No. 4, pp. 357–69.

Dreyfus, H. (1997) 'The current relevance of Merleau-Ponty's phenomenology of embodiment', paper presented to 'After Post-Modernism' Conference, University of Chicago, November.

Dreyfus, H. & Dreyfus, S. (1991) 'Towards a phenomenology of professional expertise' in *Human Studies*, Vol. 14, pp. 229–50.

Dunleavy, P. J. & Hood. D. (1994) 'From old public administration to new public management' in *Public Money and Management,* Vol. 14, No. 3, pp. 9–16.

Dupuis, A. & Thorns, D. C. (1998) 'Home, home ownership and the search for ontological security' in *Sociological Review*, Vol. 41, No. 2, pp. 23–41.

Elliot, A. (1996) *Subject to Ourselves; Social Theory, Psychoanalysis and Postmodernity*, Polity Press, Cambridge.

Ellul, J. (1967) *The Technological Society*, trans. J. Wilkinson, Vintage, New York.

England, H. (1986) *Social Work as Art: Making Sense of Good Practice*, Allen & Unwin, London.

Epstein, L. (1980) *Helping People: the Task-centered Approach*, C. V. Mosby, St Louis.

Eraut, M. (1997) 'Perspectives on defining "The Learning Society"' in *Journal of Education Policy*, Vol. 12, No. 6, pp. 551–8.

Esping-Andersen, G. (ed.) *Welfare States in Transition*, Sage, London.

Evetts, J. (1998) 'Professionalism beyond the nation-state: international systems of professional regulation in Europe' in *International Journal of Sociology and Social Policy*, Vol. 18, No. 11/12, pp. 24–31.

Ewald, F. (1991) 'Insurance and risk' in *The Foucault Effect: Studies in Governmentality*, Burchell, G., Gordon, C., & Miller, P. (eds), Harvester Wheatsheaf, Hemel Hempstead.

Feeley, M. & Simon, J. (1992) 'The new penology: notes on the emerging strategy of corrections and its implications' in *Criminology*, Vol. 30, No. 4, pp. 452–74.

Feeley, M. & Simon, J. (1994) 'Actuarial justice: the emerging new criminal law' in *The Futures of Criminology*, Nelken, D. (ed.), Sage, London.

Ferguson, H. (2001) 'Social work, individualization and life politics' in *British Journal of Social Work*, Vol. 31, No. 1, pp. 41–56.

Ferguson, H. (2003) 'Outline of a critical best practice perspective on social work and social care' in *British Journal of Social Work*, Vol. 33, No. 8, pp. 1005–24.

Feyerabend, P. (1975) *Against Method*, Verso, London.

Feyerabend, P. (1981) *Problems of Empiricism: Philosophical Papers, Volume 2*, Cambridge University Press, Cambridge.

Filer, A. (ed.) (2000) *Assessment: Social Practice and Social Product*, Falmer Press, London.

Finkel, A. M. (1996) 'Comparing risks thoughtfully' in *Risk: Health, Safety & Environment*, Vol. 7, pp. 325–34.

Fischer, R. & Kargel, H. (1997) *Social Work and Community in a Private World*, Longmans, London.

Fitzgerald, J. (1999) *Child Protection and the Computer Age: Sharing Information between Agencies by Computer*, Bridge, London.

Floersch, J. (2002) *Meds, Money, and Manners: the Case Management of Severe Mental Illness*, Columbia University Press, New York.

Foucault, M. (1979) 'Governmentality' in *Ideology and Consciousness*, No. 6, pp. 5–21.

Foucault, M. (1990) 'An aesthetics of existence', trans. Alan Sheridan, in *Michel Foucault: Politics, Philosophy, Culture; Interviews and Other Writings 1977–1984*, Kritzman, L. (ed.), Routledge, New York.

Foulkes, S. H. (1986) *Group-analytic Psychotherapy: Method and Principles*, Maresfield, London.

Fox, J. & Cooper, R. (1996) 'Cognitive processing and knowledge representation in decision making under uncertainty' in *Qualitative Theories of Decision Making*, Scholz, R. W. & Zimmer, A. C. (eds), Wiley, New York.

Franklin, J. (1998) *The Politics of the Risk Society*, Polity Press, Cambridge.

Fraser, N. & Honneth, A. (2001) *Redistribution or Recognition?: A Philosophical Exchange*, Verso, London.

Freeman, M. D. A. (1983) 'The rights of children in care' in *Providing Civil Justice for Children*, Greach, H. & Szwed, E. (eds), Edward Arnold, London.

Friedman, M. (1991) 'Beyond caring: the de-moralization of gender' in *Canadian Journal of Philosophy*, Supplementary Vol. 13, pp. 87–110.

Frisby, D. (1985a) *Fragments of Modernity*, Polity Press, Cambridge.

Frisby, D. (1985b) 'Georg Simmel: first sociologist of modernity' in *Theory, Culture & Society*, Vol. 2, No. 3, pp. 49–67.

Fritzsche, A. F. (1996) 'The moral dilemma in the social management of risks' in *Risk: Health, Safety and Environment*, Vol. 7, pp. 36–47.

Froggett, L. & Sapey, B. (1997) 'Communication, culture and competence in social work education' in *Social Work Education*, Vol. 16, No. 1, pp. 41–53.

Fukuyama, F. (1995) *Trust: The Social Virtues and the Creation of Prosperity*, Free Press, New York.

Furedi, F. (1997) *Culture of Fear: Risk Taking and the Morality of Low Expectation*, Cassell, London.

Gaba, D. M. (1992). Dynamic decision-making in anesthesiology: cognitive models and training approaches, in *Advanced Models of Cognition for Medical Training and Practice*, Evans, D. A. & Patel, V. L. (eds), Springer-Verlag, Berlin/Heidelberg.

Gambrill, E. (2003) 'Evidence-based practice: sea change or the Emperor's new clothes?' in *Journal of Social Work Education*, Vol. 39, No. 1, pp. 3–23.

Garbarino, J. & Kostelny, K. (1993) Neighborhood and community influences on parenting' in *Parenting: an Ecological Perspective*, Luster, T. & Okagaki, L. (eds), Lawrence Erlbaum Associates, Mahwah.

Garbarino, J. & Sherman, D. (1980) 'High-risk neighborhoods and high risk families: the human ecology of child maltreatment' in *Child Development*, Vol. 51, pp. 188–98.

Garland, D. (1996) 'The limits of the sovereign state' in *British Journal of Criminology*, Vol. 36, No. 4, pp. 445–71.

Garrett, P. M. (1999a) 'Producing the moral citizen: the "Looking After Children" system and the regulation of children and young people in public care' in *Critical Social Policy*, Vol. 19, No. 3, pp. 291–311.

Garrett, P. M. (1999b) 'Mapping child-care social work in the final years of the twentieth century: a critical response to the "Looking After Children" System' in *British Journal of Social Work*, Vol. 29, pp. 27–47.

Garrett, P. M. (2003a) 'The Trouble with Harry: Why the "new agenda of life-politics" fails to convince' in *British Journal of Social Work*, Vol. 33, pp. 381–97.

Garrett, P. M. (2003b) 'Swimming with dolphins: the assessment framework, New Labour and new tools for social work with children and families' in *British Journal of Social Work*, Vol. 33, No. 4, pp. 441–63.

Garrett, P. M. (2003c) *Remaking Social Work with Children and Families: a Critical Discussion of the Modernisation of Social Care*, Routledge, London.

Garrett, P. M. (2004) 'More Trouble with Harry: a rejoinder to the "life-politics" debate' in *British Journal of Social Work*, Vol. 34, pp. 577–89.

Geddes, J. (1998) 'Evidence based practice in mental health' in *Evidence Based Mental Health*, Vol. 1, No. 1, February, pp. 12–19.

Giddens, A. (1985) *The Nation State and Violence*, Polity Press, Cambridge.

Giddens, A. (1990) *The Consequences of Modernity*, Polity Press, Cambridge.

Giddens, A. (1991) *Modernity and Self Identity*, Polity Press, Cambridge.

Giddens, A. (1994a) *Beyond Left and Right*, Polity Press, Cambridge.

Giddens, A. (1994b) 'Risk, trust and reflexivity' in *Reflexive Modernization*, Beck, U., Lash, S. & Giddens, A. (eds), Polity Press, Cambridge.

Giddens, A. (1998) 'Risk society: the context of British politics' in *The Politics of Risk Society*, Franklin, J. (ed.), Polity Press, Cambridge.

Giddens, A. (1998) *The Third Way: the Renewal of Social Democracy*, Polity Press, Cambridge.

Giddens, A. (1999) 'Risk and the runaway world' in *The Reith Lectures Revisited*, London School of Economics, London.

Gigerenzer, G. & Todd, P. M. (1999) *Simple Heuristics that Make Us Smart*, Oxford University Press, Oxford.

Gillespie, L. D., Gillespie, W. J., Robertson, M. C., Lamb, S. E., Cumming, R. G. & Rowe, B. H. (2002) 'Interventions for preventing falls in elderly people' in *The Cochrane Library,* Issue 3, Update Software, Oxford.

Gilligan, C. (1982) *In a Different Voice: Psychological Theory and Women's Development*, Harvard University Press, Cambridge, MA.

Goldstein, H. (1973) *Social Work Practice: A Unitary Approach*, University of South Carolina Press, Columbia.

Gonchar, N. & Roper Adams, J. (2000) 'Living in cyberspace: recognizing the importance of the virtual world in social work assessments' in *Journal of Social Work Education*, Vol. 36, No. 3, pp. 587–96.

Gordon, C. (1991) 'Governmental rationality: an introduction' in *The Foucault Effect: Studies in Governmentality*, Burchell, G., Gordon, C. & Miller, P. (eds), Harvester Wheatsheaf, Hemel Hempstead.

Gould, N. (2003) 'The caring professions and information technology – in search of a theory' in *Information and Communication Technologies in the Welfare Services*, Harlow, E. & Webb, S. A. (eds), Jessica Kingsley, London.

Granovetter, M. (1985) 'Economic action and social structure: the problem of embeddedness' in *American Journal of Sociology*, Vol. 91, November, pp. 481–510.

Grubin, D. (1998) *Sex Offending Against Children: Understanding the Risk*, Police Research Series, Paper 99, Home Office, London.

Habermas, J. (1990). *Moral Consciousness and Communicative Action*, trans. C. Lenhardt & S. W. Nicholsen, MIT Press, Cambridge, MA.

Hacking, I. (1986) 'Making up people' in *Reconstructing Individualism*, Heller, T. C., Sosna, M., & Wellbery, E. (eds), Stanford University, Stanford.

Hadley, R. & McGrath, M. (1980) *Going Local: Neighbourhood Social Services*, Bedford Square Press, London.

Halachmi, A. & Bovaird, T. (1997) 'Process reengineering in the public sector: learning some private sector lessons' in *Technovation,* Vol. 7, No. 5, pp. 227–35.

Hammond, K. R. (1996) *Human Judgment and Social Policy: Irreducible Uncertainty: Inevitable Error and Unavoidable Injustice*, Oxford University Press, Oxford.

Hampton, K. (2001) *Developing Success Criteria for Joint Health Improvement Appointments between the NHS and Local Government*, Office for Public Management, London.

Hannah-Moffat, K. (1999) 'Moral agent or actuarial subject: risk and Canadian women's imprisonment' in *Theoretical Criminology*. Vol. 3, No. 1, pp. 71–94.

Hannah-Moffat, K. (2002) 'Governing through need: the hybridizations of risk and need in penalty', paper presented at British Society of Criminology 'Crossing Borders' Conference, University of Keele.

Hansen, L. S. (1996) *Integrative Life Planning: Critical Tasks for Career Development and Changing Life Patterns*, Jossey-Bass, New York.

Hardey, M. & Maddox, D. (2000) 'Family risk assessments – dangers, dilemmas and decisions in practice' in *Family Law*, Vol. 30, August, pp. 555–9.

Hardt, M. & Negri, A. (2000) *Empire*, Harvard University Press, Cambridge, MA.

Harris, J. (2002) 'Caring for citizenship' in *British Journal of Social Work*, Vol. 32, No. 3, pp. 267–81.

Hartley, D. (1990) 'Beyond competency: a socio-technical approach to continuing professional education' in *British Journal of In-Service Education*, Vol. 6, pp. 66–70.

Healy, K. (2000) *Social Work Practices*, Sage, London.

Healy, K. (2001) 'Reinventing critical social work: challenges from practice, context and postmodernism' in *Critical Social Work*, Vol. 2, No. 1, Spring, pp. 4–15.

Healy, K. (2002) 'Managing human services in a market environment: what role for social workers?' in *British Journal of Social Work*, Vol. 32, No. 5, pp. 527–54.

Healy, K. & Hampshire, A. (2002) 'Social capital: a useful concept for social work?' in *Australian Social Work*, Vol. 55, Issue 3, pp. 227–38.

Heidegger, M. (1977) *The Question Concerning Technology and Other Essays*, trans. W. Lovitt, Harper & Row, New York.

Heller, A. (1992) 'Modernity's pendulum' in *Thesis Eleven*, Vol. 31, No. 3, pp. 12–24.

Her Majesty's Inspectorate of Probation (1997) *Risk Management Guidance*, Home Office, London.

Hills, J., LeGrand, J. & Piachaud, D. (2002) *Understanding Social Exclusion*, Oxford University Press, Oxford.

Hindess, B. (1997) 'A society governed by contract' in *The New Contractualism?*, Davis, G., Sullivan, B., & Yeatman, A. (eds), Macmillan, Melbourne.

Hollis, F. (1964) *Casework: a Psychosocial Therapy*, Random House, New York.

Holman, B. (1988) *Putting Families First: Prevention and Child Care*, Macmillan Education, London.

Honneth, A. (1995) *The Struggle for Recognition: the Moral Grammar of Social Conflicts*, Polity Press, Cambridge.

Honneth, A. (2001) 'Recognition or redistribution? Changing perspectives on the moral order of society' in *Theory, Culture & Society*, Vol. 18, No. 2–3, pp. 43–55.

Hood, C. (1991) 'A Public Management for All Seasons?' in *Public Administration*, Vol. 69, Spring, pp. 3–19.

Hood, C. (1995) 'Contemporary public management: a new global paradigm?' in *Public Policy and Administration*, Vol. 10, No. 2, pp. 104–17.

Hood, C. (1996) *Accident and Design: Contemporary Debates on Risk Management,* UCL Press, London.

Hood, C. (2001) 'Control, bargains and cheating: the politics of public service reform', paper delivered at the Annual Meeting of the American Political Science Association, San Francisco, 30 August–2 September.

Hood, C., & Jackson, M. (1991) *Administrative Argument*, Ashgate, Aldershot.

Hood, C. & Rothstein, H. (2000) *Business Risk Management in Government: Pitfalls and Possibilities*, report commissioned for the National Audit Office.

Hood, C., Rothstein, H., & Baldwin, R. (2001) *The Government of Risk: Understanding Risk Regulation*, Oxford University Press, Oxford.

Hood, C. & Scott, C, (2000) *Regulating Government in a 'Managerial Age': Towards a Cross National Perspective*, Centre for Analysis of Risk and Regulation, London School of Economics, London.

Houston, S. (2003) 'Establishing virtue in social work: a response to McBeath and Webb' in *British Journal of Social Work*, Vol. 33, No. 6, pp. 819–24.

Houston, S. & Griffiths, H. (2000) 'Reflections on risk in child protection: is it time for a shift in paradigms?' in *Child and Family Social Work*, Vol. 5, No. 1, February, pp. 1–10.

Howe, D. (1980) 'Inflated states and empty theories in social work' in *British Journal of Social Work*, Vol. 10, pp. 317–40.

Howe, D. (1993) *On Being a Client: Understanding the Process of Counselling and Psychotherapy*, Sage, London.

Howe, D. (1996) 'Surface and depth in social-work practice' in *Social Theory, Social Change and Social Work*, Parton, N. (ed.), Routledge, London.

Howe, D. (1998) 'Psychosocial work' in *Social Work: Themes, Issues and Critical Debates*, Adams, R., Dominelli, L. & Payne, M. (eds), Macmillan (now Palgrave Macmillan), Basingstoke.

Hudson, C. G. (2000) 'At the edge of chaos: a new paradigm for social work?', in *Journal of Social Work Education*, Vol. 36, No. 2, Spring/Summer, pp. 21–34.

Hughes G. & Lewis, G. (eds) (1998), *Unsettling Welfare*, London, Routledge.

Humphrey, J. C. (2003) 'New Labour and the regulatory reform of social care' in *Critical Social Policy*, Vol. 23, No. 1, pp. 5–24.

Hutchinson, D. (1981) 'The request for placement has meaning' in *Parents of Children in Placement,* Sinanoglu, P. A. & Maluccio, A. N. (eds), Child Welfare League of America, New York.

Hutton, W. (1998) *The Stakeholding Society*, Polity Press, Cambridge.

Iacono, S. C. (1996) 'The demise of meaning-making and social agency as critical concepts in the rhetoric of an information age' in *The Information Society* Vol. 12, No. 4, pp. 449–50.

Interdepartmental Liaison Group on Risk Assessment (2000) *Use of Risk Assessment within Government Departments*, HMSO, London.

Ions, E. (1977) *Against Behaviouralism: a Critique of Behavioural Science*, Basil Blackwell, Oxford.

Jack, G. (1997) 'An ecological approach to social work with children and families' in *Children and Family Social Work*, Vol. 2, pp. 109–20.

Jack, G. (2000) 'Ecological influences on parenting and child development' in *British Journal of Social Work*, Vol. 30, pp. 703–20.

Jack, G. & Jordan, B, (1999) 'Social capital and child welfare' in *Children and Society*, Vol. 13, pp. 242–56.

Jackson, S. (1996) 'New foundations for scientific social and behavioural research: the heuristic paradigm', in *British Journal of Social Work*, Vol. 6, pp. 877–8.

Jacobs, J. (1961) *The Death and Life of Great American Cities*, Vintage Books, New York.

Jacobs, O. (1996) *The End of Certainty*, Free Press, New York.

James, A. (2002) 'The McDonaldization of social work – or come back Florence Hollis, all is (or should be) forgiven' in Lovelock, R., Lyons, K. & Powell, J. (eds), *Reflecting on Social Work: Discipline and Profession*, Dartford, Ashgate.

Jervis, P. & Richards, S. (1997) 'Public management, raising the game' in *Public Money and Management*, Vol. 3, April–June, pp. 43–58.

Jessop, B. (1999). 'The changing governance of welfare' *Social Policy and Administration*, Vol. 33, pp. 348–59.

Jones, D. (2001) 'Misjudged youth: a critique of the Audit Commission's reports on youth justice' in *British Journal of Criminology*, Vol. 41, pp. 362–80.

Jones, H. (ed.) (1975) *Towards a New Social Work*, Routledge, London.

Jones, L. (ed.) (2000) *Safe Enough? Managing Risk and Regulation*, The Fraser Institute, Vancouver.

Jordan, B. (2000) *Social Work and the Third Way: Tough Love as Social Policy*, Sage, London.

Jordan, B. (2004) 'Emancipatory social work: opportunity or oxymoron' in *British Journal of Social Work*, Vol. 34, pp. 5–19.

Joyce, P. (2001) 'Governmentality and risk: setting priorities in the new NHS' in *Sociology of Health and Illness,* Vol. 23, pp. 594–614.

Kahneman, D. & Tversky, A (1973) 'On the psychology of prediction' in *Psychological Review*, No. 80, pp. 237–51.

Katz, M. (ed.) (1993) *The 'Underclass' Debate*, Princeton University Press, Princeton.

Kemshall, H. (1996) 'Offender risk and probation practice' in *Good Practice in Risk Assessment and Risk Management*, Kemshall, H. & Pritchard, J. (eds), Jessica Kingsley, London.

Kemshall, H. (2000) 'Conflicting knowledges on risk: the case of risk knowledge in the probation service' in *Health, Risk & Society*, Vol. 2, No. 2, pp. 143–58.

Kemshall, H. (2002) *Risk, Social Policy and Welfare*, Open University Press, Buckingham.

Kemshall, H., Parton, N., Walsh, M. & Waterson, J. (1997) 'Concepts of risk in relation to organizational structure and functioning within the personal social services and probation' in *Social Policy & Administration*, Vol. 31, No. 3, pp. 213–32.

Kendall, J. (2000) 'The third sector and social care for older people in England: towards an explanation of its contrasting contribution in residential care, domiciliary care and day care', in *Civil Society Working Paper 8*, London School of Economics, London.

Kendall, J. & Knapp, M. (2000) 'Measuring the performance of voluntary organisations' in *Public Management*, Vol. 2, No 1, pp. 105–32.

Kettl, D. F. (1997) 'The global revolution in public management: driving themes, missing links' in *Journal of Policy Analysis and Management*, Vol. 16, No. 3, pp. 446–62.

King, J. (1993) 'Learning to solve the right problems: the case of nuclear power in America', *Journal of Business Ethics*, Vol. 12, pp. 105–16.

Kisthardt, W. E. & Rapp, C. A. (1992) 'Bridging the gap between principles and practice: implementing a strengths perspective in social work practice' in *Case Management and Social Work Practice*, Rose, S. M. (ed.), Longman, New York.

Klein, M. (1951) *Love, Guilt and Reparation*, Hogarth Press, London.

Knoke, D., Pappi, F., Broadbent, J. & Tsujinaka, Y. (1996) *Comparing Policy Networks*, Cambridge University Press, Cambridge.

Kwong-Leung, T. (2000) 'Asian crisis, social welfare and policy responses: Hong Kong and Korea compared' in *International Journal of Sociology and Social Policy,* Vol. 20, No, 6, pp. 49–71.

Langan, M. (2000) 'Social services: managing the Third Way' in *New Managerialism: New Welfare?*, Clarke, J. et al. (eds), Sage, London.

Lash, S. (1999) *Another Modernity: a Different Rationality*, Blackwell, Oxford.

Lash, S. & Featherstone, M. (2001) 'Recognition and difference: politics, identity, multiculture' in *Theory, Culture & Society*, Vol. 18, No. 2–3, pp. 1–19.

Lash, S. & Urry, J. (1994) *Economies of Sign and Space*, Sage, London.

Latour, B. (1987) *Science in Action*, Harvard University Press, Cambridge, MA.

Latour, B. (1988) 'The politics of explanation: an alternative' in *Knowledge and Reflexivity: New Frontiers in the Sociology of Knowledge*, Woolgar, S. (ed.), Sage, London.

Law, J. (1984) 'On the methods of long distance control: vessels, navigation and the Portuguese route to India', unpublished paper, University of Keele.

Law, J. (1994) *Organizing Modernity*, Blackwell, Oxford.

Law, J. (1997) 'Heterogeneities', paper presented at the meeting on 'Uncertainty, Knowledge and Skill', at Limburg University, Diepenbeek, Belgium.

Law, J. & Singleton, V. (2000) 'This is not an object', Centre for Science Studies and the Institute for Women's Studies, Lancaster University, www.comp.lancs.ac.uk/sociology/soc032jl.html

Lawson, H. (1985) *Reflexivity: the Post-Modern Predicament*, Hutchinson, London.

Lefort, C. (1988) *Democracy and Political Theory*, Polity Press, Cambridge.

Leidner, R. (1993) *Fast Food, Fast Talk: Service Work & the Routinization of Everyday Life*, University of California Press, Berkeley.

Leighton, D. (2002) 'Searching for politics in an uncertain world: interview with Zygmunt Bauman' in *Renewal: A Journal of Labour Politics*, Vol. 10, No. 1.

Leisering, L. (2003) 'Government and the life course' in *Handbook of the Life Course*, Mortimer, J. T. & Shanahan, M. J. (eds), Kluwer, New York.

Leuenberger, C. (2002) 'The end of socialism and the reinvention of the self: a study of the East German psychotherapeutic community in transition' in *Theory and Society*, Vol. 31, pp. 255–80.

Levinas, E. (1974) *Otherwise than Being or Beyond Essence*, Duquesne University Press, Pittsburgh.

Levitas, R. (1998) *The Inclusive Society? Social Exclusion and New Labour*, Macmillan (now Palgrave Macmillan), Basingstoke.

Levy, A. & Kahan, B. (1991) *The Pindown Experience and the Protection of Children*, Staffordshire County Council, Stafford.

Lindblom, C. E. (1979) 'Still muddling through, not yet though' in *Public Administration Review*, Vol. 39, No. 1, pp. 79–86.

Lindley, D. V. (2000) 'The philosophy of statistics' in *Journal of the Royal Statistical Society*, Series D, Vol. 49, Part 3, pp. 293–319.

Lipshitz, R. & Strauss, O. (1997) 'Coping with uncertainty: a naturalistic decision-making analysis' in *Organisational Behaviour and Human Decision Processes*, Vol. 69, No. 2, February, pp. 149–63.

Lister, R. (1998a) 'First steps towards a fairer society', in 'Guardian Society', *Guardian*, 9 June.

Lister, R. (1998b) 'From equality to social inclusion: New Labour and the welfare state' in *Critical Social Policy*, Vol. 18, No. 2, pp. 215–26.

Lister, R. (2001) 'New Labour: a study in ambiguity from a position of ambivalence' in *Critical Social Policy*, Vol. 21, No. 4, pp. 425–48.

Loewenberg, F. M. (1984) 'Professional ideology, middle range theories and knowledge building for social work practice' in *British Journal of Social Work*, Vol. 14, No. 4, pp. 309–22.

Luck, M., Pocock, R. & Tricker, M. (2000) *Market Research in Health and Social Care*, Routledge, London.

Luhmann, N. (1988) 'Familiarity, confidence, trust: problems and alternatives' in *Trust: Making and Breaking Cooperative Relations*, Gambetta, D. (ed.), Basil Blackwell, Oxford.

Luhmann, N. (1995) *Die Soziologie des Risikos*, de Gruyter, Berlin.
Luik, J. C. (2000) 'Second-hand smoke and cancer: the research evidence' in *Safe Enough? Managing Risk and Regulation*, Jones, L. (ed.), The Fraser Institute, Vancouver.
Lukacs, G. (1971) *History and Class Consciousness*, Merlin Press, London.
Lupton, C. (1998) 'Family group conferences: user involvement or family self reliance? in *British Journal of Social Work*, Vol. 28, No. 1, pp. 107–28.
Lupton, D. (1993) 'Risk as moral danger: the social and political functions of risk discourse in public health' in *International Journal of Health Services*, Vol. 23, No. 3, pp. 113–19.
Lupton, D. (1999) *Risk*, Routledge, London.
Lymbery, M. (1998) 'Care management and professional autonomy: the impact of community care legislation on social work with older people' in *British Journal of Social Work*, Vol. 28, No. 6, pp. 863–78.
Macarov, D. & Bearwald, P. (2001) 'The future of social work theory and practice' in *Journal of Social Work Theory and Practice*, Issue 3, pp. 3–13.
Macdonald, G. (1994) 'Developing empirically-based practice in probation' in *British Journal of Social Work*, Vol. 24, No. 1, pp. 405–27.
Macdonald, G. (2001) *Effective Interventions for Child Abuse and Neglect: an Evidence-based Approach to Planning and Evaluating Interventions*, John Wiley, Chichester.
Mackenzie, L., Byles, J. & Higginbotham, N. (2000) 'Designing the home falls and accidents screening tool' in *Journal of Occupational Therapy*, Vol. 63, No. 6, June, pp. 260–9.
Maddock, S. (1998) 'Making modernisation work: new narratives, change strategies and people management in the public sector' in *International Journal of Public Sector Management*, Vol. 15, No. 1, pp. 13–43.
Maddock, S. & Morgan, G. (1998) 'Barriers to transformation: beyond bureaucracy and the market conditions for collaboration in health and social care' in *International Journal of Public Sector Management*, Vol. 11, No. 4, pp. 234–51.
Malchow, H. L. (1985) 'Public gardens and social action in late Victorian London' in *Victorian Studies*, Vol. 29, No. 1, pp. 97–124.
Malone, G. (1994) 'The rise of the regulatory state in Western Europe' in *Western European Politics*, Vol. 17, No. 2, pp. 21–34.
Maluccio, A. N. (1981a) *Promoting Competence in Clients*, Free Press, New York.
Maluccio, A. N. (1981b) 'The emerging focus on parents of children in placement' in *Parents of Children in Placement*, Sinanoglu, P. A. & Maluccio, A. N. (eds), Child Welfare League of America, New York.
Mandel, M. J. (1983). 'Local roles and social networks' in *American Sociological Review*, Vol. 48, pp. 376–86.

Mandel, M. J. (1996) *The High-Risk Society: Peril and Promise in the New Economy*, Random House, New York.

Manning, N. (2001) 'Psychiatric diagnosis under conditions of uncertainty: personality disorder, science, and professional legitimacy' in *Rethinking the Sociology of Mental Health*, Busfield, J. (ed.), Blackwell, Oxford.

Manthorpe, J. et al. (1995) 'Taking a chance' in *Community Care*, 20–21 October, pp. 19–25.

Margolin, L. (1997) *Under the Cover of Kindness: the Invention of Social Work*, University Press of Virginia, Charlottesville.

Marriott, P. (2000) 'Risky business' in *Volunteering*, May, pp. 10–11.

Marris, P. (1974) *Loss and Change*, Routledge & Kegan Paul, London.

Marsh, P. (1994) 'Partnership, child protection and family group conferences: the New Zealand Children, Young Persons and their Families Act 1989' in *Journal of Child Law*, Vol. 6, No. 3, pp. 109–15.

Marshall, M., Gray, A., Lockwood, A. & Green, R. (2002) 'Case management for people with severe mental disorders' in *The Cochrane Library*, Issue 3, Update Software, Oxford.

Marthinsen, E. (2002) 'Giddens, life politics and the development of child protection services', unpublished paper, Institute of Social Work, NTNU, Trondheim, Norway.

Martin, S. (1999) 'Visions of best value: modernizing or just muddling through' in *Public Money and Management*, Vol. 19, No. 4, pp. 57–61.

Martinson, R. (1974) 'What works? Questions and answers about prison reform' in *The Public Interest*, Vol. 35, pp. 22–54.

Matthies, A. L. (2001) 'Social work research and local policies: assisting social sustainability', paper presented at 'Researching Social Work Practices' Conference, Helsinki, 24–25 October.

May, T., Harocopos, A. & Hough, M. (2000) *For Love or Money: Pimps and the Management of Sex Work*, Police Research Series, Paper 134, Home Office, London.

McAuliffe, D. & Coleman, A. (1999) ' "Damned if we do and damned if we don't": exposing ethical tensions in field research' in *Australian Social Work*, Vol. 52, No. 4, pp. 56–64.

McBeath, G. B. & Webb, S. A. (1991a) 'Child protection language as professional ideology in social work' in *Social Work and Social Sciences Review*, Vol. 2, No. 2, pp. 122–45.

McBeath, G. B. & Webb, S. A. (1991b) 'Social work, modernity and post modernity' in *Sociological Review*, Vol. 39, No. 4, pp. 745–64.

McBeath, G. B. & Webb, S. A. (1997) 'Community care: a unity of state and care? Some political and philosophical considerations' in *Concepts of Care*, Hugman, R., Peelo, M. & Soothill, K. (eds), Edward Arnold, London.

McBeath, G. B. & Webb, S. A. (2002) 'Virtue ethics and social work: being lucky, realistic, and not doing one's duty' in *British Journal of Social Work*, Vol. 32, No. 8, pp. 1015–36.

McDonald, T. P., Poertner, J. & Harris, G. (2001) 'Predicting placement in foster care: a comparison of logistic regression and neural network analysis' in *Journal of Social Service Research*, Vol. 28, No. 2, pp. 1–20.

McGuire, J. B. (1997) 'Evidence based approaches in mental health settings' in *Children & Society*, Vol. 11, No. 2, pp. 89–96.

McLaughlin, J. (2001) 'EBM and risk – rhetorical resources in the articulation of professional identity' in *Journal of Management in Medicine*, Vol. 15, No. 5, pp. 352–63.

McLeod, H. (1974) *Class and Religion in the Late Victorian City*, Croom Helm, London.

McLuhan, M. (1964) *Understanding Media*, McGraw-Hill, New York.

McMahon, A. (1998) *Damned if You Do, Damned if You Don't: Working in Child Welfare*, Ashgate, Sydney.

McMahon, T. (2002) 'Strengths, justice and collective action: what social work and community welfare can offer Australian Indigenous Education', paper presented to National Indigenous Education Conference, Townesville, Australia, July.

Mead, L. (1986) *Beyond Entitlement: the Social Obligations of Citizenship*, Free Press, New York.

Mead, L. (1989) 'The logic of workfare: the underclass and work policy' in *Annals of the American Academy of Political and Social Science*, Vol. 501, January.

Means, R. (2000) 'The risk/dependency model' in *The Blackwell Encyclopaedia of Social Work*, Davies, M. (ed.), Blackwell, Oxford.

Meyer, C. H. (1985) 'Social support and social workers: collaboration or conflict?' in *Social Work*, Vol. 30, pp. 291–302.

Meyer, P. (1983) *The Child and the State: the Intervention of the State in Family Life*, Cambridge University Press, Cambridge.

Middleton, L. (1999) 'Could do better' in *Professional Social Work*, November, pp. 8–9.

Midgley, M. (1996) *Utopias, Dolphins and Computers: Problems of Philosophical Plumbing*, Routledge, London.

Millham, S. et al. (1986) *Lost in Care: the Problems of Maintaining Links between Children in Care and Their Families*, Gower, Aldershot.

Misztal, B. A. (1996) *Trust in Modern Societies*, Polity Press, Cambridge.

Mitchell, D. (1999) *Governmentality: Power and Rule in Modern Society*, Sage, London.

Monaghan, L., Bloor, M., Dobash, R. P. & Dobash, R. E. (2000) 'Drug-taking, "risk boundaries" and social identity: bodybuilders' talk about ephedrine and nubain' in *Sociological Research Online*, Vol. 5, No. 2.

Moren, S. & Blom, B. (2003) 'Explaining human change: on generative mechanisms in social work practice' in *Journal of Critical Realism*, Vol. 2, No. 1, pp. 45–58.

Morgan, B. (1996) 'Community care and social work with adults' in *Social Work Competences*, Vass, A. (ed.), Sage, London.

Morris, K., Marsh, P. & Wiffin, J. (1998) *Family Group Conferences – a Training Pack*, Family Rights Group, London.

Moxley, D. P. (1989) *The Practice of Case Management in the Human Services*, Sage, London.

Mullaly, B. (2002) *Challenging Oppression: a Critical Social Work Approach*, Oxford University Press, New York.

Munro, E. (1998) *Understanding Social Work: an Empirical Approach*, Athlone Press, London.

Murray, C. (1990) *The Emerging British Underclass*, Institute of Economic Affairs, London.

Nash, M. & Savage, S. P. (1995) 'Criminal justice managers: setting targets or becoming targeted?' in *International Journal of Public Sector Management*, Vol. 8, No. 1, pp. 4–10.

National Audit Office (2000) *Supporting Innovation: Managing Risk in Government Departments*, HMSO, London.

National Audit Office (2001) *Joining Up to Improve Public Services*, HMSO, London.

National Children's Bureau (1999) *Family Group Conferences*, Highlight No. 169, Library & Information Service, National Children's Bureau, London.

Neal, M. (2000) 'Risk aversion: the rise of an ideology' in *Safe Enough? Managing Risk and Regulation*, Jones, L. (ed.), The Fraser Institute, Vancouver.

Neal, M., & Davies, J. C. H. (1998) *The Corporation under Siege: Exposing the Devices Used by Activists and Regulators in the Non-Risk Society*, SAU, London.

Netten, A. & Curtis, L. (2000) *Unit Costs of Health and Social Care 2000*, Personal Social Services Research Unit, University of Kent, Canterbury.

Newman, T. (1999) *Evidence-based Child Care Practice*, Highlight No. 170, National Children's Bureau, London.

Newton, K. (1997) 'Social capital and democracy' in *American Behavioural Scientist*, Vol. 40, No. 5, pp. 575–86.

Nisbett, R. E. & Ross, L (1980) *Human Inference: Strategies and Shortcomings of Social Judgement*, Prentice-Hall, Englewood Cliffs.

O'Malley, P. (1996) 'Risk and responsibility' in *Foucault and Political Rationality*, Barry, A., Osborne, T. & Rose, N. (eds), UCL Press, London.

O'Malley, P. (2000) 'Uncertain subjects: risks, liberalism and contract' in *Economy and Society*, Vol. 29, No. 4, pp. 460–84.

O'Melia, M. & Miley, K. K. (2002) *Pathways to Power: Readings in Contextual Social Work Practice*, Allyn & Bacon, New York.

Olsen, J. P. (1996) 'Norway: slow learner – or another triumph of the tortoise?' in *Lessons from Experience*, Olsen, J. P. & Peters, B. G. (eds), Scandinavian University Press, Oslo.

Orme, J. (2001) 'Regulation or fragmentation? Directions for social work under New Labour' in *British Journal of Social Work*, Vol. 31, pp. 611–24.

Orme, J. (2002) 'Social work: gender, care and justice' in *British Journal of Social Work*, Vol. 32, No. 6, pp. 799–814.

Orme, J. & Glastonbury, B. (1993) *Care Management: Tasks & Workloads*, Macmillan (now Palgrave Macmillan), London.

Osborne, S. (1996) *Managing in the Voluntary Sector: a Handbook for Managers in Charitable and Non-Profit Organisations*, International Thomson Business Press, London.

Osborne, S. (1997) 'Managing the co-ordination of social services in the mixed economy of welfare: competition, co-operation or common cause?' in *British Journal of Management*, Vol. 8, No. 1, pp. 317–28.

Pahl, R. (1998) 'Friendship: the social glue of contemporary society' in *The Politics of Risk Society*, Franklin, J. (ed.), Polity Press, Cambridge.

Parker, J. (1989) *Women and Welfare: Ten Victorian Women in Public Social Service*, Macmillan (now Palgrave Macmillan), Basingstoke and London.

Parker, R. (1990) *Safeguarding Standards*, National Institute for Social Work, London.

Parsloe, P. (1967) 'Meeting the needs of the disturbed child' in *British Journal of Psychiatric Social Work*, Vol. 9, No. 2, pp. 90–6.

Parton, N. (1996) 'Social work, risk and the "blaming system"' in *Social Theory, Social Change and Social Work*, Parton, N. (ed.), Routledge, London.

Parton, N. (1998) 'Risk, advanced liberalism and child welfare: the need to rediscover uncertainty and ambiguity' in *British Journal of Social Work*, Vol. 28, pp. 5–27.

Parton, N. (2003) 'Rethinking professional practice: the contributions of social constructionism and the feminist "ethics of care"' in *British Journal of Social Work*, Vol. 33, No. 1, pp. 1–16.

Parton, N. and O'Byrne, P. (2000) *Constructive Social Work: Towards a New Practice*, Macmillan (now Palgrave Macmillan), London.

Pasquino, P. (1978) 'Theatrum politicum: the genealogy of capital, police and the state of prosperity' in *Ideology & Consciousness*, No. 4, Autumn, pp. 41–72.

Patmore, C., Qureshi, H. & Nicholas, E. (2000) 'Consulting older community care clients about their services: some lessons for researchers and service managers' in *Research, Policy and Planning*, Vol. 18, No. 1, pp. 4–11.

Patterson, L. (2002) 'From welfare to work: women lone parents and neo-liberalism', paper presented at Social Policy Research Centre, University of New South Wales, Sydney, June.

Payne, J. L. (1998) *Overcoming Welfare: Expecting More From the Poor and From Ourselves*, Basic Books, New York.

Pearson, C. (2000) Money talks? Competing discourses in the implementation of direct payments' in *Critical Social Policy*, Vol. 20, No. 4, pp. 459–78.

Peggs, K. (2000) 'Which pension? Women, risk and pension choice' in *Sociological Review*, Vol. 41, pp. 349–64.

Performance & Innovation Unit (2000) *Better Policy Delivery and Design: a Discussion Paper*, Cabinet Office, London.

Perhac, R. M. (1996) 'Does risk aversion make a case for conservativism?' in *Risk: Health, Safety & Environment*, Vol. 7, Fall, pp. 297–307.

Perlman, H. H. (1957a) *Casework, a Problem-Solving Process*, University of Chicago Press, Chicago.

Perlman, H. H. (1957b) 'Freud's contribution to social welfare' in *Social Service Review*, Vol. 31, No. 2, pp. 192–202.

Perri 6 & Peck, E. (2004) 'New Labour's modernisation in the public sector: a neo-Durkheimian approach and the case of mental health services' in *Social Administration*, Vol. 82, No. 1, pp. 83–108.

Peters, M. A. (2001) 'Neoliberalism and the governance of welfare', in Special Issue on Neoliberalism, Cheyne, C. (ed.), *A Journal for South Pacific Cultural Studies*, Vol. 38.

Peters, M. A., Fitzsimons, P. & Marshall, J. (1999) 'Education and managerialism in a global context' in *Education and Globalization: Critical Concepts*, Torres, C. & Burbules, N. (eds), Routledge, London.

Peters, M. A. and Marshall, J. D. (2001) 'Introduction: New Zealand, neo-liberalism and the knowledge economy' in *Access: Critical Perspectives on Cultural and Policy Studies in Education*, Vol. 19, No. 2, pp. 1–8.

Phillips, J. & Waterson, J. (2002) 'Care management and social work: a case study of the role of social work in hospital discharge to residential or nursing home care' in *European Journal of Social Work*, Vol. 5, No. 2, pp. 171–86.

Phoenix, J. (2002) 'In the name of protection: youth prostitution policy reforms in England and Wales' in *Critical Social Policy*, Vol. 22, No. 2, pp. 353–75.

Pidgeon, N. F. (1991) 'Safety culture and risk management in organizations' in *Journal of Cross-Cultural Psychology*, Vol. 22, No. 1, pp. 129–40.

Pierson, J. (2002) *Tackling Social Exclusion*, Routledge, London.

Pinker, R. (1983) 'Social welfare and the education of social workers' in *Approaches to Social Welfare*, Bean, P. & MacPherson, P. (eds), Routledge & Kegan Paul, London.

Player, S. & Pollock, A. M. (2001) 'Long-term care: from public responsibility to private good', in *Critical Social Policy*, Vol. 21, No. 2, pp. 231–45.

Portney, K. E. & Berry, J. M. (1997) 'Mobilizing minority communities: social capital and participation in urban neighborhoods' in *American Behavioural Scientist*, Vol. 40, No. 5, pp. 632–44.

Postle, K. (2002) 'Working "between the idea and the reality": ambiguities and tensions in care managers' work' in *British Journal of Social Work*, Vol. 32, No. 3, pp. 335–51.

Powell, F. (1998) 'The professional challenges of reflexive modernization: social work in Ireland' in *British Journal of Social Work*, Vol. 28, pp. 311–28.

Powell, M. (1999) *New Labour, New Welfare State?*, Policy Press, Bristol.

Powell, M. (2000) 'New Labour and the third way in the British welfare state: a new and distinctive approach?' in *Critical Social Policy*, Vol. 20, No. 1, pp. 39–60.

Powell, M. (2002) 'In search of the new politics: concepts and measures of the Third Way', paper presented to ECPR Joint Sessions of Workshops, Turin, 22–27 March.

Powell, W. W. (1990) 'Neither market nor hierarchy: network forms of organization' in *Research in Organizational Behavior*, Vol. 12, Staw, B. M.. & Cummings, L. L. (eds), JAI Press, Greenwich, CT, pp. 295–336.

Power, M. (1997) *The Audit Society: Rituals of Verification*, Oxford University Press, Oxford.

Prins, H. (1999) *Will They Do It Again? Risk Assessment and Management in Criminal Justice and Psychiatry*, Routledge, London.

Putnam, R. D. (1993) *Making Democracy Work*, with Robert Leonardi and Raffaella Y. Nanetti, Princeton University Press, Princeton.

Putnam, R. D. (1995) 'Bowling alone: America's declining social capital' in *Journal of Democracy*, Vol. 6, No. 1, pp. 65–78.

Putnam, R. D. (2000) *Bowling Alone: the Collapse and Revival of American Community*, Simon & Schuster, New York.

Ratcliffe, T. A. (1956) 'Relationship therapy and casework' in *British Journal of Psychiatric Social Work*, Vol. 5, No. 1, pp. 1–15.

Ratcliffe, T. A. (1957) 'The problem family' in *Report of a Conference at Worcester*, Institute for the Study and Treatment of Delinquency, King's College, London.

Ratcliffe, T. A. & Jones, E. V. (1956) 'Intensive casework in a community setting' in *Case Conference*, Vol. 2, No. 1, pp. 17–21.

Rawls, J. (1971) *A Theory of Justice*, Harvard University Press, Cambridge, MA.

Reddy, S. (1996) 'Claims to expert knowledge and the subversion of democracy: the triumph of risk over uncertainty' in *Economy and Society*, Vol. 25, No. 2, pp. 222–54.

Rehmann-Sutter, C. (1998) 'Involving others: towards an ethical concept of risk' in *Risk: Health, Safety & Environment*, Vol. 9, Spring, pp. 11–19.

Reich, A. (2000) 'Researching neoliberal reforms in child protection agencies: a quest for the new century', paper presented to Adult Education Research Conference, Victoria, British Columbia.

Reid, W. J. (1994) 'The empirical practice movement' in *Social Services Review*, Vol. 68, pp. 165–84.

Reid, W. J. (2000) *The Task Planner*, Columbia University Press, New York.

Relph, B. & Webb, S. A. (2003) 'Internet child abuse' in *Information and Communication Technologies in the Welfare Services*, Harlow, E. & Webb, S. A. (eds), Jessica Kingsley, London.

Report of the Inquiry into the Care and Treatment of Christopher Clunis (1994) Chairman, J. H. Ritchie, HMSO, London.

Rhodes, R. A. W. (1997) *Understanding Governance*, Open University Press, Buckingham.

Rhodes, T. & Cusick, L. (2000) 'Love and intimacy in relationship risk management: HIV positive people and their sexual partners' in *Sociology of Health and Illness*, Vol. 22, No. 1, pp. 1–26.

Richards, S. (2001) *Four Types of Joined up Government and the Problem of Accountability*, Report for the National Audit Office, HMSO, London.

Rittel, H. W. J. & Webber, M. M. (1973) 'Dilemmas in a general theory of planning' in *Policy Sciences*, Vol. 4, pp. 155–69.

Roback, P. J. & Welch, S. M. (2001) 'Classification trees for decision making in the social services with application to welfare recidivism' in *Journal of Social Service Review*, Vol. 27, No. 3, pp. 45–57.

Robards, K. J. & Gillespie, D. F. (2000) 'Revolutionizing the social work curriculum: adding modeling to the systems paradigm' in *Journal of Social Work Education*, Vol. 36, No. 3, pp. 80–96.

Rohlin, M. & Mileman, P. A. (2000) 'Decision analysis in dentistry – the last 30 years' in *Journal of Dentistry*, Vol. 28, No. 7, pp. 453–68.

Rose, N. (1985) *The Psychological Complex*, Routledge & Kegan Paul, London.

Rose, N. (1991) 'Governing the enterprising self' in *The Values of the Enterprise Culture*, Heelas, P. & Morris, P. (eds), Unwin Hyman, London.

Rose, N. (1993) 'Government, authority and expertise in advanced liberalism' in *Economy and Society*, Vol. 22, No. 1, pp. 283–99.

Rose, N. (1996a) 'The death of the social? Refiguring the territory of government' in *Economy and Society*, Vol. 25, No. 3, pp. 327–56.

Rose, N. (1996b) 'Governing "advanced" liberal democracies' in *Foucault and Political Reason: Liberalism, Neo-liberalism and Rationalities of Government*, Barry, A., Osborne, T. & Rose, N. (eds), UCL Press, London.

Rose, N. (1999) *Powers of Freedom: Reframing Political Thought*, Cambridge University Press, Cambridge.

Rose, N. & Miller, P. (1992) 'Political power beyond the state: problematics of government' in *British Journal of Sociology*, Vol. 43, No. 2, pp. 172–205.

Ross, E. (1982) ' "Fierce questions and taunts": married life in working class London' in *Feminist Studies*, Vol. 8, No. 3, pp. 570–87.

Ross, L. (1977) 'The intuitive psychologist and his shortcomings' in *Advances in Experimental Social Psychology*, Berkowitz, L. (ed.), Academic Press, New York.

Ross, L. (1997) 'What is an assessment? Service users, their carers and the community care assessment visit' in *Social Services Review*, Vol. 4, pp. 26–38.

Rudolph, S. M. & Epstein, M. H. (2000) 'Empowering children and families through strengths-based assessment' in *Reclaiming Children and Youth*, Vol. 8, No. 4, pp. 207–32.

Rummery, K. & Glendinning, C. (2000) *Primary Care and Social Services: Developing New Partnerships for Older People*, Radcliffe, Abingdon.

Sackett, D. L. (1996a) 'Evidence based medicine: what is it and what it isn't' in *British Journal of Medicine*, 312, pp. 71–2.

Sackett, D. L. (1996b) *Evidence Based Medicine*, NHS Research and Development Centre for Evidence Based Medicine, Oxford.

Salauroo, M. & Burnes, B. (1998) 'The impact of a market system on the public sector: a study of organizational change in the NHS' in *International Journal of Public Sector Management*, Vol. 11, No. 6, pp. 451–67.

Saleebey, D. (ed.) (1992). *The Strengths Perspective in Social Work Practice*, Longman, New York.

Saleebey, D. (2001) *Human Behaviour and Social Environments: a Biopsychosocial Approach*, Columbia University Press, New York.

Sanderson, I. (2002) 'Making sense of "what works": evidence-based policy making as instrumental rationality', paper presented to Political Studies Association Annual Conference, Aberdeen, April.

Sapey, B. (1997) 'Social work tomorrow: towards a critical understanding of technology in social work' in *British Journal of Social Work*, Vol. 27, No. 6, pp. 803–14.

Sarasin, F. P. (1999) 'Decision analysis and the implementation of evidence-based medicine' in *Monthly Journal of the Association of Physicians*, Vol. 92, No. 11, pp. 669–71.

Sargent, K. (1999) 'Assessing risks for children' in *Risk Assessment in Social Care and Social Work*, Parsloe, P. (ed.), Jessica Kingsley, London.

Sarre, R. (2001) 'Beyond "what works?" A 25-year Jubilee retrospective of Robert Martinson's famous article' in *Criminology*, Vol. 34, No. 1, pp. 134–42.

Schlesinger, M. (2002) 'A loss of faith: the sources of reduced political legitimacy for the American medical profession' in *The Milbank Quarterly*, Vol. 80, No. 2, pp.22–35.

Schmidt, H. G., Norman, G. R., & Boshuizen, H. P. A. (1990) 'A cognitive perspective on medical expertise – theory and implications' in *Academic Medicine*, Vol. 65, No. 10, pp. 611–21.

School, A. (2001) 'An Inspector Calls: a practical look at social care inspection' in *British Journal of Social Work*, Vol. 31, No. 1, pp. 161–8.

Schwartz, A. E. (2002) 'Societal value and the funding of kinship care' in *Social Sciences Review*, Vol. 76, pp. 430–59.

Scourfield, J. & Welsh, I. (2003) 'Risk, reflexivity and social control in child protection: new times or same old story' in *Critical Social Policy*, Vol. 23, No. 3, pp. 398–420.

Scriven, M. (1997) 'Truth and objectivity in evaluation' in *Evaluation for the 21st Century: a Handbook*, Chelimsky, E. & Shadish, W. R. (eds), Sage, London.

Seligman, A. (1998) 'Researching the voluntary sector', Keynote speech given at the 4th Conference of National Council of Voluntary Organizations, Loughborough.

Sellars, W. (1956) 'Empiricism and the philosophy of mind' in *Minnesota Studies in the Philosophy of Science, Volume I: The Foundations of Science and the Concepts of Psychology and Psychoanalysis*, Feigl, H. & Scriven, M. (eds), University of Minnesota Press, Minneapolis, pp. 253–329.

Sennett, R. (1980) *Authority*, Vintage, New York.

Sennett, R. (1994) *Flesh and Stone: The Body and the City in Western Civilization*, Faber, London.

Sennett, R. (1998) *The Corrosion of Character: the Personal Consequences of Work in the New Capitalism*, W. W. Norton, New York.

Sennett, R. (2003) *Respect: the Formation of Character in an Age of Inequality*, Allen Lane, London.

Sevenhuijsen, S. (2000) 'Caring in the Third Way: the relation between obligation, responsibility and care in Third Way discourse' in *Critical Social Policy*, Vol. 20, No. 1, pp. 5–38.

Shaw, J. (1974) *The Self in Social Work*, Routledge & Kegan Paul, London.

Shaw, M. (1994) *Global Society and International Relations*, Polity Press, Cambridge.

Sheldon, B. (1979) 'Not proven: the case of social work effectiveness' in *Community Care*, 14 June.

Sheldon, B. (1982) *Behaviour Modification*, Tavistock, London.

Sheldon, B. (2001) 'The validity of evidence-based practice in social work: a reply to Stephen Webb' in *British Journal of Social Work*, Vol. 30, No. 5, pp. 801–10.

Sheppard, M. & Ryan, K. (2003) 'Practitioners as rule using analysts: a further development of process knowledge in social work' in *British Journal of Social Work*, Vol. 33, No. 2, pp. 157–76.

Shils, E. (1981) *Tradition*, University of Chicago Press, Chicago.

Shiva, V. (1998) 'Reductionist science as epistemological violence' in *Science, Hegemony and Violence*, Nandy, A. (ed.), Oxford University Press, Oxford.

Shrader-Frechette, K. S. (1995) 'Evaluating the expertise of experts' in *Risk: Health, Safety and Environment*, Vol. 6, Autumn, pp. 239–45.

Siddall, A. (2000) 'From Beveridge to Best Value: transitions in welfare provision' in *Management, Social Work and Change*, Harlow, E. & Lawler, J. (eds), Ashgate, Aldershot.

Simmel, G. (1971) 'The metropolis and mental life' in *Georg Simmel: On Individuality and Social Forms*, Levine, D. N. (ed.), University of Chicago Press, Chicago (originally published in 1903).

Simon, H. A. (1975) *Models of Man: Social and Rational*, John Wiley, Chichester.

Simon, H. A. (1987) 'Rational decision making in business organizations' in *Advances in Behavioral Economics, Vol 1*, Green, L. & Kagel, J. H. (eds), Ablex, Norwood, NJ.

Simon, H. A. (1991) 'Cognitive architectures and rational analysis: comment' in *Architectures for Intelligence*, VanLehn, K. (ed.), Lawrence Erlbaum Associates, Hillsdale.

Simon, J. (1988) 'The ideological effect of actuarial practices' in *Law and Society Review*, No. 22, pp. 771–800.

Simpson, L. C. (1995) *Technology, Time and the Conversations of Modernity*, Routledge, London.

Simpson, L. C. (2001) *The Unfinished Project: Toward a Postmetaphysical Humanism*, Routledge, New York.

Sinfield, A. (1970) 'Which way for social work?' in *The Fifth Social Service*, Townsend, P. (ed.), Fabian Books, London.

Skehill, C. (1999) 'Reflexive modernity and social work in Ireland: a response to Powell' in *British Journal of Social Work*, Vol. 29, pp. 797–809.

Skynner, A. C. R. (1967) 'Diagnosis, consultation and co-ordination of treatment' in *Report for the National Association of Mental Health Inter-Clinic Conference*, NAMH, London.

Slater, D. & Tonkiss, F. (2000) *Market Societies and Modern Social Thought*, Polity Press, Cambridge.

Slovic, P. (1999) 'Trust, emotion, sex, politics and science: surveying the risk-assessment battlefield' in *Risk Analysis*, Vol. 19, No. 4, pp. 689–701.

Smale, G., Tuson, G., Biehal, N. & Marsh, P. (1993) *Empowerment, Assessment and the Skilled Worker*, HMSO, London.

Smith, A. (1974) *The Theory of Moral Sentiments*, MacFie, A. & Raphael, D. (eds), Clarendon Press, London.

Smith, A. (1990) 'Comment [on Efron's "Why isn't everyone a Bayesian?"]' in *Readings in Uncertain Reasoning*, Shafter, G. & Pearl, J. (eds), MIT Press, Cambridge, MA.

Smith, C. (2001) 'Trust and confidence: possibilities for social work in "High Modernity"' in *British Journal of Social Work*, Vol. 31, pp. 287–305.

Smith, C. (2002) 'The sequestration of experience: rights talk and moral thinking in "late modernity"' in *Sociology*, Vol. 36, No. 1, pp. 43–66.

Smith, D. (1987) 'The limits of positivism in social work research' in *British Journal of Social Work*, Vol. 17, No. 4, pp. 401–16.

Smith, D. & McCloskey, J. (1998) 'Risk communication and the social amplification of public sector risk' in *Public Money and Management*, Oct.–Dec., pp. 41–50.

Smith, N. H. (2002) *Charles Taylor: Meanings, Morality and Modernity*, Polity Press, Cambridge.

Specht, H. & Courtney, M. (1994). *Unfaithful Angels: How Social Work Has Abandoned Its Mission*, Free Press, New York.

Stack, C. (1974) *All Our Kin: Strategies for Survival in a Black Community*, Harper & Row, New York.

Stalker, K. (2003) 'Managing risk and uncertainty in social work: a literature review' in *Journal of Social Work*, Vol. 3, No. 2, pp. 211–34.

Starr, C. & Whipple, C. (1980) 'Risks of risk decisions' in *Science*, Vol. 298, pp. 1115–19.

Stenson, K. & Sullivan, R. R. (2001) *Crime, Risk and Justice: The Politics of Crime Control in Liberal Democracies*, Willan, Exeter.

Stevenson, O. & Parsloe, P. (1978) *Social Services Teams: the Practitioners' View*, HMSO, London.

Stower, S. (1998) 'Measuring risk in a children's unit: developing a local strategy for health, safety and risk management at Queen's Medical Centre, Nottingham' in *International Journal of Health Care Quality Assurance*, Vol. 11, No. 7, pp. 232–7.

Strathern, M. (1992) *After Nature: English Kinship in the Late Twentieth Century*, Cambridge University Press, Cambridge.

Sunesson, S., Blomberg, S., Edebalk, P. G., Harrysson, L., Magnusson, J., Meeuwisse, A., Petersson J. & Salonen, T. (1998) 'The flight from universalism' in *European Journal of Social Work*, Vol. 1, Issue 1, March, pp. 19–29.

Sztompka, P. (1999) *Trust: a Sociological Theory*, Cambridge University Press, Cambridge.

Tanner, D. (1998) 'The jeopardy of risk' in *Practice*, Vol. 10, No. 1, pp. 15–28.

Taylor, C. (1985) *Philosophical Papers, Vol. 1: Human Agency and Language*, Cambridge University Press, Cambridge.

Taylor, C. (1989) *Sources of the Self: the Making of Modern Identity*, Cambridge University Press, Cambridge.

Taylor, C. (1992) *The Ethics of Authenticity*, Harvard University Press, Cambridge, MA.

Taylor, C., & White, S. (2001). 'Knowledge, truth and reflexivity: the problem of judgement in social work' in *Journal of Social Work*, Vol. 1, No. 1, pp. 37–59.

Taylor-Gooby, P. (1999) 'Risk and the welfare state' in *British Journal of Sociology*, Vol. 50, No. 2, pp. 177–94.

Taylor-Gooby, P. (2000), 'Risk and welfare' in *Risk, Trust and Welfare*, Taylor-Gooby, P. (ed.), Macmillan (now Palgrave Macmillan), London.

Tesoriero, F. (1999) 'Will social work contribute to social development into the new millennium?' in *Australian Social Work*, Vol. 52, No. 2, pp. 11–17.

Testa, M. F. (2001) 'Kinship care and permanency' in *Journal of Social Service Research*, Vol. 28, No. pp. 17–25.

Thompson, P. B. & Dean, W. (1996) 'Competing conceptions of risk' in *Risk: Health, Safety & Environment*, Vol. 7, pp. 361–74.

Thorburn, J. (1989) 'What kind of permanence?' in *Child Care: Concerns and Conflicts*, Morgan, S. & Righton, P. (eds), Hodder & Stoughton, London.

Thorpe, D. (1997) 'Regulating late-modern childrearing in Ireland' in *Economic and Social Review*, Vol. 28, pp. 63–84.

Thyer, B. A. (2001). 'Evidence-based approaches to community practice' in *Social Work Practice: Treating Common Client Problems*, Briggs, H. E. & Corcoran, K. (eds), Lyceum, Chicago.

Tilbury, C. (2004) 'The influence of performance management on child welfare policy and practice' in *British Journal of Social Work*, Vol. 34, pp. 225–41.

Timms, N. (1959) 'Theorizing about social casework' in *British Journal of Psychiatric Social Work*, Vol. 5, No. 2, pp. 156–68.

Timms, N. (1964) *Social Casework: Principles and Practice*, Routledge & Kegan Paul, London.

Todorov, T. (2002) *Imperfect Garden: the Legacy of Humanism*, Princeton University Press, Princeton.

TOPPS (1999) *Modernizing the Social Care Workforce*, Consultation document, October, Leeds.

Touraine, A. (1995) *Critique of Modernity*, Blackwell, Oxford.

Trinder, L. (ed.) (2000) *Evidence Based Practice: a Critical Appraisal*, Blackwell Science, Oxford.

Trotter, C. (1999) 'Don't throw the baby out with the bath water – in defence of problem solving' in *Australian Social Work*, Vol. 52, No. 4, pp. 80–91.

Tuddenham, R. (2000) 'Beyond defensible decision-making: towards reflexive assessment of risk and dangerousness' in *Probation Journal*, Vol. 47, No. 3, September, pp. 173–83.

Tversky, A. and Kahneman, D. (1986) 'Rational choice and the framing of decisions' in *Journal of Business*, Vol. 59, No. 4, pp. 251–78.

Twigg, J. & Adkin, K. (1994) *Carers Perceived: Policy and Practice in Informal Care*, Open University Press, Buckingham.

Tyson, K. (1995) *New Foundations for Scientific Social and Behavioral Research: the Heuristic Paradigm*, Prentice-Hall, Englewood Cliffs.

Van der Veen, R. (2000) 'Reflexive modernization and social solidarity: notes on the future of the modern welfare state' in *The Netherlands Journal of Social Sciences*, Vol. 36, No. 1, pp. 89–105.

Vaughan, E. & Seifert, M. (1992) 'Variability in the framing of risk issues' in *Journal of Social Issues*, Vol. 48, No. 4, pp. 119–35.

Vourlekis, B. S. & Greene, R. R. (1992) *Social Work Case Management*, Aldine de Gruyter, New York.

Wacquant, L. (1999) 'How penal common sense comes to Europeans: notes on the Transatlantic diffusion of neoliberal doxa' in *European Societies*, 1–3, Fall, pp. 319–52.

Wagner, P. (1994) *A Sociology of Modernity: Liberty and Discipline*, Routledge, London.

Walters, W. (2000) *Unemployment and Government: Genealogies of the Social*, Cambridge University Press, Cambridge.

Warren, K. & Knox, K. (2000) 'Offense cycles, thresholds and bifurcations: applying dynamical systems theory to the behaviors of adolescent sex offenders' in *Journal of Social Service Research,* Vol. 27, No. 1, pp. 2–17.

Waterson, J. (1999) 'Redefining community care social work: needs or risks led?' in *Health and Social Care in the Community*, Vol. 7, No. 4, pp. 276–9.

Webb, J. (2004) 'Organizations, self-identities and the New Economy' in *Sociology*, Vol. 38, No. 4, pp. 719–38.

Webb, S. A. (1996) 'Forgetting ourselves? Social work values, liberal education and modernity' in *Studies in the Education of Adults*, Vol. 28, No. 2, pp. 224–40.

Webb, S. A. (2001) 'Considerations on the validity of evidence-based practice in social work' in *British Journal of Social Work*, Vol. 31, No. 4, pp. 57–79.

Webb, S. A. (2002) 'Evidence-based practice and decision analysis in social work: an implementation model' in *Journal of Social Work*, Vol. 2, No. 1, pp. 45–64.

Webb, S. A. (2007) 'The comfort of strangers: the emergence of social work in late Victorian England' in *European Journal of Social Work*, Vol. 10.

Webb, S. A. & McBeath, G. B. (1989) 'A political critique of Kantian ethics in social work' in *British Journal of Social Work*, Vol. 19, pp. 491–506.

Welshman, J. (1999) 'The social history of social work: the issue of the "problem family", 1940–70' in *British Journal of Social Work*, Vol. 29, pp. 475–6.

White, M. S. (1980) 'The role of parental visiting in permanency planning for children' in *Social Welfare Forum*, Columbia University Press, New York.

White, S. (1997) 'Beyond retroduction? Hermeneutics, reflexivity and social work practice' in *British Journal of Social Work*, Vol. 27, pp. 739–53.

White, S. K. (1990) *The Recent Work of Jürgen Habermas: Reason, Justice and Modernity*, Cambridge University Press, Cambridge.

White, T. (1992) 'Contracting and agreements with the SSD: a voluntary sector view' in *Purchasing and Providing Social Services in the 1990s*, Allen, I. (ed.), Policy Studies Institute, London.

Williams, F. (1999) 'Good-enough principles for welfare' in *Journal of Social Policy*, Vol. 28, No. 4, pp. 667–87.

Williams, F. (2000) 'Travels with Nanny, Destination Good Enough: A Personal/Intellectual Journey through the Welfare State', Inaugural Lecture, University of Leeds, 11 May, www.leeds.ac.uk/sociology/inaugural/

Williams, F. (2004) 'What matters is who works: why every child matters to New Labour: commentary on the DfES Green Paper *Every Child Matters*' in *Critical Social Policy*, Vol. 24, No. 3, pp. 406–27.

Williams, R. (1966) *Culture and Society: 1780–1950*, Penguin, Harmondsworth.

Williams, R. (1997) *Hegel's Ethics of Recognition*, University of California Press, Berkeley.

Wilson, K., Sykes, J., Sinclair, I. & Gibbs, I. (2002) 'Kinship care versus stranger foster care' in *Adoption and Fostering*, Vol. 26, No 2, pp. 12–18.

Wilson, W. J. (1987) *The Truly Disadvantaged*, Chicago University Press, Chicago.

Winch, G. W. (1995) 'Developing consensus: reflections on a model-supported decision process' in *Management Decision*, Vol. 33, No. 6, pp. 22–31.

Wing, H. (1992) 'The role of inspection and evaluation in social care' in *Quality Counts: Achieving Quality in Social Care Services*, Kelly, D. & Barr, B. (eds), Whiting & Birch, London.

Winnicot, D. W. (1957) *The Child, the Family and the Outside World*, Tavistock, London.

Wistow, G., Knapp, M., Hardy, B. & Allen, C. (1994) *Social Care in a Mixed Economy*, Open University Press, Buckingham.

Wittel, A. (2001) 'Towards a network sociality' in *Theory, Culture & Society*, Vol. 18, No. 6, pp. 51–76.

Woollacott, M. (1998) 'The politics of prevention' in *The Politics of Risk Society*, Franklin, J. (ed.), Polity Press, Cambridge.

Wu, G. (1999) 'Anxiety and decision making with delayed resolution of uncertainty' in *Theory and Decision*, Vol. 46, No. 2, pp. 159–98.

Wulczyn, F., Kogan, J. & Jones Harden, B. (2003) 'Placement stability and movement trajectories' in *Social Service Review*, Vol. 77, pp. 212–36.

Yankelovich, D. (1991) *Coming to Public Judgment: Making Democracy Work in a Complex World*, Syracuse University Press, Syracuse.

Yelloly, M. A. (1980) *Social Work Theory and Psychoanalysis*, Van Nostrand Reinhold, New York.

Young, J. (1999a) *The Exclusive Society*, Sage, London.

Young, J. (1999b) 'Cannibalism and bulimia: patterns of social control in late modernity' in *Theoretical Criminology*, Vol. 3, No. 4, pp. 87–407.

Younghusband, E. (1978) *Social Work in Britain: 1950–1975, Volume 2*, George Allen & Unwin, London.

Yudice, G. (1995) 'Civil society, consumption, and governmentality in an age of global restructuring' in *Social Text*, Vol. 45, pp. 1–26.

Zanagger, P. & Detsky, A. (2000) 'Computer-assisted decision analysis in orthopedics – resurfacing the patella in total knee arthroplasty as an example' in *Journal of Arthroplasty*, Vol. 15, No. 3, pp. 283–8.

Index

4885